Sapphistry

THE BOOK OF LESBIAN SEXUALITY

Dedication

This book is dedicated to Marsha Seeley, one of the most creative and hardworking women I know. She led the first discussion groups on lesbian sexuality, and later on I was privileged to work with her. We have led several groups together, in addition to doing presentations at various women's spaces and conferences. Marsha has my undying admiration for her ability to deal with hostile crowds, malfunctioning movie projectors, my procrastination, and bad service in restaurants. She has my gratitude for all the encouragement she gave me, though I called a lot of it "meddling" and "prodding" at the time. Most of the philosophy behind this book, the didactic information, and the communication exercises were developed in conjunction with her. I am sure she won't agree with everything in it and will inform me of her reservations immediately. That is the beauty of our friendship. Marsha, I love you.

The author would like to express special appreciation to Emily Rosenberg for her thorough, painstaking and erotic indexing.

Sapphistry

THE BOOK OF LESBIAN SEXUALITY

by

PAT CALIFIA

THIRD EDITION, REVISED

the
Naiad
Press
inc.

1988

lovingly illustrated by Tee Corinne

About the Author

I came out in 1971 in Salt Lake City, Utah. I was 17, living in a college dormitory, and madly in love with a broad-shouldered, brilliant woman who lived down the hall. She was alarmed by my adolescent passion and insisted that any relationship between us must be platonic. She also insisted on remaining my best friend. I spent a miserable winter trekking through snow and ice to my classes, coming home to my room, staying up late to write reams of frustrated poetry, and ingesting whatever foreign substance I thought would help my pain. The pressures of school, an inchoate and nonconforming sexual identity, my disapproving Mormon family, and unrequited love combined to force me out of school with a nervous breakdown.

I went on public assistance and moved into the Women's Center, and I tried to heal myself and acquire the skills I needed to cope with a hostile, male-dominated world. I realized that there were no individual solutions. There simply was not any room in the system for women, especially lesbians. I had to become involved in political activity, or I would not survive. While I lived in Salt Lake, I was involved in consciousness-raising work for the ERA, founding a Women's Center, anti-war activities, self-health, and housing for poor people and minorities.

In the winter of 1973, there was a three-day blizzard that completely buried my roommate's car. She had the flu, and I had to dig it out. While I plied my shovel, I decided that one more winter in Deseret would do me in. A few months later, I met a dyke from San Francisco who offered me sanctuary. Before the year was over, I had quit my $1.60-an-hour job in the bindery, packed my books and blue jeans and t-shirts, and bought a one-way ticket on a Greyhound bus. It was the best decision I ever made.

I knew living in Salt Lake was making me hate myself, but I didn't know how bad it was until I escaped. I kept feeling waves of tension melt away. I couldn't believe how many lesbians there were and what a difference it made to be able to see them and talk to them and know I was one of them. They seemed so sophisticated and cosmopolitan to me that I was intimidated and tried to keep a low profile until I knew I wouldn't make a fool out of myself by speaking out. The biggest lesbian group at the time was Daughters of Bilitis, so I joined that group and did some volunteer work for them. Within six months, I realized that almost every dyke I met came from some place just as benighted and backward as Utah, so I happily began to debate and argue and pontificate again and felt much more like my old self.

After working on the San Francisco Sex Information switchboard, I became interested in sex education. Lesbians never called the switchboard, so a friend and I began to lead groups on lesbian sexuality. *Sapphistry* is a result of this work. I also began to write about women's culture, feminist politics and erotica. Some of my work got published in feminist, lesbian or gay magazines, including *Vector, Sisters, Focus, Black Maria, The Lesbian Tide, The Advocate,* and *Heresies.*

I am working on a degree in psychology. My areas of interest are sex therapy, counseling sexual minorities, and sex research. I've done research on lesbian sexuality, some of which has been published in the *Journal of Homosexuality, 4*(3), 1979.

My plans for the future are to continue to develop my career as a freelance writer and to obtain a license that will allow me to do counseling. I imagine I will continue to be interested in the area of human sexuality, especially the issue of sexual variation, from a feminist perspective.

Pat Califia
January 1980

About the Artist

Tee Corinne, 36, is a fourth-generation Floridian, second-generation artist (mother), Double Scorpio, with a Master of Fine Arts degree from Pratt Institute, 1968. Some of her credits include the *Cunt Coloring Book,* the *Sinister Wisdom* Poster, *I Am My Lover* (portions), *A Woman's Touch* (portions), and most of the Naiad Press covers. She was one of the ten artists honored in the Great American Lesbian Art Show, L.A. Women's Building, May 1980.

About the Illustrations

The illustrations are done as a series of homages to women artists who have created images of women making love together. Most of the material appeared in books published in Paris in limited editions. The bodies in each drawing were done from tracings of the individual woman's work. The style of the series as a whole is closest to that of Gerda Wegener's 1917 colored prints. Many of the background details came from the work of other women graphic artists. Special thanks are due the staff of the Institute for Sex Research, Bloomington, Indiana, for their help in locating many of the original illustrators and examples of their work.

Table of Contents

Foreword

The fact that sex is a learned process, not something that just comes naturally, is hard for some people to grasp. To be sure, the instinct is there, but putting the instinct together with another person benefits immeasurably through positive infomation. Pat Califia's book gives to the Lesbian comprehensive and honest sex-positive information about sex between women. But even more, through it we become aware of the need for communication on all levels, of the need for respecting our diversity and our right to choose both life and sexual styles, and of the dangers of conformity.

The book Del Martin and I wrote in 1972, *Lesbian/Woman,* was the first to deal forthrightly, and from a Lesbian point of view, with what Lesbians did sexually. In retrospect, we probably should have expanded more on the "how to" aspects. For Lesbians, like non-Gay women, have grown up in a society which denigrates their sexuality, and most need endorsement, encouragement and instruction to make their sex lives free and joyous. *Sapphistry* fulfills this need.

Looking back over 25 years in the Lesbian, Gay and Feminist movements, it is revealing that for the first 13 of those years the subject of sex between women was almost never discussed among friends and acquaintances—and I suspect among some lovers. Del and I were two of the founders of the Daughters of Bilitis in 1955. Over the years we acted as peer counselors (and active listeners) to thousands of Lesbians. Yet sexual problems, or fears, or questions about how to do it, never came up. They must have been there (we had problems, and *Sapphistry,* had it been available 25 years ago, would have been of great help to us). But so great was the taboo against talking about sex, the fear of invading our own, or another's, privacy, that it was as if it didn't exist.

It wasn't until 1968, when the National Sex Forum was started in San Francisco, that talk about sexuality, or any orientation, began to be a little easier for women. As the Forum became known, I began to get anonymous phone calls from women asking "how do you do it." Unfortunately, it wasn't possible at that time to go into all the details over the phone, and for the most part, the women were still too scared to come into the office for a face-to-face chat.

The Feminist movement and the escalation of information about human sexuality as a whole have changed all this. Women, both Gay and non-Gay, now feel far more free to seek out groups dealing with sexuality. And courses such as those given by the National Sex Forum have proliferated throughout the country, making accurate and positive sex information much more available. Eventually some books which dealt exclusively with Lesbian sexuality were written, but only within the last five years, and only a few. *Sapphistry* fills a need that has never before been met. *Loving Women* by the Nomadic Sisters was the first "sex manual" for Lesbians. A loving, feminist book with excellent illustrations, it concentrates on the more common methods of Lesbian lovemaking. *The Joy of Lesbian Sex* by Dr. Emily L. Sisley and Bertha Harris covers a broad swath of information, but in some places it is judgmental and tends to portray Lesbians as super-women—which we aren't. Lesbians *do* have sexual hang-ups, there *are* pre-orgasmic Lesbians—almost all of us have suffered to some degree from society's anti-sexual bias and the mythology that women (including Lesbians) are not sexual.

This mythology, incidentally, is still alive and flourishing despite the work of Alfred C. Kinsey, Masters and Johnson, and others. Virtually every book on human sexuality (those used as textbooks by medical schools and many other professional schools) still proclaims the un-fact that Lesbians are really not so much interested in sex or orgasm as they are in hugging and kissing a lot. This kind of misinformation is a direct attack on all women's sexuality. As you might have guessed, these misstatements come from male writers and are contained in the few paragraphs devoted to "facts" about Lesbians within a much longer discussion of male homosexuality.

Sapphistry not only discusses the broad range of sexual behavior possible between women, but it does so in a non-judgmental and realistic way. Pat Califia understands the need for communication, for caring and for sharing between women. She also understands the diversity of Lesbians, and that what *you* choose to do sexually is okay. There are no performance standards.

Our sexuality is a basic part of our being. Exploring our sexuality with our partners, or with ourselves, nourishes and nurtures us. It gives us joy, physical release, a feeling of well-being which serves to strengthen us as we go out into the world to fight those other battles so necessary to insure the freedom of us all from the bigotry, hatred and misunderstanding of those who would deny us not only our sexuality but our very right to existence.

So read, sisters, and learn about yourselves. Knowledge makes us stronger, able to make good choices, sure of our feelings. It is because Lesbians are strong, loving and aware, that we can make the difference in the struggle to change our world as we now know it into our vision of how it should be, a world free of oppression and bigotry, a world free for all of us to be who we are.

Phyllis Lyon, D.A.

Introduction

I could not have written this book without believing it was important. I want to thank all the women who shared this belief with me and encouraged and supported my efforts. Their support came in many forms—dinners, proofreading, money, conversation, drawings, arguments, photographs, orgasms. Without the nurturance and criticism I received from this wonderful network, I could not have sustained the level of commitment necessary to finish the book.

Each time I encountered an obstacle, I had to reassess my attraction to this project. I came to realize that there are two reasons why it seemed so necessary for me to write this book.

The first reason is the invisibility of lesbianism in our culture. During childhood and adolescence, I was constantly aware of a vague sensation of being different from everyone else I knew. I could not pinpoint or describe this difference, but it seemed to isolate me from other people. When I examined the lives of the adults closest to me, I became distressed and anxious because I could not imagine myself marrying or having children. Women's lives seemed unnecessarily limited and frustrating to me. By the time I was 13, I had read *The Feminine Mystique.* (It was the only literature to find its way from the women's movement to my tiny drugstore in Utah.) Understanding the mechanism which turned women into second-class citizens made me feel less crazy and isolated, but it didn't give me a clue about what to do with my passion.

When I left my parents' home to attend college, I met other feminists for the first time. I also met other lesbians. When I realized that this was a choice available to me, I felt an immediate rush of relief. So *that* was it. How simple! Loving other women, making love with other women . . . it was a perfect solution. When I thought of the time I had wasted in self-hate, doubt and despair, I was furious.

The majority culture controls us by limiting our vision and denying us all possible images of the women we might become. This book carries a subversive message. It presents an alternative to conformity.

I have another, more immediate reason for writing this book. When I came out, I rejected all the judeo-christian, psychoanalytic myths about lesbians—that we wanted to be men, that we hated children, that we could be cured by a talented male lover. It was more difficult to ferret out and avoid another set of misconceptions about lesbians. I call them "pro-lesbian myths."

The most popular pro-lesbian myth is the assumption that two women know exactly how to please one another sexually. When I was a fledgling dyke, this sounded good to me. I was terrified of sex and clung to anything that made it sound less threatening. I ignored some of the implications that accompanied this reassuring generalization. One was that all women have the same pattern of sexual response and the same sexual preferences. The other was a message that talking about sex should be unnecessary.

This particular pro-lesbian myth eventually caused me a lot of misery. When I finally started actually having sex with other women, I couldn't have orgasms with them. It bothered me, but I didn't want to admit to myself just how much it bothered me. I told myself that women didn't get hung up on orgasms the way men did because sex shouldn't be genitally oriented (more pro-lesbian propaganda) and went on to other lovers.

The more often this experience was repeated, the more I panicked. Was there something wrong with my genitals? Was there something wrong with my head? Was there something wrong with being a lesbian? My lovers were hurt or angry when I explained to them that the evening had been pleasant but, no, I hadn't come. I began to fake orgasms, hoping that a real one would magically appear. Then I was really in trouble. In an egalitarian, nonoppressive relationship with another woman (which is the only kind of relationship women can possibly have), faking orgasms was unheard of. I didn't know any *straight* women who faked orgasms.

I began a frantic search for information. I started with the clinical literature in the university library. It was no help at all. I was beyond caring if cunnilingus represented a neurotic fear of penetration and pregnancy. I just wanted to know how the hell anybody managed to get off on it. Some straight friends gave me some pseudo-lesbian pornography. It aroused me fiercely, made me feel a little sick, and told me nothing about lesbian orgasms. I used it to enhance my masturbation fantasies, then began to wonder if I couldn't come with partners because I masturbated too often. I ripped off a copy of *The Joy of Sex* because I was too embarrassed and too broke to buy it, figuring that a hip, liberated sex manual might have something in it that would help me. I was informed on page 239 that women who do not have orgasms reliably should consider having a lesbian affair.

I finally picked the oldest, wisest lesbian I knew and blurted out my problem to her. She stared into her beer for what seemed like hours, then gave me a suspicious once-over. "Are you sure you're a lesbian?" she demanded.

I have heard other women recount similar experiences. Good sex does *not* automatically result every time two women (or more) reach for each other. We need to stop buying the romantic fantasy that a lover who really cares about us can sense what pleases us and provide it without a murmur of xiii

direction. We also need to stop fragmenting our sisterhood by dictating standards of sexual behavior to each other.

This book is a resource designed for use within the lesbian community. I have tried not to label any form of sexual activity as politically incorrect, aesthetically displeasing, or morally wrong. I prefer to make information available, covering as many topics as possible, and encourage you to use it to make your own choices. My experience is that when someone tries to make me feel guilty about the route I take to pleasure, they want some control over my life. I would like to see that happen less often. I think we all need more permission to explore various sexual options and more freedom to experiment with our fantasies.

I have been told that sexuality is a frivolous issue. I don't agree. It is true that our sexuality has been derided and distorted. However, I think we have overreacted to this oppression by refusing to acknowledge the sexual component of lesbianism. We are not simply arch-feminists. We are women who think about touching each other, who undress each other and explore the sensual possibilities of our own and our lovers' bodies.

It is difficult to combat misogyny on a large scale if it fluorishes within us. We can confront our internalized hostility and heal the damage done by a society that fears and hates the body. Our sexuality can be a source of pleasure, nourishment and strength. This book is an attack on the repression and colonization of women's sexuality. It is intended to strengthen us and prepare us for a long, difficult struggle for liberation.

HOMAGE TO

Mariette Lydis
1894-1970

Painter and Illustrator, born in Austria

1
The Erotic Imagination

Our sexual experiences are both limited and enhanced by the erotic imagination each of us possesses. This imagination determines which women will attract us, the sensations we will desire and pursue, the scents or fabrics or sounds we find arousing, and the experiments we will perform. These mental images or visualizations of sexual activity are enjoyable both for their own sake and for the events they lead us to create. We draw upon many diverse sources to obtain raw material for the erotic imagination to play with—things we see when we open a door without knocking, whispered conversation at the next table, stories we read, pictures we see, suggestions made by an uninhibited lover. If our sources are limited or expurgated, our erotic aspirations are also cramped and censored.

Our awareness of the erotic imagination and the uses we make of it vary from woman to woman. Some lesbians enjoy creating rich, complex scenarios which can be acted out with a lover or used to intensify masturbation. Other women prefer fantasies which are more closely connected to reality. They conjure up experiences they would like to have with a woman they have just met, or they recreate special encounters from the past. Some lesbians are not conscious of any erotic fantasies that have characters or plots. When they masturbate or have sex with a partner, they may see patterns or colors or hear snatches of music.

A sexual experience is produced by interactions between our fantasies, our emotional reactions and physical sensation. It is difficult—perhaps impossible—to become turned on if our feelings and our imagination are not engaged and active. This book starts with a section on fantasies and erotica because so much of our sexuality begins in our hearts and minds.

Sexual Fantasies

Telling yourself a risque story is one way to use your erotic imagination. Women who enjoy fantasizing are sometimes surprised by the exotic or arbitrary quality of their private erotic musings. Here are some examples of sexual fantasies that lesbians have written down for me. It is obvious that sexual fantasies are highly individualized and very diverse.

My lover and I lie in the sun, stretched on a flat rock by a swimming hole. Then we dive in and under, swimming naked in the stream. We play, stroke each other, kiss, all with the water flowing around us. Later that night we lie by a very warm fire, comfortably tired, and there in the open make love. The firelight illuminates her body and warms mine. After kissing her genitals lovingly, we drink cool stream water from a canteen.

*

Imagining that a woman is finger-fucking me, and that it goes on and on and on till I have an orgasm (can't accomplish this in reality).

*

My favorite fantasies usually involve sexual relations with someone I have not yet had an actual physical experience with. Once I am involved, I no longer have fantasies. If I'm not completely satisfied with the reality of a relationship, I fantasize other relationships with other people.

*

I enjoy imagining walking into a room where a group of six to eight women (in various stages of undress) meet me. Two or three walk over to me and start fondling, kissing, stroking me, while the others are lying down, legs spread, and exposing themselves, inviting me closer. The woman attending me (standing) brings me to orgasm while I am fingering two of the women. Then I walk over to each of the other reclining women (one at a time) and give them each the kind of attention they ask for.

*

Being made love to by another woman while I am partially restricted from movement. Gentle lovemaking, long high excitement levels. Using some kind of sensuous food (avocado, papaya, strawberries) for tactile sensations, lubrication.

*

Two men on the BART notice each other. One starts masturbating himself discreetly. the other notices and is turned on too. They move closer together and masturbate each other, no one else realizing what is happening, until they achieve orgasm.

*

My lover has a camper with a bed in the back. I have been fantasizing about getting it on with her while parked on a busy city street—maybe late afternoon and early evening. I like the idea of people being very close but not knowing what is going on.

*

Having a strange, older, authoritative woman making love to me.

*

That I have a penis/clitoris and can penetrate my partner.

*

Being made love to by two women at the same time, being very passive and very much the center of attention and activity.

*

This fantasy is for when being made love to. The woman making love to me is whipping me. There is an audience. This may take place in an old-fashioned girls' school, where she is the teacher, or in a theatre, with us on stage.

*

Myself and three women on a stage. The audience is comprised of women. We are naked on a raised platform. One woman has her fingers in my vagina, her tongue is licking my clitoris. One woman is sucking my breasts. One woman is lying, her cunt on my face, I'm sucking her and my hands are stroking her breasts. She is moaning.

*

I hypnotize my partner and she performs to my pleasure. She is less inhibited.

*

Imagining my lover tasting me while I masturbate.

*

Most of my fantasies, oddly enough, involve men. Taboo situations—like the back seat of a car or my favorite, which is a gang rape situation in a field of grass at night—all young boys.

*

I am an Amazon warrior who has been wounded in battle (with men). I land on an island in a boat I've been drifting in and am discovered by the local group of Amazons. One of these women takes me tenderly out of the boat and begins to make love to me, nursing me back to consciousness. The rest of the Amazons lovingly watch, begin to get turned on too and start making love with each other.

*

I don't fantasize much, but a brief one I have sometimes, when I'm masturbating and having trouble coming is that I'm letting go, losing control, to such a degree that I urinate copiously.

*

Having a woman put her hand down inside the front of my jeans and play with my pussy and talk erotically at the same time.

*

Oh, it's weird. That I'm working in a lesbian whorehouse (I have been a prostitute in the past, but for men, of course) and a customer chooses me and starts to work me up, but I can't really respond freely and she orders me to take off my panties, which I do (I have on a short negligee). We go into a private room. She orders me to lie down and she brings me just short of orgasm manually and then stops and orders me to go down on her, which I do (very enthusiastically, I may add). She comes and leaves. I'm going crazy, still haven't come. I go out into the parlor and begin to talk with another customer, who hasn't decided who to choose. I sit on her lap and start rubbing myself on her leg. We go off into the private room and she ties me up and goes down on me after teasing me for some time. I reach an explosive climax and she pays with a credit card. (Probably stolen, but you can't have everything.)

*

Being done from the back and the front at the same time!

*

Being with my woman on a rainy/snowy weekend in a small warm cabin, sharing the pleasure and satisfaction in lovemaking, in whatever turns us on at the time. I, in my new relationship, fantasize a lot about sex, because I feel I am making *love* to a woman I have deep emotion for. This feeling just seems to bring me closer to her.

*

I'm lying nude on the sand on my back with my legs up and spread. While I'm sleeping, a guy comes along and starts to suck my cunt. I wake up but pretend I'm sleeping. A crowd gathers. I keep my eyes closed. He begins to fuck me. The crowd begins to do various sexual activities. I open my eyes and finish the fuck that way, enjoying every minute of it.

*

My fantasies usually consist of planning what I want to do in bed that night.

*

Someone making love to me for hours, letting me direct, giving me all the sensuous things I ask for.

*

In my fantasy I have a red sports car and go every day to sit in front of a factory where a tall brunette with large breasts leaves work. One day it rains and I offer her a ride home. She accepts and somehow I give her something to knock her out and an aphrodisiac, then take her to a big castle-like building and put her through sexual machinery. It's important to add that the woman MUST be a brunette, and that I'm always dressed in leather.

*

The whole world watching me come.

*

I meet a stranger through some encounter or other. Sometimes I have my shirt open or something. I am very aggressive sexually with the other woman, usually reaching for her breasts at an early stage. She gets turned on and so do I. Almost immediately, we are both naked and come at the same time.

*

Making love amidst a hundred cats, or in furs and silks and satins.

*

To lie down in a vary warm room without my clothes on, to be massaged with oil all over my body, ending with my genitals until I come.

*

Screwing a man while he's being screwed.

*

My most common one is where my partner and I are in the 69 position on our sides and we both are coming at the same time. We are rocking each other rhythmically and it's all spontaneous.

*

Standing in the middle of an open field of grass about four acres in size with woods surrounding it and a warm breeze blowing, with no clothes on, masturbating and then tumbling to the ground when I was just about to come and climax by rolling around on/in mother earth's soft mattress of grass and soil and leaves.

*

Walking down the street, and a car full of seductive women pulls up next to me and says, "Hey, cutie, why don't you come for a ride." And I say, "Who, me?" and they say, "Yeah, you, we watched you walking and couldn't control ourselves. Hop in, we'll take care of you."

*

Being in a dimly lit room with a big bed, fireplace, silk sheets, and a woman, maybe more than one. Everyone moving with pleasure on the brink of orgasm. Then multiple orgasms occurring, alternating. I love to see a woman come.

*

Making love with a woman out in nature, in trees, in the morning—and at night in a tent, while it's raining.

*

I would like to see my wife/lover masturbate.

*

Having a woman wake me up from a deep sleep by gently making love to me. I am very passive and nude. She is dressed.

*

My lover's pretty purple labia, so long and juicy and ready to be loved, and her great breasts, slim hips and easy smile.

*

I had a wonderful fantasy about my going to the South Pacific, settling on an island and writing. I envisioned staying at a tavern where the owner is a dark, tall woman. Continental, well-educated, independent. We become friends. I spend time in the tavern pursuing my drunken poetic license. Until we have a rift one day. I go away crushed, silent, to a cottage. The climax comes when I am hurt and/or sick in some manner and she comes to my rescue, lovingly. Fade out or I lie in her arms being cared for tenderly.

*

A bunch of fine women (about 12) are in my harem in the country by the beach—all Amazons! No clothes—they are all sucking my fingers and toes and nose and ears and vagina and clitoris and asshole and I come for hours . . . days . . . weeks . . . .

*

I have an ongoing, serial-like fantasy which has been a part of my daily life since about 1970. It is the only one I have which will create actual physical excitement, similar to the excitement of being held and caressed. It has to do with two imaginary gay men who live together and are in love. They are very much into role-playing. I am not very concerned with the "masculine" partner, but it sexually excites me to fantasize about the "feminine" one— his reactions, behavior, etc. I enjoy "watching" him being loved in a way in which he is definitely being dominated (but never actually abused), enjoying anal penetration (in a variety of positions), and in general, his getting into a feminine role. (A brief daydream of him just washing dishes can give me intense excitement.)

*

My fantasies seldom involve sex—they are more likely to involve sharing and loving in a relationship.

*

Oh wow, love to see her with a garter belt on and nothing else but stockings. Turns me on so fast. (I am blushing.)

*

My only current fantasy is having sex with my former partner. In the fantasy we are gentle and tender and we keep repeating each other's names. I am also very turned on by sexual sounds like gasping, sighing, grunting.

*

This is a hard one. But I must say that animals are real sexual/sensual to me, and so I fantasize my cat licking my clit with its rough tongue. This works real well for me, and when the cats were smaller and I'd be sitting in a chair (near floor level) beating off with my hand, they'd think it was something to attack, and just watching them get ready to pounce was exciting.

*

I like to imagine the "discharge" that appears when I'm excited as being so profuse that there is enough to cover my whole body and my partner's body and we roll and slide and glory in it, licking each other all over.

7

*

Warm moist lips covering mine and deep french kissing.

*

Riding a horse and coming.

*

Sliding up and down a passionate sweaty body.

*

I come home from work and find my woman in a flimsy nightie. I grab her at the door and pull her down on top of me. We start making love right there on the floor. She runs away and tells me we have to eat dinner and if I'm good she'll give it to me after she does the dishes. While we are eating, I don't take my eyes off her chest or her parts below. She gets up and goes into the closet and bends over just enough so that I can see her pubic hair and her ass. At that I get very excited and start to grab her again, but with no luck. She's even madder now that I tried to force her a second time. Then she tries to punish me by saying since you tried twice you're not getting it at all. Then I tell her that suits me fine and I don't want it anyway. After a little silence she then feels bad for getting me all upset and tries to make up with me. First she'll pretend to drop her fork under the table and when she gets down there, she'll open my pants and stick her tongue inside me. We end by making love under the table.

*

I am in a very beautiful room with lots of velvet pillows and draperies around. I am tied spread-eagled on a waterbed. At the four corners of the bed are four women, each with a giant plume. We are all naked except for high heel shoes and garters. They tickle me with the feathers while I writhe and screech. Then one of them jumps on the bed and eats me till I come. We are all laughing and then I'm untied and we all tumble on the bed—laughing, hugging, tickling one another. By the way, I am a queen and they are my maids-in-waiting.

*

Watching two women make love in a situation where it is okay for me to watch and get turned on.

*

Trying on beautiful clothes with a woman friend/lover—each of us sees the other in beautiful, soft, shiny, cool, cottony clothes and in various states of undress. We're free to touch each other's hair, breasts, etc. but can't have any explicitly sexual experience at that time, so the excitement builds to incredible peaks.

* *

I am in a woman's bar with some friends. This woman is suddenly there. I don't see her come in nor has she been in the bar beforehand. She is tall

(5'8" or so), dark-haired (short hair) with deep blue eyes. We notice each other at the same time. She asks me to dance, and from the first moment we touch we are instantly hot for each other. We go into the bathroom (in the bar) into one of the stalls and lock the door. There is no toilet—only a little room with carpeting. She takes off my pants and starts to play with my clit with her fingers and tongue. She sticks her tongue into my vagina and out again and keeps playing with me until I come. Then I do the same to her. We make plans to go out (to dinner or something—I can't remember) the next night. She leaves first—goes back upstairs (the bathroom is downstairs) and out of the bar. I go back and join my friends. No one is the wiser. I am extremely pleased with both her and myself.

*

That someone is getting me off and I have no choice but to get off—sort of forced to but not in an unkind way.

*

My lover is on a high and narrow bench, padded and comfortable. She is tied at wrists and ankles—with arms and legs apart. Slowly, very softly and lightly I kiss her everywhere—alternating with stroking her body with a soft feather. She is driven to frenzy but cannot escape the sweet torture.

*

I am drinking red wine and from time to time I pour from the jug toward her mouth. Sometimes I give her wine directly from my mouth. After a lengthy period of stimulation and seductive teasing she has a great orgasm with much moaning and thrashing about. I find this very exciting and masturbate to an exhaustive climax. (I like to trade places in this fantasy, too.)

*

Meeting someone I know at their place or mine—someone I'm attracted to. We both feel loose and free and are having fun. We feel comfortable together. We are playing some sexual games with innuendoes and eyes meeting and looking away—both shy and yet aggressive. We start teasing each other. We may get into some massage or wrestling. We both realize we have overwhelming sexual feelings for each other and a desire to be close. We make love and it is free and beautiful and just like the first time I fell in love.

*

   Some women responded to my question about their favorite sexual fantasy as follows:

*

Don't have any one favorite sexual fantasy; don't usually fantasize about sex—mostly just about being close, if at all.

*

I'm not sexually oriented and never fantasize. I just don't think about it unless I'm doing it.

No favorite—I like the real thing better.

*

I have no favorite fantasy—I've acted them all out.

Common Concerns about Sexual Fantasies

One woman refused to describe her favorite sexual fantasy. She told me, "No—it's too sick." Her reaction makes it clear that the content of our fantasies can cause anxiety or other negative feelings. If you think some of your fantasies are questionable, reading about the images other women find erotic may alleviate some of your anxiety. It is probable that you are not the first or only lesbian to enjoy a particular fantasy.

It is important to remember the essential difference between an arousing daydream and a real sexual encounter: in the fantasy, you are in complete control. That makes it possible to enjoy visualizing yourself doing things that might turn you off or terrify you if they really happened. The mind has an ability to juxtapose sensations and techniques without limiting itself to the stimulation you usually find pleasurable. Thus, there is nothing illogical about the woman who enjoys fantasizing herself reaching multiple orgasms during vaginal penetration even though she can't reach climax that way during lovemaking.

When you are directing your own home movie, you can take good care of yourself as a character in the drama. In the privacy of your own imagination, you can enjoy the idea of being overpowered or of someone desiring you so intensely that they take you despite protests and resistance. Fantasies about seduction or rape are very common and are often disturbing to the women who have them.

A popular belief spread by armchair psychologists is that fantasies reveal our "true" selves. Thus, a person who has a rich fantasy life must be "repressing" a lot of hostility, sexual tension, frustration, or desire. According to this reasoning, a woman who has fantasies about having sex with men (or women or animals) must be repressing a genuine urge to experience that type of sex. When this theory is applied to fantasies about rape or other acts of violence, it has disastrous consequences for women. Most feminists have struggled against the pervasive myth that the victim of a sexual assault is the one who should be held responsible and blamed for its occurrence. It is very difficult to fight this callous ideology and insist on the definition of rape as an unsolicited and unwelcome act of aggression.

Perhaps fantasies do tell us something about our unrealized selves. It is difficult to prove or disprove this possibility, since the theory assumes unconscious mechanisms that repress unacceptable desires and resolve that repression via fantasies and dreams. The existence or nonexistence of an unconscious mechanism cannot be demonstrated. In the absence of empirical evidence, it seems cruel and foolish to insist on a straightforward correlation between fantasies and behavior. The primary purpose for fantasizing is to turn yourself on.

The symbolic meaning of rape in the context of a sexual fantasy is so different from the physical fact of rape that it seems unfair to call them the same thing. Being out of control or being possessed are states of mind that we frequently experience during sex. Being tied up, being forced to have sex, having an older or more authoritative partner, being ordered around, or being drugged or hypnotized—these events can all serve as metaphors for abandoning ourselves to sexual pleasure.

Heterosexual activity is another common fantasy theme that can give lesbians a lot of concern. Rather than implying that you are "really" heterosexual, these fantasies may represent a search for novelty and forbidden fruit. Some women simply do not enjoy fantasizing about activities they actually engage in. They want to feel a little wicked and perverse when they start constructing an evening of autoerotic entertainment. After so many years of being voyeurized and exploited for the pleasure of heterosexuals, it seems only fair that some of us should obtain some gratification out of voyeurizing and "exploiting" them.

Group sex, bondage, animals and spanking are other themes that have a high guilt potential. It can be very upsetting to have your most original and potent fantasy become a source of tension and uneasiness. Trying to suppress a fantasy you feel bad about usually won't make it go away, so do just the opposite. Embrace it. Let the fantasy run its course and become as wild and extreme as it possibly can. Embroider it, turn it loose, revel in it. At the same time, give yourself permission to have and enjoy other fantasies. If you have another plot to switch to when the original fantasy becomes distressing, you won't feel stuck or obsessed.

Trust yourself. You will know when you are enjoying a fantasy for its own sake and when it represents something you may want to play around if an opportunity presents itself. Don't discount the variety of sexual fantasies quoted earlier. Given this variation in plot and characters, it would be unrealistic to label some fantasy content acceptable and other content unacceptable. In all sexual matters, diversity and individuality seem to be the norm, not conformity and homogeneity.

Also keep in mind that not having fantasies can be as frequent a source of concern as having the "wrong" kind. Women who aren't aware of having erotic fantasies may wonder if they are missing something. They may have been told they are undersexed or uptight, or even been accused of lying when they told a partner or friend they did not fantasize. The truth is that some women are not aroused by mental images of sexual activity. They are aroused by what really happens to them—the texture of their lover's fur coat, kisses, the sound of quickened breathing.

If you don't have sexual fantasies and you feel ambivalent about it, remember the woman who couldn't write down her favorite sexual fantasy because it was "too sick." It seems as if it doesn't matter what we feel bad about as long as we feel bad about something. If you do have fantasies, you're oversexed or a mass of carefully concealed perversions and twitches. If you don't have them, you must be inhibited or repressed.

This is a double bind. Nobody wins. The only solution is to go after what we enjoy and forget about what we've heard we should enjoy.

Actualizing Fantasies

You may have had the following experience. You and your partner are having a fine sensual time together. In the middle of fooling around, she asks you, "What are you thinking about?" You respond that you were fantasizing. When pressed for details, you say that you were imagining the two of you in a different setting, or perhaps you were thinking about another woman (either real or imaginary). Your partner is hurt and angry and accuses you of mental infidelity. The lovemaking session terminates in hostility.

Even women who have no guilt about fantasizing during masturbation or in nonsexual situations (at work, on the bus, waiting in line at the grocery store) may be dubious about fantasizing during sex with a partner. Does it mean you don't love the woman you are with, or is she somehow deficient in skill if you need to fantasize when you are with her?

Fantasies can heighten sexual tension quickly and effectively. This does not necessarily mean there is anything wrong with your partner. The two of you may be tired, and using fantasies can be easier than exerting a lot of physical energy. In this instance, fantasizing becomes another technique to be used like nipple tweaking or anal stimulation whenever it seems desirable. For some women, fantasy is an integral part of any sexual experience. An attempt to quit fantasizing would inhibit their enjoyment. The mind and the body are not two completely separate entities. If you stop breathing, making noises or moving your hips during sex, you can halt building excitement. An erotic mental image can also be an essential part of your reaction to what your lover's hand or mouth is doing.

For that reason, if your partner confesses to indulging in erotic fantasies when she is with you, you may feel flattered instead of jealous. Of course you need to feel free to ask for reassurance that she does, indeed, desire you and wants to be with you rather than Amelia Earhart. (But would you really deny anyone you love an opportunity to get something together with Amelia?) Once you feel soothed and comforted, you can be very pleased with yourself for being sexy enought to provoke all those lascivious images.

If this doesn't work, and it continues to bother you to hear the details of your partner's fantasies, maybe it would be better not to ask her about them. It can be all right to allow each other some privacy and some space to be different. You can give each other validation and affectionate support without having identical patterns of sexual response. It helps if you can trust each other enough to believe that real problems will be brought up and dealt with honestly.

If hearing about your partner's fantasies doesn't make you jealous but arouses you or makes you curious, there's no reason to ignore them or leave them out of your lovemaking. Exploring fantasies by acting them out can be a very exciting experience.

This can happen in a variety of ways. First of all, you don't necessarily need a partner to actualize your fantasies. You may not be in a relationship, or your lover may be unwilling to participate. You can use most of the suggestions that follow during masturbation. This is a nice way to express appreciation for yourself, and at the very least it is a pleasant alternative to an evening of television.

If you do have a partner and you have never discussed the subject before, try broaching the topic when you are not in bed. If you're already involved in sex, she may have developed some expectations about what is going to happen. A suggestion that you get into a discussion of your sexual fantasies can be disconcerting. She is less likely to feel threatened or inadequate if you start talking about it over breakfast.

You can begin by asking her if she has any favorite fantasies and telling her about one of yours. Swap stories. If one of you doesn't have fantasies of her own, she can share parts of erotic books or poses in photographs that she finds exciting. If it hasn't already occurred to her, suggest that it might be fun to try playing with some of these ideas the next time you make love or whenever you're both in the mood. The conversation will have given you each enough information to create something alluring and thrilling for your partner.

There are a variety of ways to use this information to enrich your sexuality. You may want to tell her erotic stories while she masturbates or improvise a dialogue while the two of you pleasure each other. The available roles are infinite. You can be two women in a harem, a school teacher and a student, mistress and slave, passengers on an airplane, Amazon warriors, guerilla fighters, pagan priestesses, prostitute and client—anything you want to try out or try on.

You may experience some hesitancy about getting completely into your role. It is exhilarating to conquer shyness and forget you are playing a part. A responsive audience can make all the difference. Since you are each other's audience, show your appreciation. Throw each other good lines and compliments.

Costumes can help bring a role to life. You don't have to rent theatre sets or wardrobes to be able to play dress-up. Thrift stores are excellent sources of cheap fantasy drag. If you find a long dress, satin vest, or elegant suit that is slightly stained or has a tiny cigarette burn, buy it anyway. It's only for wearing at home. Picking out items you are going to use only for sex can make you feel very decadent and sensuous.

You may want to experiment with makeup. Look for bargain counters in large department stores. You can often get out-of-fashion cosmetics for mere spare change. You don't have to use them in a traditional feminine way (although that can be a lot of fun if it isn't something you have to do to get a job or a date). You can create a new personality for yourself or make up for the role of alien or vampire. Water-soluble fingerpaints can be used as body paint. (While decorating yourself or a lover, be careful not to get it in your eyes or crotch.)

The setting is important in some fantasies. This can take some extra work. Don't get obsessive about turning your studio apartment into a replica of Queen Elizabeth I's court. It's much easier to be suggestive. Limiting visibility can be a big help. Douse the lights and rely on candles. Details will be muted. If she is hopelessly realistic, take off her glasses. Your sofa can become the back seat of a car. A few extra pillows can make a bed into a nest. Drape sheets over your kitchen table and hide underneath it. You are trapped by a raging blizzard inside a tiny igloo. Never mind if it's silly. The point is to change your frame of reference.

If you want to create a really powerful illusion, blindfold your lover. She then becomes dependent on your voice and your touch to define her reality. Strip her. Tell her what you are going to do—and do something else. Surprise her (pleasantly, of course) with novel sensations. You can make a mitten out of rabbit fur or velvet and alternate its caresses with the feel of your bare hand. Ice cubes are startling and can be used to tease, provided she can tolerate the sensation. Follow the ice cubes with warm oil and a careful massage.

Acting out fantasies works best when all parties involved feel good about themselves and the relationship and are in a playful mood. Even with these prerequisites, it is possible for strong, unexpected feelings to intrude on

14

your theater. Be sensitive to one another. The leftover anger from bad sexual experiences or sorrow over old rejections and pain can be triggered unintentionally in the course of the game. These feelings may be intense, but it isn't necessarily bad that they surface. In fact, the experience can be cathartic, enabling you to finish with the past and leave it behind.

The most fascinating and beguiling fantasies are not always the most lighthearted ones. There is nothing wrong with exploring the darker or more dangerous side of your eroticism. You should be aware that these scenarios are likely to create more aftershocks than the ones suitable for production by Walt Disney. It would be unfair to embark upon such a voyage without warning your companion or companions that the trip may be hazardous. They will be better prepared to help you process what you learn about yourself if they have advance notice that those skills may be needed.

Whatever level you choose for your exploration of fantasy, remember that trust is essential to the creation of intimacy. Just having sex with another woman makes us very vulnerable. When we share our private erotic images, we take an even bigger risk. Do only what feels exciting and fun, and deserve each other's trust.

Erotica

According to the stereotypical view of women, we do not respond to explicit visual representations of sexual activity. This belief is based on the assumption that women place a higher priority on relationships than they do on sex (which follows from the notion that hot sex and close relationships are mutually exclusive categories). It also reflects a fear of what might happen if women started valuing sexual pleasure as much as or more than social stability. Consequently, the producers of traditional erotica assume their audience is male. Oddly enough, some feminists also believe that explicit erotica has little or no appeal for women simply because we are women.

My experience contradicts this stereotype. True, I have met women who don't get any pleasure out of looking at explicit photographs or movies or reading sexy episodes in novels. I don't wish to invalidate their experience. But I have also met other lesbians who use and enjoy a wide variety of erotica. Their favorites range from simple-minded peep shows you can see for a quarter in adult bookstores to the lyricism of June Arnold's *Sister Gin*. Is the former group of women better feminists or lesbians than the latter group?

Some form of censorship has always existed. The controversy over what types and quantities of erotic materials ought to be available, where it ought to be available, and to whom, has currently become very important to a segment of the women's movement.

In the midst of this debate, the terms "erotica" and "pornography" are often used as if they referred to two different types of sexually explicit material. Material that has some aesthetic value or is created by women is often referred to as "erotica." "Pornography" is used as a label for material intended for a male audience and reflecting sexist images of sexuality. These definitions are subjective, which means they inevitably fluctuate from woman to woman. Some sexually explicit material created by men—the paintings of Toulouse Lautrec, the poetry of Louys—can hardly be called pornographic. Some commercial, traditional erotica is produced by women photographers and writers, and some women buy it.

Because I feel that the terms "erotica" and "pornography" are not specific and imply moral judgments which are not universal, I will use the term "erotica" to refer to all material which includes or contains explicit descriptions or representations of sexual activity.

All erotica is a challenge to the puritanical bias of our culture. It threatens those institutions or individuals who want sexuality to serve and come under the control of the state. Any group that wishes to exercise fascistic control over people's lives attempts to control their sexuality. An essential part of that control is the suppression of explicit images of sexual acts, expecially those sexual acts that promote pleasure over conformity or suggest variation and individuality. Generally speaking, the more closely pornography conforms to the party line on acceptable sexual behavior, the more it is tolerated. Genuinely subversive erotica is often never allowed to come into being or circulate.

The bulk of erotica, that material which is most readily available, is difficult to defend. It is full of misinformation about sex. It often portrays women as the victims of violence or coercion and implies that women are not serious when they refuse sexual advances and that they enjoy being forced into sex. Some of it portrays children or animals being used in exploitive ways. However, there is a minority trend in erotica toward representing human sexuality in a positive and accurate way. This type of erotica seeks to make sexual variation more visible and functions as an underground source of information about erotic nonconformity. Some erotica serves as yet another function, which is to organize members of sexual minorities into subcultures where they can meet and support one another. Gay men and lesbians no longer need to resort to ads to find friends and lovers if they live in large cities. However, homosexuality is not the only form of deviant sexuality that exists. Sadomasochists, transvestites and transsexuals, pedophiles, and prostitutes are some of the groups that are beginning to organize and claim the right to be open about their sexual style and preferences. They cannot organize through the straight press.

Feminists and lesbians obviously cannot support anti-pornography movements if these movements are motivated by a desire to stamp out sexual variation. In the case of a gay newspaper being busted for obscenity, it seems fairly clear that homophobia is at work. I think we have more trouble recognizing our own prejudices and antagonism toward groups that make us feel uncomfortable because their sexuality is so different from our own. Instead of recognizing potential allies in our struggle against sex roles and heterosexism, we attack people who are less well organized and self-aware than lesbian feminists. Is a lesbian organization which rejects a transsexual member behaving any differently from a group of heterosexual women who reject a lesbian? Is a group of feminists attempting to ban sadomasochistic pornography behaving any differently from a church group trying to prevent sex education films from being shown in the classroom? These questions deserve more than cursory thought.

There is ostensibly an ideological difference between the feminist antipornography movement and right-wing attempts to enforce censorship. Politically conservative groups are opposed to any representation of human sexuality, especially those that have the potential to create social change. They tend to oppose pre- or nonmarital sex, birth control, abortion, sex education, and gay rights in addition to pornography. The feminist groups are primarily concerned with sexist images of woman-as-victim and the dissemination of permissive images of violent sex. They feel that violent pornography can cause or contribute to sexual assault upon women and abusive treatment of children.

It is difficult to demonstrate a causal relationship between violent visual images and sexual assault. Dubious evidence exists in support of and in disagreement with this contention. It is certainly true that the society as a whole has a terrible record on the issues of rape and child abuse. It is clear that we badly need more general public education on these issues, more protection for victims and more effective ways of dealing with individuals who are potential or actual rapists or child abusers. It is not clear that simply removing certain types of erotica from the market will have any effect at all on our culture's confused treatment of sexual violence. It may be that energy spent on attacking pornography could be better spent agitating for nonsexist sex education, creating feminist erotica, operating crisis hotlines for parents who are afraid they will abuse their children or need assistance to stop doing so, opening rape centers and lobbying for legislation which will give victims of sexual assault recourse and protection from their assailants.

Not all of the erotica labeled "violent" by feminist anti-pornography groups depicts nonconsensual activity. Sadomasochistic images come most frequently under attack. The argument for this seems to be, "No one would really consent to being tied up, spanked, insulted or whipped. Therefore, this pornography is violent.'' This is reminiscent of the myth of the seductive homosexual, always on the lookout for innocents to prey upon and recruit into a deviant lifestyle. Obviously no one would seek out a homosexual experience on their own initiative. Picketing sadomasochistic movies or confusing this kind of erotica with wifebeating and rape is the result of a similar kind of reasoning. Individuals who explore their sado-masochistic fantasies are as stigmatized and persecuted as homosexuals, perhaps more so. What does their private, consensual activity have to do with sexual terrorism of women and children? When feminist anti-pornography groups focus on sadomasochistic erotica, are they eradicating aggression and violence, or are they contributing to the oppression of a group on the sexual fringe? It seems relevant to point out that some lesbians are part of the sadomasochistic subculture. This form of sexual behavior is not confined to heterosexuals, bisexuals, or gay men.

Child pornography is another big issue with the anti-pornography movement. As in the case of rape, it is difficult to see how eliminating the images will eliminate the act. The coercive use of children as sexual objects goes on regardless of whether or not there are magazines which document the fantasy of sex between adults and young people. Historically, movements to protect children from the sexual depredations of adults have focused on gay men. They thus supplement rather than challenge enforcement of mandatory heterosexuality.

Is a boy of 17 who seeks out older men for sex a child? Is a girl in high school who knows she is a lesbian a child? When children of two and three years of age are prevented from exploring their own genitals and told not to ask questions about their own bodies, who is being protected and what threatens them? Legally, young people are not entitled to any kind of sexual expression. The juvenile justice system often deals harshly with young people whose only "crime" is their homosexuality. Will the anti-pornography movement create a climate in which children can explore their own sexuality with whomever and however they choose? Will it guarantee them the information and security they need to make those choices? Or will it create a more repressive climate in which even less information about sexuality is available and even less sexual variation is tolerated?

When a well organized, right-wing movement is flourishing and clamoring for stricter censorship and harsher laws governing sexual conduct, it seems dangerous for feminists to work in tandem with or parallel to it. When the law is allowed to make distinctions between acceptable erotica and pornography which can be banned, the results are reactionary. Courts are notorious for their stubborn support of the conservative and repressive elements of society. Obscenity trials are usually vehicles for suppressing social criticism or sexual deviation.

Given the obnoxious nature of most traditional erotica, attacks against it are quite tempting. Quick victories are possible. Unfortunately, it is much easier to close down an adult bookstore or an x-rated movie theater than it is to alter entrenched attitudes about sexuality. Every tactic that can be used to close down such an establishment can be used to close down a gay bar. Any law that can be used to shut down the producers of traditional erotica can be used against lesbian newspapers and feminist erotica.

The position of sexual minorities in America is not secure. Gay people have created a small and tenuous culture which amounts to a ghetto. Any laws which make more sexual oppression possible will be used first against groups which cannot defend themselves. There are sexual minorities who will come under attack before gay men and lesbians, but we are not immune from persecution.

Rather than run the risk of inciting or encouraging such persecution, we could work for greater sexual freedom and more positive attitudes toward nonreproductive modes of sexual expression.

Favorite Sexual Experiences

Lesbians have recently started to create their own erotica. A wide variety of literature and art that celebrates our woman-to-woman experience is coming into being. This is one of the most healthy and courageous events in lesbian history. It seems to me that we need more, new and different kinds of erotica rather than less or no erotica. If we incorporate sexuality into our poetry, songs, weaving, architecture, pottery and painting, and share what we create, the lesbian environment will be much more beautiful and vigorous.

When I asked women to write down their favorite sexual fantasies, I also asked them to describe a favorite sexual experience. Some of these descriptions are included here as examples of lesbian erotica. It was interesting to note how many different criteria women used for selecting a particular experience as their favorite. Sometimes they wrote something down because it was a first time or an experiment with something new and different. For other women, the intimacy, trust and love they had with a particular partner made the experience their favorite. Other women remembered experiences that made them laugh, or recorded times in their lives when sexuality and spirituality merged.

*

The girl I loved in '66 had a heater in her bedroom and a mattress on the floor. We always made love in front of that heater, where it was very warm, and a soft light came from inside it. I will never forget receiving the first sex of my life in that hot, firelit room and the way our skin felt to the touch because of the heater's breath. As we would turn and roll around, the play of different temperatures on our flesh intensified our excitement until it was unreal.

*

Alone with her, we dance to soft music, undress each other, dance in the nude, fall into bed, kiss all over, touch, rub each other, roll around. Sometimes she has an orgasm. I never have with anyone (male or female) but only when I masturbate. This disturbs neither of us.

*

I was masturbating my lover and the phone rang. She answered it and had great difficulty talking because she was so close to coming. The person on the phone was a dyke who knew what we were doing, so to be funny she just kept on the phone as long as possible. My lover finally hung up abruptly. I just was laughing and trying even harder to make her come.

*

When I get really turned on, I switch into automatic pilot and my body takes over. Sometimes I am amazed at how I feel and act—it is completely unself-conscious and spontaneous. It feels like I am a big, twisting snake and the boundaries between my lover and me are disintegrating. It doesn't really matter what is actually occurring at that time—everything feels wonderful, and having an orgasm doesn't matter.

*

It was with a woman who was a sorority sister of mine, with whom I had a loving relationship for about a year. We're still very good friends, and when you stop to think about it, what we had, considering I was her first woman lover, it was pretty amazing. The experience that stands out: It was late April—early May. We were eating lunch in the house dining room and we were so aroused by each other that we threw some blankets in the car and on our way up to the park stopped for wine. We parked the car and walked way up into the hills until we found a soft, secluded spot by a tree. We made love—alternating giving pleasure with our tongues—in the hot sun with the sound of birds and insects all around us, matting down the high green grass to make a nest. I can remember leaving at dusk and smiling at the mark left by our loving. It was so clean—so uncomplicated—and heightened by the fact that we were outdoors.

*

A full body-to-body massage with scented body oil—all in front of a real log fire in the fireplace; the whole evening for loving, nothing rushed, no expectancy pressures; both partners fully satisfied; next day—a walk on the beach!

*

One of my most favorite sexual experiences with my present lover is the aftermath. After fucking, I usually go down on her/take a fingerful of come, rub it on her clit, and suck it off . . . I want as much of her in me as I can get.

*

One night we got into bed and wrestled by candlelight. We did not touch each other's genitals. We communicated by touch but not sexually. The next morning, we made love and were very warm and gentle toward each other. We experimented with different techniques. It was the romping the night before that let us be free with each other the next morning.

*

Lying half-awake on a Saturday morning to discover she has begun to kiss my shoulders and work her way down my spine. To feel her fingers begin to stroke and caress my labia. Feeling my juices run warm and moist out of my vagina. To have her roll me onto my back and begin caressing my body and self to a state of full awareness. The ecstasy of feeling her lips brush across my tummy, her tongue darting along my thighs, feeling her body weight nudging my legs apart, fingers separating my pubic hairs and finally her tongue caressing my clitoris. All the warm and wonderful ecstasy of her mouth along my labia, clitoris and into my vagina—exploding (literally and figuratively) with an orgasm so intense while holding her close to me so she might also feel its magnitude.

*

My favorite sex experience was one long weekend where my lover and I told each other our favorite sex fantasies and spent the weekend playing them out. Much to our delight, we both had similar fantasies—so it was terrific. I've never felt as open or free before (or since) that weekend.

*

Making love in the moonlight. I'd like to try it out-of-doors if I can ever find a place where it's safe. Meanwhile, I make do with moonlight coming through a window. The light almost puts me into a trance. It's an odd ef-effect. I love it.

*

We knew each other before, but we had seldom spoken to one another before that lesbian/feminist meeting. Just as it was breaking up, she asked me about something I had said, and I told her that the answer was a long story. We eventually ended up at my apartment, where we talked of politics and revolution for hours. As we got more and more excited about the conversation, we got very turned on to each other. The excitement increased as we held each other and made out. The conversation reached its climax as we began to make love. The lovemaking conveyed an intensity of purpose as if to involve the other in our dreams and aspirations. Orgasm brought release from mental as well as physical tensions.

*

Watching sexual partner masturbate while I was making love to her.

*

I love to have much body contact during sex. That's why I prefer tribadism (clitoral), which usually leads to a long-lasting plateau experience (which is for me more important than the orgasmic peak).

*

I like to be fucking a woman with my finger(s), me kneeling between her legs, and I'm sitting up and just watching her squirm, feeling good because of me, writhing in sexual joy.

*

Making love to more than one woman at the same time—it was a trip— especially since I loved them both and they loved me—the combination of emotional/physical satisfaction was incredible.

*

Getting stoned. Crawling into a tiny tent with my lover. Thunderstorms and lightning shake and illuminate the tent. We are one with the universe and the storm.

*

Dancing close to a woman; being so aroused by it to the point of orgasm.

*

My brand new lover and I had gone out of town to a state park and rented a cabin. We spent an entire afternoon and evening in bed, learning about each other. It was cool and rained all day long. We talked about preferences, dislikes, and hangups we each had and what really turned us on. It was the first time I had felt comfortable (she's only my second lover), since I felt very inexperienced and she definitely *wasn't!* I learned with her that I didn't need to apologize for being inexperienced and awkward. That wasn't important to her, *I* was. Wow! A whole new experience! Not at all like my experience with men.

*

I like to make love in the summer because then our bodies perspire and slide around together. There isn't anything like it!

*

One time a lover and I did tribadism up against a wall—fantastic!

*

My lover and I were at a friend's house, waiting for her to finish her bath. We were waiting in the living room. My lover was lying on the floor. Suddenly she pulled down my pants. I straddled her face, kneeling while she licked and rubbed me with her hands. Then she held my butt in her hands, licking me furiously while I came to orgasm. My friend in the bathtub talked throughout, unaware of our activity.

*

Simply holding, caressing a woman, slow, soft, all over, our bodies very close—right now I "forget" this feeling—I've been without a partner for *so* long!

*

Looking through an erotic book and becoming so turned on we practically ripped our clothes off!

*

Every once in a while, my lover and I do tribadism in a head-to-foot position—I face one way—other partner on top facing other direction—can do a lot with hands while rubbing pussies—great!

*

Cunnilingus is my favorite, both to give and receive. I love it when my woman goes down on me, and then I can do that for her. I'm a "talker" and so is my current lover, so we make a lot of noise. That heightens the enjoyment.

*

I had been physically ill for several days and was feeling rather ugly and inadequate and was unemployed and my lover came to me very passionately in the middle of the day.

*

We stripped the bed down to a bare sheet. Had liquor by the bed, candles lighted, music playing. We were fully dressed. Propped up on the bed, we began to kiss and say sexy things to each other, then began to undress each other—slowly. At one point, I took my beautiful lover to the bathtub, with only a candle. I stroked, bathed, and dried her. I was bathed warmly, slowly, and sensually next. We took the candle back to the bed. Before lying down again, I began to touch my lover's wet cunt. Pushing her back toward the bed, I began to turn around and straddle her face with my cunt. While she licked and thrust at me, I sucked and nibbled inside her lips. We labored vigorously, wildly fucking each other, squeezing each other's asses and thighs until we came together! Then we lay together and ate an ice cream bar—kissed—said good night.

*

I love to hug my woman with all my strength and feel the same type of strength directed to me.

*

The best one was when my lover woke me up in the middle of the night and made love in bed. Totally surprising and had to be extra quiet, since my parents were sleeping nearby.

*

The first with my lover. Both of us married, unhappy. Escaping for a weekend. Very close friends, sharing beliefs and hope for better treatment as women in marriage and work. Enjoying the closer we got emotionally and physically but not knowing why. Last day of three days together, waking up to roll over, hug and kiss one another and tell each other we loved each other. Not knowing what it meant but not wanting to return to the same things. She said, "What are you worried about? This is not the ending, it's only a beginning."

*

After the very first time I ate my lover, she told me she'd never been eaten like that ever, she really enjoyed *me* and complimented me a lot—this turned me on even more, and I immersed myself in simply pleasing her and was fantastically reimbursed.

*

I like getting stoned and then masturbating with my vibrator. I always have incredible orgasms—then I just lie there exhausted.

*

I was rubbing the clitoris of my lover and was so involved that I had an orgasm from the stimulation of rubbing her.

*

I had cramps one morning, and my lover made me tea and rubbed my abdomen and brushed my hair and told me how much she loved me, and I made up a poem about her and we made love and my cramps went away.

*

HOMAGE TO

Margit Gaal

active around 1921

Illustrator

2
Self-Loving

It can be difficult to believe that another woman wants to love or pleasure you if you have trouble accepting your own body or don't take much delight in your own company. Self-hate or intense self-doubt produce a craving for reassurance and approval that can never be completely satisfied. Everybody needs to feel loved and valued by other people, but a relationship founded on real insecurity can keep you forever dependent. If the relationship ends or changes drastically, you are left without inner resources, and your self-esteem will vanish.

Women are not encouraged to be self-sufficient. We are supposed to be tireless in our efforts to please and take care of other people. We aren't supposed to form opinions about ourselves—we are supposed to wait for the verdict of other people. We wind up never being sure if we are attractive, intelligent, creative, good, or worthwhile. This make it hard for us to take independent action, make demands, start new things, or get out of bad situations.

In the process of coming out as lesbians, many women come to realize the value (and difficulty) of being self-reliant. We begin to do things for ourselves that we thought husbands or daddies had to do. As we realize that other women are not really incompetent, we accept their help and learn from them. But old habits die hard. Because we feel stifled by the heterosexual world, we come to need the lesbian subculture. We may become more willing to conform to its standards and bargain for its approval than we ever were when we dealt with straight society. Loving other women is no substitute for loving yourself.

Self-love is a decision to gamble on yourself. It means taking your own word for what is real and good, and trusting your own decisions. It can free a lot of energy for tackling other projects. I can't imagine what lesbians could accomplish if we quit harassing ourselves and tearing ourselves apart. But this is where the scary part, the risk, comes in. These "other" projects waiting in the wings for us to get our act together are things we're afraid of. They're important, and therefore dangerous, because we might try and fail.

Self-acceptance isn't worth much if it won't sustain some losses or pratfalls. Insisting on maintaining your dignity at all costs is paralyzing. Mistakes are informative, and so is playing the fool.

Sexuality seems to be the territory where our anxieties and self-doubt retreat and hold fast. This chapter discusses some areas where women find it difficult to love and accept themselves.

Body Image

One of the first discoveries to come out of the early women's movement was that there is no such thing as a beautiful woman. When members of consciousness-raising groups talked to one another about their bodies, it became apparent that tall women wished they were petite, small women longed to be Amazonian, brunettes thought they would be more appealing if they were blonde, blondes thought they were boring, voluptuous women felt fat and went on endless diets trying to become slim-hipped and small-breasted, and slender women worried about being mistaken for boys.

I don't think lesbians are immune to this. It's true that we often reject stereotypical, feminine standards of appearance and prefer a more androgynous, comfortable image. But we have our own ideas about what is attractive and what isn't, and most of us still wrestle with all the awful messages we got about our female bodies when we were growing up. We show our disapproval of women who "don't look like lesbians" and madly cruise the women who personify the Superdyke Look.

Enforcement of the lesbian norm is especially painful for fat women, black and third world women, and disabled lesbians. Groups of these women have recently started to form for the purpose of giving one another support and validation.

Most of our discomfort about our bodies is misplaced and amounts to self-torture. There are lots of ways to combat "the uglies": massage, self-defense classes, more attention to nutrition and less attention to calories, different clothes, sports, masturbation, believing the compliments friends and lovers give us, enough sleep, fat liberation, good sex, ice cream, mirrors, contact with other women who want to work out of negative feelings about their own bodies, Reubens's paintings, and stubbornness.

The Female Genitals

This section is about the part of our bodies we most often despise: the vulva. Our genitals are hidden, and we are not supposed to touch them; therefore, they must be shameful. If this is not so, why are the words we hear which refer to the female genitals used as insults? Why is anything even associated with the female genitals, like menstruation, so secret and distasteful? Why do we have to be so careful about spraying and rinsing away our sexual perfume? Why are we supposed to get hurt there and bleed the first time we have sex?

As young women, we are not likely to encounter any positive images of the vulva. Traditional erotica usually puts more emphasis on being explicit than it does on being beautiful. Some commercial pornography seems to make a deliberate attempt to portray the female genitals as ugly or inferior. In medical textbooks, the diagrams of the "External Female Genitalia" are clinical rather than sensual and symmetrical rather than accurate. The inner lips are usually short and thin. The clitoris is small. The inner lips always connect with the clitoral hood. The urethra is always located exactly midway between the clitoris and the vagina.

Feminist, woman-loving-women artists have only recently begun to portray the female genitals. Their images are erotic and informative. When we look at the "cunt portraits" created by Betty Dodson, Tee Corinne, or Marilyn Gayle (among others), we see that real women do not look like the diagrams in medical textbooks or the "split beaver" in porn. Labia can be many different sizes, shapes, and textures. Clitorises can be the size of seed pearls, peas, or fingernails. Inner lips do not always merge with the clitoral hood. Hoods can be folded double, some are retractable, and some cannot be pulled back from the glans of the clitoris. The urethra varies in size and placement. In fact, there is such a wide variation in color and configuration of the genitals that it is impossible to say what a "typical" woman should look like.

These images alter the meaning of the female sex. They represent women repossessing and reclaiming their own bodies. They make it possible to celebrate the vulva and make it more difficult to deride, ignore, or blindly use it as an object.

The language we use to talk about our genitals is also changing. Women are taking over the slang terms that used to be insults. This process is similar to using the term "dyke" with pride instead of scorn. As a word becomes part of our culture and our terminology, new meanings and new contexts are added to it, until finally its connotation is permanently altered. In addition to liberating terms like "cunt" and "pussy," lesbians are using new words to describe their sexuality. The term "yoni" is a synonym for the female genitals that has recently started to appear in lesbian literature.

Your vulva is part of your body like your elbows, hands, belly button, ears, and nose. Knowing what your own genitals look like can help you feel how much a part of you your sex is and consequently how much a part of you your own sexuality is.

I was 17 the first time I looked at my own cunt. I had been masturbating since I was about two and was starting to realize I was a lesbian, so I figured I might as well add another sin to my list of crimes. Besides, I was genuinely

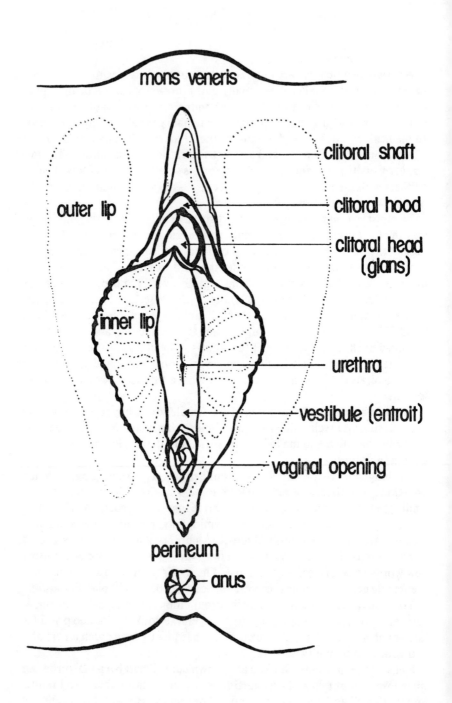

mons veneris

clitoral shaft

clitoral hood

clitoral head
(glans)

outer lip

inner lip

urethra

vestibule (entroit)

vaginal opening

perineum

anus

curious. I'd been touching myself "down there" for years to get myself off or get myself clean, and lately other people had been touching me "down there" too, and I had no idea what it was really like.

I was supposed to be writing a paper comparing Spinoza and Descartes. I knew it was going to be tough to write because I had fallen asleep in every single lecture. So I ditched the paper, spent an hour looking for a hand mirror, closed all the curtains in my dormitory room, locked the door, took off my pants, got up on the bed, and stared down at the reflection between my plump white thighs.

My initial reaction was disgust, disbelief, and disappointment. *That* wasn't the nice friendly beast my hand had snuggled up to. How could a clit be that little? How could anybody stand to put their tongue down there?

I got dressed and started to work on my paper. I couldn't concentrate. I tried to remember what I had seen. In five more minutes, I was on the bed again, taking a longer and kinder look.

I spent the whole afternoon writing my paper, getting curious, getting naked, and coming to terms with my own genitals. I didn't erase all my negative feelings about my own body in one day, but I got off to a good start.

When I told this story to friends or in discussion groups, some of the women who heard it always confided to me that they still hadn't gotten around to looking at their own genitals. Consequently, the next section is a description of a self-examination or exploration of the female genitals.

Self-Examination

Pick a day when you don't have to pack for a trip or cook dinner for guests. Find a place where you won't be disturbed for an hour and can lie down comfortably. (Some women may prefer to sit in a large chair.) Unplug the phone if you have one and put out the dog or cat. You may want to play some music, make yourself a little snack, or do other things that you find relaxing and pleasing.

It's a good idea to have some lubricant on hand. Petroleum jelly is too thick; and if you get any into your vagina, it tends to promote vaginal infections. Use a water-soluble lubricant your vagina can eliminate naturally or an oil it can absorb. KY Jelly, unscented Albolene Cream, coconut oil, baby oil, salad oil, saliva, and any lotion which does not contain perfume or alcohol are lubricants which women have recommended to me. If you're not sure about an oil or cream, put a little on the edge of one of your inner lips to test it out.

Use a mirror to examine your vulva. Take a look at the diagram and identify the different parts. Put some lubricant on your fingers and stroke yourself between the outer and inner lips. Test their sensitivity to different kinds of touches. Try pressing the outer lips together over the labia minora. Some women like to tug gently on the inner lips when they masturbate. Other women may hold their hand over the outer lips and apply pressure to them. Does it feel better to stimulate your clitoris by pressing right on the glans or above it or to one side? Is one side of your clitoris more sensitive than the other? Do you like to go around it in circles with your fingers or push down on it with your hand? The mons veneris itself can be sensitive. Knead and manipulate it. Experiment. If you masturbate in one particular way, today is the time to explore other kinds of touches.

Uncurl one of your pubic hairs and see how long it is. How does the color of your pubic hair compare to the hair on your head or under your arms? Do you think it will turn white or gray when you age, or has it already changed color compared to when you were younger?

Are your genitals all one color, or is there a gradual shading of pinks, browns and reds? Some women have dark-colored genitals, while other women are a light pink. The outer and inner lips may be a different color from the area around the vagina.

How are your genitals proportioned? Would you say your cunt is Baroque, Danish Modern, Romantic, Socialist Realist, or Cubistic? Is one inner lip longer than the other? Does your clitoris change visibly in size when you are aroused?

While you are doing the self-examination, don't leave out your anus. The perineum, that stretch of skin between vagina and anus, is often very sensitive. The anal opening itself can respond to gentle stimulation with pleasurable feelings. Some women like being touched around the outside of the sphincter muscle; other women like penetration. You may want to see what penetration feels like, if you've never experienced it during masturbation or with a partner. Generally speaking, the anus carries more tension and is less relaxed than the vagina, so go slowly. Any part of the body will relax when it is made to feel good.

Can you find your urethra? On some women, it is very visible. Other women may be able to find it by pulling up on the mons and bearing down with their stomach muscles. If you still can't find your urethra and you feel curious about it, take your mirror into the bathroom. You can sit on the edge of the bathtub and watch your genitals while you urinate. The urethra is a primary erogenous zone for some women. They may apply pressure to it during sex or masturbate by inserting a finger or smooth object a little way inside it.

Take a look at your vaginal opening. Rather than being a gaping hole, it usually appears to be soft folds of skin. It is a potential space rather than a tube or tunnel. Use some more lubricant and experiment with stimulating the opening. Do you enjoy penetration? The opening itself and the part of the vagina closest to it are the most sensitive areas. The deeper part of the vagina, back by the cervix, is usually sensitive only to pressure and pain. Some women find that the anus is more sensitive than the vagina.

You may want to conclude your self-examination by masturbating. If you are an artist, you may feel like drawing your own portrait. Some lesbians who are textile artists have made wall hangings, quilts, or embroidered capes depicting the vulva. You may want to write a description of your cunt in prose or poetry.

Next time you masturbate, take time to taste and smell your own vaginal lubrication. Some women find that a fear of smelling or tasting bad prevents them from relaxing with a partner. This can be especially inhibiting if your partner wants to eat you. The only way to alleviate that anxiety is to smell and taste your own sexual juices.

If you are curious about the sexual organs that can't be seen with a hand mirror, you may want to take a self-health class at a feminist clinic. A few clinics sometimes offer groups for lesbians, and most of them do not treat their lesbian clients in a homophobic way. Part of the self-health class is learning how to insert a plastic speculum into your vagina, lock it into place, and find your own cervix. You can look at your cervix in a mirror by shining a flashlight into the vagina. Seeing this little pink mushroom can be thrilling. Birth control pamphlets don't do it justice.

Knowledge is power; and the more knowledge we have about our own bodies, the more powerful we feel!

Kegels

Kegels are exercises that can increase awareness of and control over the genitals. They were developed by a Dr. Arnold Kegel to help women who had trouble controling urination. The women who did them kept reporting that they were experiencing increased sexual pleasure as well. Kegels involve contracting the pubococcygeus (PC) muscle. This muscle runs from the pubic bone in front to the tail bone in back. It's like a sling or saddle that we sit in. Besides controlling the urethra, the PC muscle contracts during orgasm. Like any other muscle, it needs to be kept in tone. Kegels provide that exercise.

Many women already do a version of Kegels. They discovered the PC muscle as children, when they played at stopping and starting the flow of urine. If you don't know where your PC muscle is or what it feels like when it contracts, you can find out the next time you need to pee. When you sit on the toilet, spread your legs apart. See if you can stop the flow of urine. If you can stop and start it at will, the muscle you feel contracting is the PC muscle. If you can't find it, don't give up—try again next time you urinate.

You can also find this muscle by inserting a lubricated finger or two into your vagina and bearing down. You will probably feel a tightening inside the vagina.

There are three kinds of Kegels: slow, quick, and pull in/push out. To do a slow Kegel, tighten the PC muscle as you did to stop urine flowing. Hold it for a count of three. Relax. For quick Kegels, do just the opposite: tighten and relax the muscle as fast as you can. Most women who can find their PC muscle can do slow and quick Kegels. I have not talked to many women who can do the pull in/push out version. You are supposed to pull up the entire pelvic floor as if you were trying to suck water or air into your vagina, then push down to expel the water or air. This exercise uses abdominal muscles as well as the PC muscle. I have been able to sort of do this once or twice in the bathtub, where I could feel the water moving. If you can't do them, don't worry. Slow and quick Kegels are quite sufficient to keep the PC muscle in shape.

The textbook recommendation is to do at least 10 of each of these at five different times during the day, then increase the number you do each exercise by five each week. Most of the women I know who do Kegels do them at random times—when they're driving to work, studying for finals, watching TV, hitchhiking, or writing a book—rather than doing them a fixed number of times a day.

When you start doing them, you may not have perfect control over the muscle. It may not want to stay contracted, and you may not be able to tighten and loosen it very quickly. If you persist, after a week or two you'll notice a change.

Kegels have been useful for women who have trouble experiencing orgasm or who wish their orgasms were stronger. They can also be used to build arousal or hasten orgasms during sex with a partner or masturbation.

Masturbation

Since this is a book about *lesbian* sexuality, it may seem surprising that masturbation is discussed before sex with a partner. After all, the term "lesbian" means a woman who has sex with other women. I'm putting masturbation first because I want to challenge the traditional view that self-stimulation is not "real" sex. It is the way most of us learn about erotic sensations and develop a pattern of sexual response. It is available when partners are not, and it should not be abandoned just because you have a lover.

Women are taught that sex is something men will do to us, not for us or with us. We are told far more about venereal disease, sin, menstruation, pregnancy, and the dangers of acquiring a bad reputation than we are about health, the clitoris, masturbation, or our own orgasms. (This assumes that someone was willing to tell us something about sex. Some of us don't even get the negative information.)

This training conditions women to view their sexuality as being under another person's control. If we have sexual problems, we look for the right lover to solve them for us. If we don't have a partner, we feel undesirable and sexually frustrated.

Lesbians get this conditioning along with other women. We refuse to accept the idea that sexuality is a male province, but we sometimes expect our women lovers to take responsibility for our pleasure and our responses. We may feel that masturbation is second-rate and feel ashamed or uneasy about it. If we have a partner and continue masturbation, we may feel we are being immature or selfish.

The myth that masturbation is physically harmful has pretty much been eradicated. The myth that it saps sexual energy and makes it harder for you to have orgasms with a partner is dying a little more slowly. Of course, masturbation does remove any desire to have sex . . . for about ten minutes. The Kinsey study showed that women who masturbate are more likely to be able to climax with partners than women who do not masturbate. The best information about what we like sexually comes from ourselves. It is easier to experiment with what we like and communicate what we find out to a partner than it is to wait for her to read our minds or guess. No amount of intuition can create rapport as quickly as simply showing a lover how we masturbate.

If we weren't all so insecure about our ability as lovers, it wouldn't matter so much whose finger was on whose clit. Why should masturbation and lovemaking be two totally separate categories? Watching a lover excite herself can be very arousing. Her vulnerability and her trust in you can contribute to the turn-on. It doesn't mean you are an inadequate lover. It means you are accepting and open to exploring new erotic avenues.

Lovers who live together sometimes experience friction if one of them wants some privacy and time to masturbate, and her partner feels threatened or put off by this. If you and a lover are having other problems with your lovemaking, this is bound to create more tension. But if the sex you have together feels good and is satisfying, your disapproval of her time alone can create unnecessary problems. Every relationship threatens to subsume the identities of the individuals involved in it. The very fact that you love someone, need her, and can be hurt by her may create a need to be apart from her, make contact with your own strength and independence, and reassure yourself that you are indeed capable of standing without her. A woman who does not feel free to take that time and assert her individuality may gradually feel too pressured and smothered to enjoy sex with you.

If you don't have a partner, you may be experiencing some loneliness and dissatisfaction. Masturbation is one way to bolster your own ego and appease your sexual hunger. Desperation is rarely attractive, so why frustrate yourself until Ms. Right (or Ms. Rights) sweep you off your Frye boots and into her waterbed?

Pleasuring yourself is founded on liking your own body well enough to touch yourself and enjoy the good feelings. Everybody deserves pleasure. Why should we have to wait to enjoy ourselves until we lose 20 pounds or finish law school or meet a new woman? Masturbation is available whenever we have the time for it. You can do it in five minutes before rushing off to a doctor's appointment, or you can spend a whole evening or weekend indulging in your own whimsies. You don't have to worry about being attractive to another person or hold back energy so that she can take her turn. This is one instance when you can be selfish without hurting anybody.

There are as many different ways to masturbate as there are women who do it. Some women like to rub on pillows, chairs, bunched up bed sheets, or other objects. Some women use their hands or a finger. You can use oil or a fabric with a sensuous texture when you touch yourself. Some women like vaginal stimulation; other women don't. Light, stroking motions; firm, pressing motions; circular motions; side-to-side motions; and other combinations are all popular. Some women use electric massagers or vibrators; and other women use water from a faucet, shower head, or oral hygiene device. Some women like to include whole body stimulation or stimulation of the anus or urethra when they masturbate. Other women focus directly on the clitoris.

The position you're in can be as important as how you touch your genitals. Some women enjoy their orgasms best when they're lying on their stomachs. Other women lie on their backs or sides, sit up, kneel, or crouch. If you can have orgasms in more than one position, you know that it feels different depending on whether you're on your back, stomach or side. Having your legs together or apart affects the orgasm, too. If you masturbate in one position and use a different one with a partner, you may have difficulty experiencing orgasms with her. A change in position may help, and you can teach yourself to come in different positions by experimenting during masturbation.

If you have never had orgasms, learning how to masturbate is probably the easiest way for you to begin. It's usually easier to explore your own body and sensitivity when you're alone. You can take as much time as you like without worrying about your partner getting tired; you can do things for yourself without having to get up the nerve to ask for them; and you can stop to rest without talking about it. The main problems encountered by most women who have never had orgasms are being reluctant to touch themselves and not giving the process enough time. Some sex therapists are starting preorgasmic women's groups to provide the support which can be helpful in overcoming these obstacles. (These groups were begun by Lonnie Garfield Barbach and are described in her book *For Yourself: The Fulfillment of Female Sexuality.*)

Masturbation can be a source of energy, a free sleeping-pill, a joyous expression of self-love, and an easy way to learn about your own sexuality. It can also be a hurried, guilt-ridden experience—a last resort when no partner is available, a secret activity to be indulged in as little as possible and always with mixed emotions. The difference between the first kind of masturbation and the second kind is this: whether or not we believe that we deserve to feel good.

Sharing Masturbation with a Partner

This is a good way to learn about each other's sensitive spots and favorite strokes. If you feel hesitant or shy about letting your lover watch you masturbate, remember that it doesn't matter if you come. You're sharing information about your own body, not putting on a performance. Feel free to ask for reassurance. The first few times you share masturbation with a partner, you may want to do it in partial darkness, do it simultaneously so that neither of you feels voyeurized, or take turns—anything you feel would make you more comfortable.

When one of you feels like having sex and the other one is too tired or just not in the mood, suggest that you share masturbation. You can hold your friend, caress her, or simply be with her as she pleasures herself. You may find yourself getting turned on enough to forget why you were too tired.

Some women hesitate to touch their own genitals or breasts during sex with a partner for fear of hurting her feelings. It would be nice if we could feel free to enjoy our own as well as our lover's touches. Adding an extra pair of hands multiplies the sensations possible. You may also feel guilty about paying too much attention to yourself and feel that you should be touching her. There is time enough to do both. Remember that watching another woman as she becomes aroused and reaches orgasm can be as exciting as climaxing yourself. The pleasure of being able to watch others enjoying sex is one that is denied to most of us in this culture.

If you have a close relationship with another woman and don't feel ready to be lovers with her or make love with her, try sharing masturbation. It's an alternative to straightforward sex and has a different effect on intimacy. If you've both been dancing together all night or watching sexy movies, why go home alone or frustrated?

Being able to masturbate during group sex is a guarantee that you won't feel cheated or left out. The energy in a group sometimes shifts, and two women may begin to focus on each other. Conversely, you may need to pull back from interaction and appreciate the experience without participating directly.

The idea of doing this is scary for many women. You can't do it without confronting any negative feelings you still have about masturbation. It's also important to trust the woman or women you are with. If a partner has told you that she stopped masturbating "at 15, when I grew up," you know better than to suggest a mutual session of jilling off. But if she seems to be open and interested in new experiences, the risk could be rewarding. If the two of you get really comfortable with each other, you could even run races.

Vibrators

These sex toys are gaining in popularity. Some women who have never had an orgasm find vibrators helpful, since they do not get tired like a hand and they provide intense stimulation. Other women may want to try water running in the bathtub or shower. (If you experiment with water, be careful not to shoot it under pressure into your vagina. This can cause injury or even death.)

A vibrator is considered by some lesbians to be one more sexual option, like using lubricants or acting out fantasies, to add more variety to sex and make it more fun. There are some myths and concerns circulating about vibrators which probably prevent some women from trying them out.

The most common myth is that a vibrator provides sensations which are so marvelous and sinfully gratifying that it will replace your partner or make it impossible for you to come using anything but a vibrator.

This is a half-truth. Vibrators do provide very strong stimulation. If you use a vibrator so long and hard that it numbs the lips of your vulva, you may have to wait several minutes for sensation to return. After sensitivity reappears, you can probably use any method you like to reach orgasm.

If a woman has never or rarely had orgasms and she discovers she can have them reliably with an electric massager, she may want to continue to use it and may be unwilling to experiment with other techniques. The experience of being able to come is so rewarding for her that she doesn't want to risk missing it even once. This woman may be "hooked" on her vibrator, but isn't the same thing true of other lesbians who experience orgasms reliably with only one technique? We don't worry about someone getting addicted to oral sex or tribadism.

If you're afraid your partner's vibrator is going to replace you, why not ask her to share it? You may like it as much as she does. View the little machine as an extension of your own body—a tool or a toy, rather than a threat or an intruder. Vibrators can be used during lovemaking in many ways. You can take turns stimulating each other, use it for all-over body massage, or use it simultaneously. If you want a vibrator the two of you can use together, get one of the long-handled models with a large, rounded head. The smaller models with pop-on attachments are usually better suited for use by one woman at a time. However, some of these vibrators come with heating attachments that feel very nice on sore muscles.

Not everybody enjoys "buzzers." Some women are turned off by the noise (although very quiet models are available) or by the idea of using a machine. Some women find the sensation unpleasant. If it seems too intense, you can try using the vibrator through a towel or clothing.

There are two kinds of vibrators: plug-in and cordless. The ones you can plug in vibrate more rapidly. The others run on batteries (and also run down). Plug-in vibrators are available from some women's businesses, large appliance stores, and department stores. Battery-operated vibrators are cheaper and can be found in any adult bookstore. They can be vagina-shaped, egg-shaped, or very slender (for anal stimulation). A variety of rubber sleeves for battery-operated vibrators is available. They are relatively cheap, and you may want to try one to see if you like the way it feels before purchasing a plug-in vibrator. Some women like to use battery-operated vibrators for anal or vaginal stimulation while they use another vibrator for clitoral stimulation.

If you become the proud owner of a "buzzer," take the same precautions with it as you would with any other electrical appliance. Never use it in or around water. You should also never use a vibrator over a skin rash, swelling, or bruise. If you are experiencing sharp pains that may be caused by torn ligaments or sprains, do not use your vibrator; it can increase the tissue damage.

If you get off on using your electric massager and start feeling guilty about it, ask yourself why you're afraid of feeling good. If you become concerned about using it exclusively, put it back in the drawer for a while and go back to your hand or teddy bear or Water-pik. You will probably discover that you haven't forgotten anything you knew before you bought the "buzzer."

38

The Sexual Response Cycle

In 1966, Masters and Johnson (now Masters and Masters) published *Human Sexual Response.* They based their description of the female sexual response cycle on actual observations of women experiencing orgasm. After centuries of "learned" debate on whether women had orgasms (or souls), and if we did, why, someone finally decided to find out the truth about women's sexuality from women. Although Masters and Johnson's use of a laboratory setting to observe human sexual behavior is still controversial, no one can doubt that the data they gathered will have far-reaching effects on the way women perceive themselves and their relationships with others.

Prior to *Human Sexual Response,* Freud's theories about female sexuality, or variations on them, were the most widely accepted standards for acceptable development and performance. He theorized that women have two separate centers of erotic feeling: the clitoris and the vagina. In childhood and early adolescence, the clitoris is the focus of a woman's sexual feelings. Freud believed that adult women transferred their sensitivity from the clitoris to the vagina and were then able to experience orgasms from penile stimulation alone. Masturbation, lesbian lovemaking, and any other sexual behavior that concentrated on the clitoris were consequently viewed as immature, neurotic, or regressive.

Masters and Johnson were not the first researchers to challenge this theory. In the 1950s, Kinsey reported that very few women were apparently able to have vaginal orgasms. It was common medical knowledge that the main body of the vagina has few nerve endings, especially in comparison with the clitoris, and it does not seem to be biologically designed as a primary erogenous zone. It was also known that all mammalian fetuses are basically female. If the gonads of fetuses with xy and xx chromosomes were removed, both would develop into female infants. The male fetus requires hormones produced by its own developing testicles to complete development as a male. The glans of the penis develops from tissue which becomes the clitoral glans in a female. They would thus seem to be homologous organs, and existence of a vaginal orgasm would logically suggest that men should experience orgasm from testicular stimulation alone. No researcher has ever demonstrated the existence of vaginal orgasms in any other mammal. Yet the Freudian theories fit society's expectations of women so well that they continue to circulate today.

The Masters and Johnson study validates what lesbians have always known and done. We may have felt bad about the kind of sex we enjoyed and bought the psychoanalytic label that told us we were immature or neurotic, but we continued to enjoy the kind of stimulation that we found most pleasurable.

There were 321 women in Masters and Johnson's sample group. Their ages ranged from 20 to 70. Some of the women had no children; some had as many as five. They observed over 4,000 orgasms which took place during heterosexual intercourse or masturbation. Three women had orgasms from breast stimulation alone. None of the women were able to have orgasms from fantasizing or reading erotic literature without additional, physical stimulation. (This doesn't mean that it can't happen, just that no instances of it were observed.)

They found that there is only one kind of orgasm. Each orgasm subjectively feels different, and women may use a wide variety of techniques to reach orgasm, but physiologically it takes place the same way each time in every woman.

Climax involves the whole body, but it does not and cannot take place without clitoral stimulation. Clitoral stimulation can be indirect and still be effective. Some women are able to reach climax by rubbing or squeezing their thighs together. Other women are able to reach orgasm during vaginal stimulation or penetration. Masters and Johnson theorize that this takes place because vaginal stimulation pulls the inner lips and can create movement of the clitoral hood. This friction of the clitoral hood against the glans can be enough to create orgasm.

Masters and Johnson coined a new term for orgasm: the sexual response cycle. They divided it into four phases: excitement, plateau, orgasm, and resolution. These phases are arbitrary and are mainly useful for descriptive purposes. Each of them is detailed below.

Excitement phase. The cycle begins the moment a woman becomes sexually aroused. A touch, a fantasy, dancing—anything that a particular woman experiences as a turn-on begins the excitement phase. This stage of the sexual response cycle can last anywhere from several minutes to an hour. Heartbeat and breathing begin to speed up. The woman may have a nipple erection (and this can happen in one nipple before the other). Toward the end of the excitement phase, the woman may begin to experience a sex flush. This is a deepening of the skin color, and in Caucasian women it looks somewhat like a rash or measles. It is not usually very apparent on dark-skinned women. Where the sex flush first appears and the pattern it spreads in vary with each individual. In some women, it never appears at all. Aside from the nipple erection, further changes may take place in the breasts. They may increase slightly in size, the pattern of veins may become clearer and stand out, and the areolae around the nipple increases in size. This may make it look as if the nipple erection has disappeared.

The genitals are also affected by the onset of arousal. In women who have had no children, the outer lips thin down and flatten. Women who have had children experience a rapid increase in size in the outer lips, due to an increased flow of blood. The labia majora may become two or three times their usual size by the end of the excitement phase. (The sexual response cycle is slightly different for women who have and women who haven't had children, because pregnancy increases the amount of blood vessels in the pelvic area.) The shaft of the clitoris increases in diameter. The inner lips begin to swell. In the vagina, lubrication begins to appear 10 to 30 seconds after any stimulation begins. Drops of clear fluid form on the vaginal walls, and the vaginal walls themselves may become a darker color. The vagina begins to dilate slightly.

It is not known exactly how vaginal lubrication is produced. The tiny drops that sweat from the walls of the vagina may appear as the result of increased blood flow into the pelvic area. The blood vessels may dilate and pass fluid into the tissues of the vagina. We do know that no fluid is secreted by the cervix. According to Masters and Johnson, the Bartholins glands at the entrance of the vagina do not contribute to vaginal lubrication; but some women who have had these glands removed say that this operation reduced the amount of vaginal lubrication.

The upper two-thirds of the vagina dilates and the uterus moves up. The walls of the vagina become thinner, stretched by the moving uterus. The upper vagina may balloon out enough to make it possible to feel the difference if you insert your fingers into your partner's vagina. It can be difficult to feel this change in your own vagina.

Plateau phase. If sexual stimulation continues to be present and the woman continues to feel turned on by that stimulation, she will enter plateau phase. This phase can last from 30 seconds to three minutes. If stimulation is halted, the body returns to excitement phase.

If the woman has a sexual flush, it spreads dramatically during this stage. It may spread down breasts, neck, and face; extend over shoulders, the inner surfaces of the arms, the stomach, thighs, buttocks and back.

Breast size may increase as much as a fourth. According to Masters and Johnson, this is especially likely in women who have breastfed children. The nipple continues to enlarge; but this is not usually apparent, since the whole nipple is erect, not just the tip of it.

The clitoris retreats up under its hood. It may not be visible. If stimulation falters or is interrupted, the clitoris may reappear, retracting again when stimulation resumes.

Breathing, heartbeat, and blood pressure continue to increase.

In childless women, the labia majora smooth out even more, making the inner lips prominent. The outer lips may swell again if plateau phase is prolonged. In women who have had children, the labia majora become swollen and engorged. This change is more visible in some women than in others. In some women, the labia majora may hang in folds. The inner lips swell and become very sensitive.

There is also a color change in the inner lips (and once again, this change is more visible in some women than in others). Masters and Johnson found that if effective, pleasurable stimulation continued after this color change, orgasm would always occur within three minutes.

The vagina continues to produce lubrication. The amount a woman lubricates and the texture and consistency of the liquid vary. Some women hardly lubricate at all; other women lubricate enough to require a towel underneath them. The longer a woman is stimulated before orgasm, the more lubrication is formed. Vaginal lubrication is also affected by the phase of the menstrual cycle.

The upper vagina balloons still further, and the lower third of the vagina reaches its point of maximum congestion. This swelling in the lower third of the vagina has sometimes been called "the orgasmic platform." In some women, you can feel it with your finger.

The uterus may start contracting late in the plateau phase. The cervix may swell slightly.

Because of increased heartbeat and breathing, the woman is usually hyperventilating at this point. If she is in a supine position (on her back), she may have spasms in the muscles of her feet. Muscular tension is building throughout the entire body, and in some women this tension produces actual cramps in the feet or calves.

Sensitivity to pain decreases. The body is able to tolerate higher levels of stimulation and continue to experience those sensations as pleasurable.

Orgasm. The orgasm lasts from 3 to 15 seconds. The clitoris has retreated under its hood. The motion of the hood being pulled back and forth over the sensitive, swollen glans produces orgasm.

Coming is a reflex, a snapping in the pelvic muscles, that sends fluid and blood out of the tissues. It is a totally involuntary action and only occurs when enough congestion exists in the pelvic tissues. Therefore, like a knee-jerk or a sneeze, it cannot be willed or forced.

During orgasm, the sex flush maintains its peak of intensity. The more intense the orgasm, the brighter the flush. The veins continue to stand out in high relief on the breasts.

The orgasm may begin with a few uterine contractions. Most of the contractions take place in the vagina at 0.8 of a second. The inner lips may be seen to contract along with the vagina, and some women feel contractions in the anal sphincter or urethra as well. The strength of these contractions depends on how far vasocongestion has progressed and how strong the pelvic muscles are. There are 3 to 15 of these contractions, and the first 5 or 6 are usually the strongest. They are particularly strong during pregnancy and are usually stronger during masturbation than during sex with a partner. Oral sex and manual stimulation of the clitoris usually result in stronger vaginal contractions than vaginal penetration.

During orgasm, the clitoris remains under its hood. The orgasm will stop if clitoral stimulation is halted.

Resolution phase. If a woman has had an orgasm, resolution will take 10 to 25 minutes. If no orgasm occurs, it may take several hours for the body to return to the same physiological conditions it was in prior to any erotic stimulation.

During resolution phase, a fine film of perspiration appears, especially in areas covered by the sex flush. This film is not related to the amount of physical effort involved in reaching orgasm. The sex flush, if any, disappears in reverse order of its appearance; the last areas to show the flush are the first areas to fade. The area around the nipples loses its erection, leaving the nipples erect; then the size of the breasts decreases over 5 to 10 minutes. The veins fade, ceasing to stand out. Finally, all vestiges of a nipple erection disappear.

After an orgasm, the clitoral glans returns to its normal position in 5 to 10 seconds. It resumes normal size in 5 to 30 minutes but remains extremely sensitive and may be painful to touch. If the woman has not had an orgasm, the clitoris remains enlarged and engorged for several hours.

The outer lips in childless women increase to normal size in one or two minutes, or in even less time. Women who have borne children find their outer lips decreasing to usual size in 10 to 15 minutes. Once again, without orgasm these changes take several hours to occur.

The inner lips return to their usual color rapidly, in a matter of seconds. The size also returns to normal in about 5 minutes.

With orgasm, the uterus descends, and the vagina returns to regular size rapidly. Without orgasm, the walls of the vagina remain swollen for 20 to 30 minutes.

Multiple Orgasms

Masters and Johnson accidentally discovered that if stimulation continued during and after orgasm, some women would have more than one orgasm within a relatively short period of time. They were curious to find out just how many orgasms women could have. By using a vibrator, some of the women they studied had 20 to 50 orgasms before they quit; and they stopped because they were tired, not because they were physically incapable of having another orgasm. Theoretically, they could have kept on climaxing forever. (Women using manual stimulation did not have as many orgasms, because their hands got tired, as a vibrator never will.)

The term "multiple orgasms" was coined to describe this phenomenon. The potential insatiability of the human female is not present in the human male. After orgasm, most men experience a refractory period. If they are stimulated during this phase, erection and orgasm will not occur. It is true that some men experience more than one orgasm during masturbation or sex with a partner, but their capacity for climaxing is considerably less than that of women.

This discovery is especially interesting after so much argument over whether women could come at all. It challenges our social sex-role and gender system which defines men as the sexual pursuers, women as the passive and unwilling prey, and homosexuality as a frustrating and inferior activity. It is convincing evidence of the power of social and cultural conditioning. Sexuality seems to be incredibly plastic. It is so amenable to manipulation that calling it a "drive" or "instinct" seems ridiculous.

The fact that multiple orgasms are a possibility does not mean that all women should have them. Lesbians I have talked to have a variety of preferences. Some of them are emotionally and physically satisfied by one orgasm and don't bother with attempting a second or third. Other women like to wait until they have gone through resolution phase before resuming masturbation or lovemaking. Some women take a quick break after their first orgasm, then start again. There were also some lesbians who liked to see how long they could tolerate stimulation and how many orgasms they could have before exhaustion set in.

In some circles, multiple orgasms have become a new sexual standard which is applied exactly the way virginity is applied in high school—to sort out who is sexually okay and who is not. Don't feel obligated to change your pattern just because the potential is there. If you didn't know you could have more than one orgasm, you may want to keep going just to see what it feels like. If it doesn't intrigue you, that's okay too.

You may have a partner who likes to have more or fewer orgasms than you do. If you are worn out or satisfied and she is still excited, maybe you can take a break and let her masturbate. It doesn't mean that you are not a good lover, just that her needs are different. Similarly, having more than one orgasm isn't selfish or self-indulgent; it's simply the pattern your body prefers.

HOMAGE TO

Gerda Wegener
1885-1940

Illustrator, born in Denmark, worked in Paris

3
Partners

Sex is treated differently from other human needs. Nobody assumes you should "intuitively" know how to cook or "automatically" know how to build a shelter. Sex is the only skill we are expected to possess without receiving any instruction. Women are led to believe that good sex happens magically and naturally if you are with someone you love. Consequently, there is a lot of talk about love in this culture, and almost none about sex.

This myth is as prevalent in the lesbian community as it is elsewhere. It has several harmful side-effects. One is that any woman who is having difficulty with the sexual aspect of her relationship may begin to wonder if her partner really cares for her. She is more likely to end the relationship than she is to deal with the problem directly. Another consequence is that many women expect a partner to be able to read their minds and sense their sexual interest (or lack of it) and locate their erogenous zones without being given any clear, verbal direction. A third result is that there's a lot of confusion between lust and romance. Some women expect sex whenever affection exists, and they express needs to their friends that their friends aren't prepared to handle. Other lesbians expect love to result from any exciting physical encounter and treat all of their sex partners like long-term lovers. The consequences are painful and confusing. This myth has yet another effect, which is to place a stigma on experimenting sexually if you aren't committed to an ongoing relationship with your partner.

We do a disservice to our partners when we close our eyes, expect them to telepathically divine our hot spots and avoid our cold spots, and judge the quality of their love by the results. We also do a disservice to fledgling dykes if we expect them to sink or swim without getting explicit information about sexuality. We need to take positive action against the anti-lesbian bias of our culture. Lesbianism is one of the most closely kept secrets of Western civilization. A woman who is frustrated with male partners may never think of assessing her feelings about women. This happens even to women who are well aware of the existence of male homosexuality, because there is almost no erotica or educational material in general circulation which presents accurate and positive images of lesbian sexuality.

The next section deals with the sexual techniques women can use to pleasure each other.

Sexual Techniques

It is impossible to describe how to make love to another woman in terms of where to touch first and what kind of touch to use. Each woman is different. The most important thing is the feeling you want to communicate. When you are touching her, she needs to feel your lust and admiration. Your hands and eyes prove that you want her. Most women need this reassurance before they can really accept pleasure. You don't have to be silent. Flatter, cajole, demand. You don't have to be polite. Bed talk can run the gamut from poetry to curses.

If she is touching you, be equally expressive. Move into her caresses. Allow your hips to dance. Let noises emerge from your belly and throat. Reach for her. Let your hands and voice ask for what you want and need. You don't have to express your arousal in ways that don't come naturally to you. Some women do a lot of moving and make a lot of noise. Other women like to hold themselves very still and center in on every little thing she's doing.

There are a hundred ways to create sensations by manipulating the flesh. You can tickle her, massage her, bite her, kiss her (all over), lick her (and blow warm air across the wet, soft place), scratch her lightly or fiercely, hold her and even hang onto her, knead and stroke and explore.

Some parts of the body are supposed to be erogenous zones for everybody—for example, the breasts. But some lesbians find it turns their partners on to suck and play with their nipples more than it turns *them* on. If your partner doesn't respond to caresses that would drive you crazy, stop pretending you are making love to yourself. Make love to *her*. Everybody has places they especially love to have touched. Sensitive areas can include the armpits, ribs, the cleft of the ass, the inner thighs, ears, feet, behind the knees or the inside of the elbow. Go hunting. You may find a spot or two she has never properly appreciated before.

Some women like to spend a lot of time on whole-body touching before they focus on genital stimulation. It can also be a turn-on to strip her as quickly as possible, tumble her onto the bed or floor, and go right for her cunt. Either pattern could get boring if it's used too often.

A description of various types of genital stimulation follows.

Manual stimulation. Manual stimulation is also called hand-crafting. It's a nice technique because hands are so intelligent and deft. There is no awkward transition from caressing your lover's breasts, neck, or thighs to caressing her genitals.

When you use this technique for the first time with a new partner, ask her if she would mind showing you what kind of strokes she likes when she

masturbates. If she doesn't feel comfortable doing that or doesn't masturbate, ask her to show you what other women have done that felt good. As
you touch her, ask her what it feels like. Explore two different areas, then
ask her which part of her genitals is the most sensitive.

Different women like varying amounts of pressure, different rates of
speed, and prefer stimulation in different areas of the vulva. Experiment
and see what she responds to. If she is lubricating freely, muscle tension is
building, and her other responses indicate she is getting close to orgasm,
focus on the one pattern that seems to be most effective. You can ask her to
put her hand over yours and guide it, if you have a hard time interpreting
her reactions.

Good positions for using this technique are lying side by side, sitting between her legs while she is on her back, sitting or kneeling behind her while
she is on her hands and knees, both of you sitting up and facing each other,
both of you standing, or cradling her in your lap.

You may want to use some artificial lubricant. This will keep you from
irritating her clitoris and labia. It will also ease any concern she has about
not lubricating quickly or copiously enough. Any of the lubricants
mentioned in the section on self-examination is fine. Some women don't
need any additional lubrication, but it can still be a pleasant treat.

Pour some of the oil or lotion into your hand, warm it, and apply it to her
body. Caress and massage her. Warm some more lubricant, and apply it
to the genitals. You may want to use only a dab and add to it when it dries
out or gets spread around—or you may want to pour a lot of lubricant on
all at once and play with the slippery, messy, wetter-than-usual feeling.

Most women do not like to be touched directly on the clitoral glans, but
some like to be stimulated quite close to it. For this reason, it's nice to have
some light to work by, especially when you're getting familiar with a new
lover's patterns.

Some lesbians think that manual stimulation is "just like masturbation"
and feel negative about it for that reason. In fact, another term for this
technique is "mutual masturbation." Since masturbation is healthy and
fun, this seems to be a poor reason not to enjoy manual stimulation. When
another woman is present, adding her imagination and talent to the experience, it's obviously a very different experience from self-stimulation.

Oral sex. Oral sex is also called cunnilingus, going down, eating someone
out, and frenching. This technique involves using your lips, tongue, and
teeth (or gums, if you can take your teeth out) to stimulate your partner's
genitals. Oral sex brings more of your senses into contact with your
partner's sexual arousal. You can smell and taste her excitement. A tongue
working in combination with the rest of the mouth creates different sensa-

tions from hands or fingers and a feeling of being sampled and savored. Because your mouth is wet, you don't have to worry about irritation or scanty lubrication.

Good positions for oral sex are lying on your stomach between her thighs while she lies on her back, kneeling at her side and bending over her while she lies on her back, kneeling at her feet while she stands and leans against the wall, or having her kneel over your face.

Here are some things to ask a new partner before you go down on her: Does she like to have her clitoris sucked, or does she find that irritating? Does she know which part of her clitoris is most sensitive—the top, one side, underneath—or what motions she likes? Does she enjoy being nibbled on, or does she want you to keep your teeth to yourself? Does she like to feel you tonguing her vagina?

When you go down on her, let your mouth express how you feel about her. If you make noises when you get turned on, these will create vibrations in your mouth that will be transmitted to her genitals. Some women find this sensation tantalizing and delicious. The area between inner and outer lips is very sensitive. Long caresses from the top of the clitoral hood down to the anus feel good there. Some women like to have their labia nibbled on or gently sucked on. Take time to appreciate all the folds and hollows of her vulva. Go easy at first, then build in intensity.

If a partner is going down on you, don't lose contact with her. Hold her head, make sounds, move, let her know what feels good and what doesn't. Most women appreciate some direction. They want to make you feel good and would rather not waste time on things that are ineffective or unpleasant.

While you are doing cunnilingus, your jaw may get tired or you may get a hair stuck on your tongue. Come up for air. Smile at her, kiss, let her caress you for a while. It can be exciting to build close to the point of orgasm, come down a little, then build back up.

The slang term for doing cunnilingus simultaneously is 69. You can have her lie on top of you facing the opposite direction so you can eat each other at the same time, or lie side by side. Lesbians who like 69 say that they get turned on thinking about their partner experiencing the same sensations that they are. They find this experience very arousing. Some of these women like to continue mutual oral sex until both partners come. Sometimes a woman may reach a point where she can't do and be done to, and she either stops stimulating her lover or asks that her lover stop stimulating her so that the most excited partner can come.

Negative feelings about oral sex are connected to negative feelings about the female genitals. If you believe that the vulva is dirty or ugly, it will be difficult for you to either go down on a partner or allow her to go down on you. There are several things you can do to change misogynistic feelings like this. One is to taste your own lubrication the next time you masturbate. Chances are it won't be unpleasant. Women taste salty and sexy. Each woman has a unique flavor and perfume. Genuinely offensive odor is usually a symptom of a vaginal infection. Another thing you can do is bathe or shower with your partner before the two of you make love. Make it a sensuous experience. Talk to her suggestively, lather her up, make sure she rinses everywhere, and dry her a bit more thoroughly than is really necessary. Some lesbians like to put flavored syrup, whipped cream, pieces of fresh fruit, guacamole, or other tasty treats in their vaginas or on the vulva before their lovers eat them out. A folded sheet can protect the bed or floor. Don't worry about the mess. The mess is half the fun.

One thing to talk about with a partner is oral sex during menstruation. Some women really like the taste of menstrual blood and are disappointed if a lover forbids them to go down on her. Other women prefer that a menstruating partner wear a tampon or diaphragm to catch the blood. Some lesbians like to use other techniques while they or their partners are bleeding.

Tribadism. A lot of women use this technique without knowing it has a name. Some slang terms are humping, grinding, and slip-and-slide. Tribadism is done by rubbing your vulva against your partner's mons veneris, hip, or thigh. Some lesbians also like to rub against their partners' buttocks or other parts of the body.

You can hold your partner in your arms to do tribadism or have her lie on her stomach while you find a place you like on her ass. You can also get into a scissors position. Lie on your backs, heads at opposite ends of the bed, and interlace your legs until you can rub against each other's genitals.

Lesbians who prefer tribadism say they love the feeling of whole-body contact. The experience of timing hip movement and feeling your partner's motions is also very erotic. Because the speed and force of motion is so important, some lesbians prefer to take turns being on top so that both partners can get off. If you do tribadism in a side-by-side position, you can still switch off and take turns coming.

This style of lovemaking gets put down for being imitative of heterosexual intercourse. There are several important differences between tribadism and straight fucking. Unlike intercourse, tribadism involves direct clitoral stimulation. There's no sexist requirement that one partner be passive. This is an active and vigorous technique and is ideal for the woman who needs to move her hips freely and rhythmically before she can come.

Tribadism is easy to do when you don't want to take off all your clothes. You may like to hold your partner down and watch her face react to the motions of your hips. Both of you can use all of your muscles and feel each other's strength. It can be fun to grease up with a lot of baby oil before you do tribadism, and turn it into a semi-wrestling match.

Vaginal stimulation or penetration. Most women find that having something inside the vagina, either moving or at rest, changes the way arousal and orgasms feel. Some lesbians don't like any penetration and experience it as distracting and annoying. Other women like a little penetration—perhaps a slight sensation of movement at the entrance or a barely perceptible feeling of fullness and pressure. Other women enjoy maximum vaginal dilation or like very vigorous and fast penetration.

Some women like to combine oral sex, manual stimulation, or tribadism with penetration. Other women like to use penetration as foreplay and stop when they get close to coming, so that they can concentrate on clitoral stimulation. A few lesbians are able to come without direct clitoral stimulation if they have the right kind of vaginal penetration.

Fingers are probably put into cunts more often than anything else. The number is often important, so ask how many. Don't assume that it feels good just because it fits. Also check on depth. Does it feel best to her just at the entrance? Does she like pressure against the back wall? Is cervical manipulation pleasurable or painful for her? The type of penetration she likes may change as she gets more turned on. Some women like more vigorous stimulation as they get closer to coming. Other women like a constant, dependable, predictable feeling.

Some lesbians also use objects to stimulate the vagina. You can use many common household objects for this purpose—brush handles, kitchen utensils, the handle of a hand mirror—anything that is clean, washable, does not have sharp edges, and is not likely to break. You can also use fruits or vegetables. It can be fun to go on a lascivious shopping expedition for a banana or zucchini of the appropriate size and shape.

Some women prefer to buy sex toys that are designed for penetration. Sex toys are easy to keep clean and can be a better fit than things you find on your dresser or in your kitchen drawers. Because they have only one purpose, you can keep them in a central location and be fairly certain of finding them when they are needed.

Many battery-operated vibrators are vagina-shaped, egg-shaped, or slim enough to fit into the anus. Some lesbians enjoy the sensation of vibration within the vagina. They say it relaxes the sphincter muscle and hastens orgasm. Other women don't care about the vibrations and never bother to turn on their vibrators or replace worn-out batteries.

If the quick humming motion of the vibrator isn't important to you, you may want to buy or make a dildo. The dildoes available in sex shops are usually phallic in appearance, so many lesbians prefer to carve or cast their own.

Dildoes are probably the most taboo sex toys a lesbian could consider using. Relatively few lesbians have even seen a dildo. This is rather funny, since nine-tenths of the world is firmly convinced that dildoes are essential to lesbian lovemaking.

A real lesbian who wants to play with a dildo has motives that would be incomprehensible to the makers of commercial erotica or to clinical psychologists. She has fantasies about it, she can think of fun things to do with it, she wants to discover new ways to tickle her partner's fancy. She knows that women don't need men to be sexual. She also knows that simply refusing to use a dildo (or any sex technique) won't rid any woman of feelings of inferiority about her gender or self-hatred about her homosexuality.

Using a dildo puts the mythology about them into perspective. It is, after all, just a piece of plastic. Whatever symbolic meaning it has is assigned by our culture.

Some dildoes come with straps or harnesses that can be used to attach them to the body. Lesbians who have used strap-on dildoes say that they make it possible to use positions that allow whole-body contact. They leave hands free to wander and make it easier to provide clitoral and vaginal stimulation simultaneously.

Any object that you put into the vagina should be used with adequate lubrication. Clean it after use. Do not put anything directly from your vagina into another woman's vagina—you can spread vaginal infections. Never put anything into your vagina that has been in someone's anus. The bacteria that grow in the rectum can cause infections in the vagina. When purchasing objects for vaginal play, be realistic about the size. Something on the small side will always fit, whereas a large object may have to be saved for those times when you are especially turned on and relaxed.

Going inside your partner makes her rather vulnerable. Some lesbians find this is a special, intense emotional experience—a demonstration of trust or a safe way to express feelings of surrender and possession.

Women who like vaginal penetration may feel ambivalent about it and wonder if it isn't "sort of heterosexual." Any technique that two women use to arouse and please one another is a *lesbian* technique. There is no reason why women can't own the insides as well as the outsides of their genitals. Vaginas don't belong to men—they belong to women!

Some lesbians who like to include vaginal stimulation in their sexual pattern find they fantasize about gender changes. These fantasies have a good chance of causing a lot of needless guilt and anxiety. In this culture, gender is a box. Women are defined by the traits they don't share with men. This creates repressed possibilities, whole wilderness areas full of potential experience that we all have a deep hunger to explore. Why should anybody have to be one gender all the time or be a woman according to this culture's definition of womanliness? I see nothing wrong with fantasizing that you are an alien from another planet, a hermaphrodite, a gay man, a boa constrictor, a virgin, or anything else that pops into your head.

Anal sex. The anus is the body's most stigmatized orifice. It is supposed to be the most secret, dirty, nasty and unacceptable part of the body. Consequently, strong feelings of shame and privacy are closely connected to the anus. Because excretion is such a ritualized, secretive and obsessive process in our culture, a lot of fear of losing control is also connected with the anus. Including the anus in sex play can bring up all these feelings. Lesbians who enjoy anal sex say that, as with vaginal penetration, anal stimulation changes the way arousal and orgasms feel.

You can combine clitoral and anal stimulation; clitoral, vaginal and anal stimulation; alternate filling the anus and vagina, or penetrate both and temporarily ignore the clitoris. See how much variety having one more hole to play with can add to your repertoire?

Some things you can do to make the anus feel good are tickling the outside, blowing on it, licking it, applying pressure to it, inserting a finger or object, or creating friction inside it. The burden of its bad reputation makes the anus very tense, so treat it lovingly. The perineum—the skin between vagina and anus—is very sensitive. Many women love to be stroked there as preparation for anal play. If you apply pressure to or penetrate the asshole, use a thick lubricant. Petroleum jelly is okay for anal use. If you are using a greased-up object, be sure it won't slip out of your hand. Something with a flared base is best. It is difficult to retrieve objects lost in the rectum.

Once something is inside the rectum, you may feel some contractions and a sensation of discomfort. Try deep breathing and relaxing. If there is no motion or friction, just pressure, your anus will gradually open up and stop contracting. Movement in and out of the anus will be more comfortable then.

Most of us are taught that piss and shit are dirty. Many women find they have to get over a fear of piss to be able to go down on another woman. A similar barrier exists with anal sex. Phobic feelings about shit prevent many women from viewing the anus as an erogenous zone.

Why do we have such different feelings about taking in nourishment and the processes our bodies use to eliminate poisons or cool off? Eating, pissing, sweating, and shitting all feel good to a healthy person. The negative feelings we have about shit seem out of proportion to its real nature. Shit is a substance not unlike mud. It has its own smell and consistency, just like any other substance. Small children have to be taught that it is ugly and nauseating. I suspect that if shit smelled like violets, we would think violets were weeds.

Paranoia about seeing or touching shit is usually justified by identifying it with disease. Communicable diseases can be passed on during anal sex, especially during oral contact. But if your partner is healthy to begin with, you have little to worry about. If your partner has an infectious disease, you run a risk of catching it no matter what kind of sex you have.

There are ways to get around negative feelings about the anus and excrement, if you want to experiment with anal sex. The outer anus can be cleaned with warm water. Inserting a finger will usually not bring you into contact with feces, since they are stored inches away from the anal opening. If you like, your partner can take an enema (a pint of warm water should do) to clean out the rectum.

Some women who try anal sex decide they don't like the way it feels. Other women enjoy the vulnerability, the slight discomfort, and the feeling of being nasty or naughty or the fantasy of losing control. It's something to ask a new partner about, especially if you like doing it. Many lesbians who feel no qualms about asking for other kinds of sex will hesitate to suggest anal play.

Simultaneous orgasm. There is a tendency to view simultaneous orgasm as an extra-special event. Its occurrence is supposed to indicate that you and your partner are very close, exceptionally attuned to one another, and extremely knowledgeable about each other's responses. This is sometimes an accurate description of the situation. However, simultaneous orgasms are just as likely to happen by accident.

Working for simultaneous orgasms can sometimes interfere with good sex. Having a goal can create performance anxiety and kill spontaneity. If you can't get the timing right, the woman who comes first may agonize over her lack of self-control, while the woman who came second chides herself for being too inhibited.

Some lesbians have a lot of fun doing their favorite thing simultaneously and seeing who can hold out the longest, or trying to come together. I think the deciding factor is how much you and your partner invest in the outcome. If it doesn't really matter and you can enjoy it no matter who comes first or together, any simultaneous orgasms that do happen are a nice bonus.

A word of caution: Before you moan, "Wow, another simultaneous orgasm!" and roll over to snore, check it out. Make sure the earth moved for both of you.

Lesbian Relationships

It has often been said that lesbians are free to form intimate relationships which are supportive of personal growth and tailored to individual needs, because no institutions exist to dictate and enforce any particular type of lesbian relationship. It is true that the phrases "community property," "alimony," "child support" and "adultery" have no legal meaning when applied to a lesbian couple. However, in the absence of governmental agencies and institutionalized religion, lesbians have developed their own social and cultural mores. The opinions and traditions of our own subculture can acquire more power over our behavior than the larger society. After all, if we become outlaws within our own community, where will we go?

Standards of acceptable sexual conduct vary from city to city. If the lesbian population is large enough, standards also vary from clique to clique. There are conservative communities where promiscuity is frowned upon. Women who like to have sex with many different partners may feel pressured into giving lip service to monogamy (they are only "looking for the right woman") and may conceal their sexual activity or curb it. Single lesbians may feel unwelcome at social events because everyone else is tightly coupled. In circles where monogamy is frowned upon as being old-fashioned and politically suspect, a woman with just one lover may feel guilty and apologetic. If she forces herself to be nonmonogamous, she may suffer from jealousy and insecurity. A sexually active lesbian who is manipulative and somewhat callous of her partners' feelings may escape criticism by labeling her behavior as a reaction to possessive or conservative lovers.

In addition to community mores, the types of relationships we form are limited by our social skills, the available opportunities to meet other lesbians, our private morality, the level of experience and degree of familiarity with our own needs, and the preferences of the women we relate to.

It can be very difficult to sort out the pros and cons of monogamy, non-monogamy and celibacy, and decide which is right for you at any given point in your life. This decision is complicated by the fact that another woman (or other women's) feelings are affected by what you do. Each of these three basic choices is discussed below. Because this is a book about sexuality, I've focused on the erotic aspects of each type of relationship. There's more to a relationship than sex, of course. Getting close to another woman usually involves talking and making decisions about money, whether or not you are going to live together, who you will socialize with and where, housework, what each of you will disclose to the outside world about your relationship, and a million other things. A whole book could (and should) be written about lesbian relationships.

Monogamy. For some lesbians a pledge of fidelity is the prerequisite of any serious, worthwhile relationship. They believe that sexual exclusivity is part of really loving someone. Monogamy is the most socially acceptable form of sexual behavior. Some women feel that they need not abandon standards of sexual conduct they learned as young people just because they are lesbians. Some monogamous lesbian couples feel the need to celebrate their relationship with a marriage performed by gay clergy or to recite their own vows to a private gathering of friends.

There are varying degrees of monogamy. Some women have a more stringent notion of it than others. There are lesbian couples who do not socialize individually, dance with or flirt with other women. Other couples agree that their outside relationships can be intimate and even romantic, provided they do not include sex. Still other couples make special agreements to cover exceptions to the rule. These exceptions can include visits out of town, the return of a former (and still desirable) lover, group sex parties, or short-term infatuations with handsome strangers.

Monogamy can provide a lot of stability and security. It offers an opportunity for two women to become very familiar with each other's personalities histories and sexuality. Some lesbians feel monogamy makes it easier to make long-term plans with a lover. This familiarity can be safe and reassuring and foster deep intimacy. However, such a relationship runs the risk of becoming boring and predictable. Monogamous couples often make deliberate changes in their routine to keep some mystery and excitement in their romance. Frequent vacations, changes in personal appearance, new hobbies, or new sexual adventures are things some couples try. The important thing is to let your partner know you don't take her for granted.

Monogamy does not guarantee that you will never be lonely, bored, or worried. No relationship can. There's no guarantee that monogamy will eliminate jealousy from your life either. There are two kinds of jealousy. One is a feeling of insecurity about your relationship. You may ask yourself, "Does she still want and need me?" When this happens, it's usually easy to get the reassurance you need. But the second kind of jealousy is insecurity about your own worth. If you start to wonder whether you are desirable or lovable, the most patient and comforting lover in the world cannot quiet your doubts.

Generally speaking, monogamy works best if there is lots of agreement over basic sexual preferences and life goals. You will probably need to have support and assistance from the outside to keep your relationship together. Some couples find it helpful to see a counselor at regular intervals to make sure their communication stays open and grievances get settled. Socializing with other couples can also be helpful. Some lesbians have joint checking accounts or make agreements to purchase household items together to strengthen their ties.

Nonmonogamy. Promiscuity has a bad name. The word implies a lack of discrimination and finer feelings. Actually, the length of a relationship is not always a gauge of its quality. Some lesbians feel it would be a shame not to enjoy the women who are available for a night or a week of love as well as the women who are available in perpetuity. There are several kinds of nonmonogamous relationships.

Some lesbians have one primary partner (with whom they may or may not live) and form secondary, more casual liaisons with other women. There are three problems with this kind of relationship. The first is finding a lover who feels good about your relating sexually to other women. The second is working out your own feelings about her other lovers or her lack of other lovers. The third problem is dealing with the way your "casual liaisons" feel about this arrangement. This pattern is attractive because it represents a compromise between rigid, complete monogamy and being single. Ideally, both women have the benefits of stability and intimacy with a lover they feel very much attached to, and the excitement of occasional (or regular) affairs.

Some lesbians don't like the idea of categorizing their partners as being more or less important, primary or secondary. They think of themselves as single and avoid any appearance of being coupled. These women encounter some prejudice based on the notion that refusing to form permanent relationships is a sign of immaturity. Lesbians who are coupled may feel threatened by single lesbians and avoid getting close to them.

Other lesbians have primary relationships with more than one partner. Three or more women may agree to consider themselves a romantic and sexual unit. This arrangement sometimes evolves out of a couple if both partners fall in love with the same woman and she is equally attracted to both of them. Triangles and other polygons raise a few eyebrows, since most of us are conditioned to think of erotic energy as a current that flows between two women—no more and no less.

Any form of nonmonogamy is no insurance against loneliness. You can have twenty lovers and still wind up spending Saturday night alone. When you feel lonely and depressed, it's easy to get suckered in by the myth that couples always take good care of each other and keep each other perfect company. It just isn't so. It's very possible to feel unloved and alone with your best friend sitting right next to you. Good friends and lovers can cushion the bumps, but they can't eliminate them.

Nonmonogamy works best for two kinds of lesbians: those women who get turned on rather than angry when they hear about a lover's erotic exploits, and those women who don't particularly need to know about their lover's erotic exploits. Spiritual and financial independence are also helpful.

Celibacy. A deliberate decision to cultivate your own company and give yourself a vacation from sex is sometimes wise. For some lesbians, being celibate means giving up orgasms altogether. Other lesbians continue to enjoy masturbation while they forego romantic entanglements. I have met couples as well as individual lesbians who chose to be celibate for specified periods of time, and one couple that decided to eliminate sex from their relationship permanently. Some of these couples were engaged in conflicts they needed to resolve before they could be sexual again. Others wanted to intensify their desire for each other and felt that abstinence would provoke appetite. Others found that they felt so guilty about having sex that it created tension which disturbed an otherwise pleasant and rewarding companionship.

Generally speaking, celibate women get even less support than single lesbians. Everybody seems to assume that if you're alive and well you're having sex with somebody, and masturbation still doesn't count as "real sex" in most circles. Friends may try matchmaking or offer subtler forms of criticism.

Trust your own judgment. No one else can really tell you what is best for you. Lesbians I have talked to mention many positive aspects of celibacy. They speak of being able to spend more time alone, thinking or reading or working; paying more attention to friends; assessing old habits and ways of relating to other women; healing old hurts; and learning how to be self-sufficient.

Contracts. When you form a relationship with another woman or other women, think of the process as negotiating a contract rather than enforcing standards or issuing ultimatums. Remember that she has her own set of preferences and needs that probably don't coincide with yours. Beware of someone who makes you feel there is no room for compromise or who makes you feel that your preferences are unreasonable or wrong. There may be too much difference between you to form a close relationship. Some women find it helpful to actually write out the terms of their contract and may make an agreement to evaluate and renegotiate it after a certain period of time.

Role-Playing

Within the lesbian community, it is a cliche that role-playing used to flourish but has vanished now that we've all joined the women's movement.

58

It is true that novels like *The Well of Loneliness* and movies like *The Fox* or *The Killing of Sister George* seem a little strange, inaccurate or funny to modern lesbians because they portray relationships organized around rather extreme or ritualistic butch/femme roles. However, I suspect that the flat statement "Lesbians don't role-play" qualifies as a myth.

Creating a public persona in the lesbian subculture is an important part of coming out. It used to be taken for granted that a young lesbian would decide whether to emphasize the masculine or the feminine aspects of her personality and appearance. This whole process still exists, though in a slightly altered form. The costumes have changed, the social mannerisms and etiquette have altered, but the continuum of masculininty and femininity continues to have meaning in the lesbian world. Most modern lesbians can tell you (if pressed) which of their acquaintances are butch and which are femme. Some women, of course, escape categorization.

Not only do the roles still exist—values are attached to them. Today's lesbian subculture puts a high value on sexual aggressiveness, independence, competence, a confrontive personality, and the possession of "non-traditional" job skills. There is much more tolerance for women who dress on the butchy side than there is for women who turn up at the bar in skirts, too much jewelry, or the least trace of makeup. It is infinitely more desir-able to be known as a woman who is sexually active and experienced than to have a reputation for passivity or naivete. Femmes are suspect. They may not really be lesbians. They are viewed as being more prone to emotional upsets and more likely to defect than butches. This value system makes women who are typed as femmes feel angry and sometimes worthless.

Role-playing has many purposes and functions. It can be a game—a form of erotic theater. Some lesbians consciously manipulate their drag and behavior and create or choose the most appropriate setting to bring some fantasy character to life. By acting out a part of your personality that's normally kept under wraps, you can explore new experiences and try out new situations. Used this way, a role can be adopted for one dance, an evening, or be reserved for use with one particular partner. You may want to acquire new insight into yourself or simply intensify your pleasure for an hour. Of course, masculinity and femininity are not the only dimensions of such a role.

A role adopted during social interactions may or may not carry over into sex. The woman who teaches self-defense, drives a motorcycle, wires her own stereo and buys all your drinks may want you to throw her down on the floor and call all the shots. The belle who lets you take her out to din-ner, waits for you to tell the cab driver where to go, and hands you her key to open the door may drag you inside and pounce on you at the foot of the stairs. It is more common for women to try to signal via their dress and

mannerisms what they are into sexually. These signals are difficult to interpret, since many lesbians are a little shy about being sexually active, and our
community doesn't have a well-developed code to guide our erotic negotiations.

Some women find that dressing or acting in a way which they conceive of
as being masculine or feminine is an essential part of their self-image. They
do not feel comfortable or genuine unless they can look and move in a way
that is consistent with their preferred role, and they have little or no desire
to alter the characteristics of that role. Some of these lesbians have ambigu-
ous feelings about their gender and might be labeled transsexual. Others
may find their preferred costume has an erotic value and could perhaps be
defined as transvestites. Still others are simply lesbians who are into role-
playing. They select their sexual partners and lovers from members of the
complementary role.

Lesbians who consciously engage in role-playing are an embarrassment
to the lesbian/feminist community. They are often treated like oddities or
family secrets. Some women suspect them of being apolitical or hetero-
imitative. Women who do not conform to the feminine stereotype are often
treated badly outside the lesbian community as well. They are subject to
harassment on the street and frequently suffer job discrimination or
housing discrimination. Their problems are sometimes ignored by other
lesbians, who feel that they would receive better treatment if they dressed or
acted in a "more appropriate" way.

I sometimes think that these lesbians get criticized so much simply because they are more accessible than patriarchal institutions. Two women
who choose to relate to each other as butch and femme are not necessarily
oppressing one another. They have found a system that works well for
them, gratifies their sexual fantasies, and utilizes the best of their individual
abilities. Role-playing in the lesbian community operates with a lot more
flexibility than gender and sex-role stereotyping in the larger society. It
takes some complicated mental gymnastics to accuse any woman who prefers other women as sexual partners of imitating heterosexuals. A femme
woman who wants a butch woman lover would not be satisfied with a male
partner. She wants a particular type of woman. She is a lesbian.

The whole issue of role-playing has become divisive. Older and younger
lesbians have trouble communicating with each other because we have different rules for developing, expressing, and changing sexual roles. A
lesbian who has been out two years has a lot to learn about her own culture
and its past from a lesbian who has been out twenty years. Older lesbians
should not be isolated from new developments and current events created
by women who are their cultural and political descendants. It would be
healthy for our community if we could surmount all such differences.

Finding Partners

A lesbian's first problem centers on finding out she's gay. Her second problem is finding out who else is.

We often use the phrase "lesbian community" without much sense of what it is, how it developed, and what its limitations are. In urban centers, the lesbian community consists of formal organizations created to take action on various lesbian issues, bars or restaurants which cater to a lesbian clientele, private social networks or "friendship families," and the parts of the gay male subculture which tolerate or welcome lesbian participation. Even in large cities, other lesbians can be hard to find if you don't know where to start looking. Outside of large cities, lesbianism is nearly invisible. Identifying other lesbians is a dangerous and difficult process. Rural communities of lesbians tend to be composed of groups of women who organized in the city, raised money, bought land, and moved to the country together. Sometimes the isolated lesbian's only contact with other lesbians is through the printed word—magazines, newspapers, penpals, or letters from organizations.

If you are having trouble finding a lesbian community in your area, ask yourself whether it is reasonable to expect to find one. Many lesbians choose to move to a city that has lesbian bars and political activity because they cannot tolerate isolation. This process can be difficult and scary. Gay organizations do their best to cope with the housing, employment, and social needs of newcomers, but this is an enormous task. Despite the financial and emotional problems involved in relocating, it can be rewarding. Many lesbians find that their feelings of depression and self-hatred were caused by feeling alone and being surrounded by people who ignored, invalidated, or attacked their sexuality.

Simply finding groups of other lesbians can solve many women's social difficulties. They are able to use the skills they learned in childhood and adolescence to make friends, meet lovers, and form support networks. Other lesbians have a harder time of it. Some women become aware of their homosexuality (or at least an absence of heterosexuality) at a very early age. They may isolate themselves or be isolated from their peers because they cannot fake an interest in the opposite sex. Adolescents who are sexually active are often treated harshly. Gay teenagers have little opportunity to learn how to date, make friends, or begin and end romantic involvements. Consequently, some lesbians find they have feelings of low self-esteem, awkwardness, or neediness that interfere with forming adult relationships.

Social skills can be learned at any point in your life. In fact, as we meet and deal with new situations, most of us acquire new social skills throughout our lives. There are several things lesbians commonly do to make it easier to find partners.

To begin with, realize that most of the women you meet will have had the same feminine conditioning that you did. This means that most women find it very difficult to make the first move. The lady who sits next to you all night without saying a word may be dying for you to ask her if she's having a good time or invite her to dance. It isn't easy. You don't know in advance whether she'll say yes or no. But somebody has to get things started, and it's better strategy to pick women you find attractive and approach them than it is to wait for someone to approach you. You won't die if she says no. Your feelings may be hurt, your self-confidence may be impaired, but you will still be around to try again. So don't ever give up—try again. A rejection may have nothing to do with you. She may already be involved. She may not be feeling like company. On some other evening, your invitation might have been accepted.

Take it slow. Be as relaxed as possible. Don't ask someone to dance and then ask her to go home with you and stay forever. Once you've made the initial move, don't be afraid to wait for her to pursue the relationship. If it's too one-sided, you'll do all the work, and you'll never be sure of her feelings for you.

You will probably be more relaxed and rejections will sting a little less if you are feeling good yourself and have other sources of emotional support. It takes more than a lover to make a rich, rewarding life. Bring the other things that make you happy into your environment. Be aware that it is often more important to have friends than it is to have a lover. Friends are a source of comfort and fun. They can help you out of the miseries, introduce you to new people they meet, and generally make your life easier. Friends are people you can give your attention and affection, and sometimes not being able to give love is as painful as not receiving it.

If, when you meet a woman who interests you, you are at a loss for what to say to her or where to take her, consider what you would do if she were your friend. Ask her about her life, her work, her plans for the future, where and when she came out. Invite her to do things you think are fun and interesting. If it seems too scary to ask her out on an official date, create a group event. Invite her to a picnic on the beach, a movie, a museum, an evening of dancing, and invite your other friends as well.

It is generally a bad idea to do anything if your only reason for doing it is to meet a sex partner or lover. That includes going to a bar, joining a group, playing on a team, and going to a party. You will feel pressured, look uncomfortable, and have a lousy time. You are more likely to meet women you have things in common with if you choose events that you can enjoy for their own sake.

You may find that you don't have the ability or knowledge you need to make the best of a certain social situation. For instance, it's hard to have a good time in a bar if you don't know how to dance, play pool or pinball, or make small-talk. If you don't know how, ask. She may not know how to dance or play pool either, but she'll have fun trying with somebody who doesn't come on like an expert. Know-it-alls are boring and irritating. If you're in a discussion group that wanders onto topics you're unfamiliar with, corner somebody and ask her for a reading list—or better yet, would she take you home and loan you some books that would inform you on the subject matter?

Taking the initiative is a big challenge. Going new places, introducing yourself, calling another woman up and making plans to do things with her involves taking risks with your pride. But there are two ways to never find friends or lovers. One is to stay home. The other is to go someplace, stick to yourself and look miserable. Go after what you want!

HOMAGE TO

Gerda Wegener
1885-1940

Illustrator, born in Denmark, worked in Paris

4

Communication

Several things can stop us from communicating as clearly as we'd like to about sexual issues and needs. First of all, we aren't given the background or the vocabulary we need to feel comfortable discussing sex. Some of us do not know exactly what we want from a lover and are afraid to appear inexperienced or naive. Other lesbians may have trouble verbalizing their preferences because they feel some guilt or discomfort about them. Fear that a partner will feel threatened or reject us can be another big obstacle to open communication about sex.

This chapter describes four different exercises that individual lesbians, pairs or groups of lesbians can use to enhance their communication skills.

Sex Terms

One difficulty lesbians encounter when they start discussing sexuality is the language itself. There are two sets of words available for exchanging sexual information. There are medical or clinical terms like clitoris, vagina, tribadism, and cunnilingus; and there is a slang vocabulary, which includes words like dyke, cunt, and finger-fucking. Many women feel awkward using clinical sex terms because they sound cold and most of them are rather long. The slang terms have frequently been used to express contempt for sex and women, which makes them offensive to many lesbians.

In addition to this problem, almost everyone has a set of sex terms that they automatically react negatively to. The words themselves trigger a bad feeling when they are used, regardless of who uses them or in what context they appear. These words are said to have a "charge" on them—a charge of negative energy.

Some lesbians deal with these difficulties by never using explicit terms to talk about sex. They rely on euphemisms like "it" or "down there" and communicate their desires with nonverbal signals like noises, eye contact, body movement, and facial expressions. With an exceptionally intuitive partner, or after a lot of trial and error, the message gets across. Some degree of misunderstanding is inevitable. This communication system makes it impossible to answer direct questions about sex and puts a lot of responsibility for detective work on your partner.

Direct communication saves time and energy that can be used to enhance the sexual experience. Individual lesbians and lesbians as a group need to develop a vocabulary of sex terms we can enjoy using. There are two ways to construct or enlarge a lesbian vocabulary of sex terms. Words that have been used in anti-sex, anti-lesbian ways can be co-opted. By using these terms with pride, lesbians can liberate them and change their meaning. The word "dyke" has already been transformed this way. Several terms for the female genitals, including "cunt," are also passing into the lesbian language. We can also make up our own terms. "Lesbiate," "feminate" and dyking it" are newly coined, feminist terms for lesbian lovemaking. "Rubbing up" is a woman-created term for masturbation.

To do the sex terms exercise, take three sheets of paper. Label one of them "female genitals," another "masturbation," and a third "lesbian sexuality." Take each sheet of paper in turn and write down all the words or phrases you can think of that fit under each heading. Don't censor yourself—write down all the terms you know about or use, pleasant and unpleasant, pro-woman and homophobic.

After you have completed your list, go through and rate each term. Which of them do you use and feel comfortable with? Which ones do you feel neutral about? Which terms have a negative charge for you? See how many of the terms are slang, how many are medical terminology, and how many are of lesbian manufacture. What do you have the most words to talk about? What do you have the fewest words to talk about?

This exercise can make you aware of the contents of your own sex terms vocabulary. It can also point out which words have a negative charge for you. If another woman uses those terms, you may have a hard time listening to her or supporting her right to express herself. Everyone has a different set of sex terms they feel comfortable using. This vocabulary varies with age, class, cultural background, and race. To forbid or discourage the use of any sex term may make it more difficult than it already is for some women to talk about sex.

If you are having a conversation about sex with another lesbian and she seems ill at east, try using the same terminology she does. It's probable that she will experience this as validating and relax a little more about talking to you.

Sensitivity Diagram

Trace the diagram of the vulva on a piece of white paper. Use crayons, colored pencils, felt-tip markers or paints to color the tracing according to your own genital sensitivity. You may want to use darker shades of one color for very sensitive areas and lighter shades for areas that are less sensitive, or you may want to use more than one color.

It can be fun to do this with a partner. If you take turns doing show-and-tell, it's a low-pressured way of finding out where and how you both like to be touched.

This exercise requires you to be very specific about your own body. It may be difficult to focus in on exactly how you masturbate or exactly where you want a partner to begin and end up.

As you explain your drawing, you may find it necessary to add information about how your sensitivity changes as you get turned on, whether you like your vibrator in a different place from where you like her tongue, and how much penetration (if any) you find enjoyable.

Sex Histories

You can write this exercise down for your own information or share it with others you are close to. This is a good way to connect your past, the way you currently express your sexuality, and the changes you would like to make in the future. Knowing what we were first told about sex and what early experiences we had with it sometimes makes our adult attitudes and needs more comprehensible.

To do your sex history, answer the following questions:

1. What is the earliest sexual experience, feeling or thought you can remember? How did you feel about it at the time?

2. As a young person, what did you do when you wanted to know more about sex?

3. What were some of the messages you got about your sexuality while you were growing up?

4. Did you masturbate as a child or explore sex with other children? Ever get caught? Did you have any consensual or nonconsensual experiences with adults?

5. Do you have orgasms now? If you do, what do they feel like? How many do you like to have during masturbation and during sex with a partner? If you don't have orgasms, describe how you experience your sexuality without them. Are you interested in having them? If you are, what do you think might help them to happen?

6. What was your first sexual experience with another woman like? If you have never had a sexual experience with another woman, describe your fantasy of what this would be like.

7. If you have had a sexual experience with another woman, how do your early experiences compare with the way you have sex with other women now?

8. How long have you gone without having sex with another person? Without masturbating? How did you feel about this experience?

9. What is the greatest number of sex partners you have had in the shortest amount of time?

10. What is the most unusual thing you've ever done sexually? How did you feel about it at the time? How do you feel about it now?

11. What part does masturbation play in your sexuality today? How do you masturbate now (if you do)? If you don't masturbate, how do you feel about that?

12. If you could change anything in your current sexual pattern, what would you do?

13. What keeps you from getting what you want?

If you choose to share this exercise with another person, read the material on ground rules before you take each other's sex histories.

Ground Rules

These guidelines are intended to provide a safe framework within which honest communication can take place. They are a revised version of ground rules created by the staff of the Resource Center for Human Relations in Oakland, California. Conversations between friends or lovers, conflict negotiations, or group discussions can be facilitated by use of these suggestions.

1. *Speak from your own experience.* It is often easier to make broad, general statements (such as "Lesbians tend to be monogamous.") than it is to make a personal statement that has some risk attached to it (such as "I don't want you to have an affair with Suzy."). Generalizations can't be proved or disproved, so they sidetrack discussions. Begin your statements with the word "I." Talk about your own experiences and take responsibility for your own feelings.

2. *Listen and respond without making judgments on the other woman's experience.* One way to avoid hearing statements that make us uncomfortable is to label the speaker as immature, weird, or unimportant. You don't have to agree with what another woman is saying, but it is important to understand the content of her message. Rather than saying, "It's really strange of you to feel that way," try, "What you're saying is making me a little nervous."

3. *Respect confidentiality.* Sexual information can be volatile. Don't solicit someone's trust and confidence unless you merit it. Using secrets to get revenge or score social points will destroy your credibility.

4. *Maintain a cycle of communication.* The cycle of communication has four stages:

  a. The speaker sends a message to her listener, being as clear and direct as possible.

  b. The listener receives the message, paying close attention to what is being said.

  c. The listener acknowledges the message.

  d. If the message is understood, the listener responds appropriately to its content. If the message is not understood, the listener paraphrases (repeats what she heard) to give the speaker a chance to verify or correct it.

If communication gets snarled and you can't figure out why, try checking the cycle to see where it broke down. Common problems with each phase are (1) It's obvious that someone who isn't being clear and direct has little chance of being understood. A deliberate attempt to be confusing or vague is manipulative and dishonest. (2) If the listener is inattentive or hostile, the message will either go right by her or get badly distorted. (3) If the listener isn't acknowledging the speaker—saying "uh huh," nodding, or using eye contact—she may give up or feel so discouraged that the quality of the message will suffer. Nothing is quite so embarrassing as exposing your feelings to a person who may be computing the value of *pi* or making out her grocery list. (4) If you don't bother to paraphrase when you receive the message, you may respond to something the speaker didn't say. Check on the accuracy of your understanding.

Paying close attention to the communication cycle slows things down. This can be very helpful in minimizing tension and anxiety. If something is important, it is worth taking enough time to discuss completely and carefully. With sexual issues, more than information is being exchanged. Women's feelings are at stake.

5. *Feel free to talk about anything.* Give each other permission to explore the variety and diversity of lesbian sexuality. Women have been silent on this subject for so long that we really know very little about it. It would be silly to limit the scope of your discussion in advance or assume that certain topics need never come up between lesbians. Every lesbian knows what it feels like to censor herself in self-defense. Do you want to do that to another woman? Support other lesbians, not for conformity but for honesty.

HOMAGE TO

Suzanne Ballivet

active around 1945

Illustrator

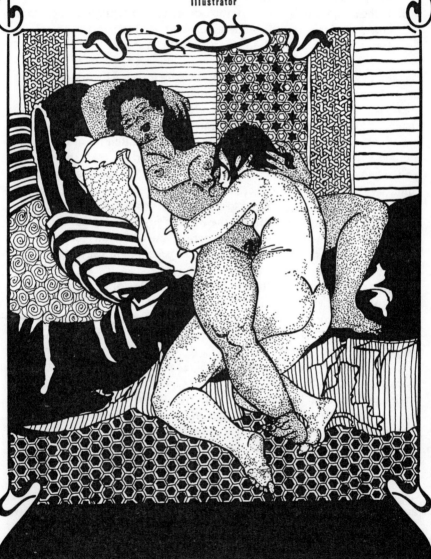

5

Common Sexual Concerns

This culture puts a high value on work that results in a tangible product, and self-sacrifice for the sake of a long-term goal. Any activity that has no purpose beyond the pleasure involved in participating in it is suspect. We tend to view our bodies as machines and pay as little attention to them as possible to keep them functioning. Genuine relaxation is rare. Sensuality has become a luxury.

When something goes wrong with our bodies, we tend to think of the problem as an illness or a failure. We are more likely to take a drug (prescribed or self-selected) than we are to assess the quality of our lives. We may feel guilty for "giving in to it" and push ourselves even harder.

A sexual problem is not always an illness or a failure. Lots of things can put the mind and body out of harmony and create a temporary state where sex is problematic. Starting work on a new job, taking exams, or expecting a visit from difficult relatives are examples of common preoccupations. Sometimes our bodies are simply not equal to the demands we put on them. In that case, it makes more sense to improve nutrition, rest and play more often, and reduce stress than it does to feel guilty or ingest pharmaceuticals.

Since many of us are ill-informed about our physical selves and a little paranoid about our bodies, once a sexual problem pops up it causes a lot of anxiety. Negative feelings we have about our lesbianism and doubts about our self-worth come to the surface. Being worried about the problem can create tension that gets in the way of sexual pleasure. This makes it more likely that the problem will recur. If this process isn't interrupted, a minor snag can become a major roadblock. This vicious cycle can be broken by taking the pressure off. You don't have to perform, and you don't have to be perfect.

Some sexual problems are caused or exacerbated by lack of information. Knowing more about other lesbians' sexuality, female anatomy and physiology can sometimes point the way out of a sexual difficulty.

Some of the more common sexual concerns lesbians can have are discussed below. Specific suggestions for ways to cope with or change the situation are included. There are probably some concerns that are not mentioned. I hope we will begin to talk more about our anxieties and sexual difficulties within the lesbian community and share information on how to deal with them. We know more about our own sexuality than most

71

researchers or therapists, and we could do a lot to reassure and help one another.

Concerns About Orgasm

Nobody knows how many women have never experienced an orgasm or are unable to climax during sex with a partner. Kinsey (1953) found that one out of four married women did not experience orgasm during sexual intercourse. This figure may have little or no significance to lesbians, who use different sexual techniques. In the time that has elapsed since Kinsey's study, sex education has become more widespread, and the feminist movement has agitated for a woman's right to control her own body and sexual experiences. In my recent study on lesbian sexuality (1979), seven respondents (2%) of a sample of 286 lesbians had never experienced orgasm. This statistic cannot be used to predict anything about lesbians in general. (This is because the population of lesbians is hidden, and no one knows what characteristics a sample of lesbians would have to have to be representative of all lesbians.) However, it does verify that some lesbians do not have orgasms.

This is not necessarily a problem. Some women feel that focusing on orgasm is antithetical to sensuality and relaxed lovemaking. They feel satisfied if a sexual experience is loving, tender, or creates other good feelings, and are not disappointed by lack of a sexual climax.

There are also lesbians who feel that a sexual encounter without orgasms is unsatisfying and pointless. If such a woman is confronted with a partner who doesn't come and doesn't care, she may have a lot of trouble accepting her partner's attitude. She may try desperately to "make" her partner come, feel inadequate if it doesn't happen, and accuse her partner of withholding trust or affection.

In a trusting and open relationship, partners can communicate their sexual satisfaction—or lack of it. A woman who is pressuring her partner to come may be experiencing lots of anxiety about the quality of her lovemaking. She may need reassurance that her lover is happy and pleased with her and would communicate her distress if any problems occurred.

If you and your lover(s) are engaged in a conflict over this issue, work extra hard to keep your sexual communication clear. It sometimes helps if the nonorgasmic partner lets her lover know when she is ready to stop having sex or to take a break. Many lesbians use orgasms to time the tempo or the end of a sexual encounter. Without orgasms, they are not sure when to begin, leave off, speed up or slow down.

Some lesbians feel frustrated because they never or rarely experience orgasms. They may not be sure exactly what an orgasm feels like or why everybody makes such a fuss about it, but they would like to have a choice. How do women learn how to have orgasms? In my study on lesbian sexuality, 152 respondents (53.1% of the sample) reported that they experienced their first orgasm during masturbation. It is usually easier to learn how to have an orgasm during masturbation than it is during sex with a partner. When you are alone, there is no need to worry about how much time you are taking, whether or not your partner is bored, or whether or not you are doing it in the right way. There is no pause between desire and gratification. You can do what you imagine you might like as soon as it comes into your head. You don't have to get up the nerve to describe your fantasy to another person. You also don't need to worry about how you'll look if you lose control. There is no one to watch or judge, just you, alone.

Some women find it hard to masturbate with their hands or fingers because they get tired and feel numb. It is sometimes helpful to try using an electric vibrator, which does not get tired and provides very strong stimulation. Once you know what an orgasm feels like, it makes it easier to learn to masturbate with your hand or climax with a partner. Don't forget that you can also use the vibrator when you are with a partner.

Some women feel very shy about touching themselves and want more subtle stimulation. It sometimes works to try masturbating in the bathtub by letting a gentle stream of warm water fall on your genitals. This is a very soothing and cleansing experience.

It can be difficult to break established patterns and habits. Some women are surprised by the number of obstacles they confront in learning how to have an orgasm. It can be hard to find the time necessary to experiment with different ways to get turned on. Old hurts and fears may surface, making the learning process even more formidable. For these women, there are groups available to provide a support structure and dispense information about female sexuality. They are usually called *pre*-orgasmic women's groups, rather than *non*-orgasmic women's groups, because of their phenominally high success rate. You can locate such a group through a women's switchboard or a clinic specializing in sex therapy.

If you have more questions about pre-orgasmic women's groups, read Lonnie Garfield Barbach's book, *For Yourself: The Fulfillment of Female Sexuality.* She is one of the women who created this process. In *For Yourself,* she describes the groups and the experiences of lesbian, bisexual and heterosexual women who have been part of them.

Some lesbians can masturbate to orgasm with ease but have difficulty when they are with another woman. Support groups similar to pre-orgasmic women's groups exist to help women change this sexual pattern.

During masturbation, a woman finds out which position or positions are most comfortable and pleasure-enhancing for her. She also finds out whether she likes masturbating with one finger or her whole hand, whether or not she likes penetration, and lots of other things. Lesbians who don't come with a partner are often keeping this information to themselves. They may be reluctant to share it out of modesty, embarrassment or a fear of making their partners feel bad.

Masturbation and sex with a partner need not be totally separate realms. Showing your partner how you masturbate can be very rewarding. Once she knows what your body is used to and likes, she can duplicate that particular pattern of stimulation. However, she should not be made responsible for your orgasm. If you are making love and want to come, go ahead and touch your own genitals. There is no need for you to be frustrated until she "learns to do it right." If you know you can come whenever you want to, whether a partner is there or not, it takes a lot of pressure off both of you. She will feel freer to experiment and play with you. You will feel less need to keep constant track of everything and wonder when, if ever, *it* is going to happen.

Lesbians who have tried this process report that at some point they are pleasantly surprised to have an orgasm while a partner is stimulating them. After that, they don't necessarily abandon masturbation and restrict themselves to partner stimulation. However, having orgasms with a partner becomes progressively easier.

Some lesbian who are able to have orgasms during masturbation and with a partner still have concerns about orgasms. They would like to expand their range of choices and be able to come using a technique they don't currently experience orgasm with. Perhaps such a woman has a lover who really enjoys oral sex. She would like to understand her lover's enthusiasm and benefit from it. But with other lovers, she has experienced orgasm as a result of manual stimulation. She feels frustrated because she can't experience something that has her curious and titillated.

It is often helpful to use masturbation as a way of altering your sexual response. Try fantasizing about the technique in question when you stimulate yourself. In the beginning, you may include only a few images of the new technique in your usual favorite fantasy. As time goes on, you may be preoccupied by new fantasies which focus almost exclusively on that technique. You can also try to duplicate the sensations you imagine it produces. If you want to learn how to come during oral sex, try using the tip of one finger and lots of lubricant, and imagine your finger is a tongue. If you want to learn how to come during tribadism, try rubbing against your whole hand or a folded up pillow.

When you have sex with a partner, don't restrict yourself to the new technique. Include it as part of an experience you are more familiar with. It's important that you not feel trapped or pressured. You need to know you can have good sex without being able to get off on a predetermined technique.

The first time you come will probably be unexpected, and the orgasm will feel different from the one you are used to. Using a different position or technique changes the way an orgasm feels. Part of learning how to come in a new way is becoming accustomed to the uniqueness of a new pleasure.

Conflicts About Technique

It is reasonable to assume that there are some sexual techniques that do not turn you on or that you actively dislike. If you are sexually active with multiple partners, chances are that you will run into a woman who prefers the things that you do not. This is a potentially explosive situation. Flexibility has a certain value when it comes to sex (and probably the rest of life, too). I would estimate this value as being equivalent to that of a good woman, who Proverbs 31:10 informs me is more precious than rubies.

If you are willing to do only those things that you know you enjoy, you may be limiting your choice of partners. By refusing to negotiate, you limit the range of your erotic experiences. If both of you start from the position that a sexual experience should be pleasurable for all parties involved, the chances are good that you can work something out.

Talk about it. Try to avoid judging each other's experiences and needs, and don't deny that a difference exists. The section on communication contains suggestions that may make this discussion a little easier.

There are lots of possible outcomes. There may be some technique that neither of you have had a lot of experience with but both of you would like to investigate. You may decide to masturbate together. You may invite a third party to join you. You may also decide to confront your reluctance and try her favorite technique.

If you agree upon the latter option, there are some things you can do to make it a good experience rather than an ordeal. Be clear about why you don't get turned on to or like a particular technique. Do you have concerns about hygiene? Take a bath or shower together. Ask her to douche or take an enema. Do you think it's too kinky, weird, or wrong? Remember that that is the prevailing attitude toward lesbianism. If both of you can get pleasure out of doing something and you don't intend to harm anyone in the process, how is it wrong or bad? Do you worry about doing it right? Tell her you are anxious because it is a new experience. Ask her to tell you how other women have done it. She should let you know what feels good and how good it feels while you are doing it.

Remember that it is also fine to decide not to have sex.

Different Levels of Sexual Need

Some lesbians want or need to have sex oftener than other lesbians. The range of sexual frequency is wide. Some lesbians I have talked to don't need to have sex oftener than once every few months. Others prefer to have sex at least once a day. This difference often causes problems in relationships, especially if there is a large difference and the relationship is monogamous.

If you and your partner(s) have conflicts over different levels of sexual need, you may be able to work out a compromise that will minimize tension. One possibility is for each of you to change your sexual patterns a little bit. The partner who needs to have sex more often may decide she can do without sex some of the time. The partner who needs to have sex less often may decide to put a higher priority on lovemaking and allot more time for erotic activity with her lover. Another possibility is for the partner with a higher level of need to find other outlets. She may decide to masturbate more often. If your relationship is nonmonogamous, she may find other partners, either for casual sex or ongoing relationships.

It will be easier to discuss this issue if you can avoid putting a value judgment on needing more or less sex. Try to find a solution that will enable both of you to get what you want, rather than arguing over which of you has the best sexual pattern. A woman who needs sex more often than her lover should not be shamed by implications that she is a lesbian nymphomaniac. A woman who needs sex less often than her lover should not be put on the defensive with accusations that she is repressed or inhibited.

If the difference is too great and your contract is not flexible enough to accommodate this difference, your relationship will cease to exist. Relationships end in many ways. Sometimes (rarely) partners agree to separate because their feelings for each other have changed and they do not blame each other for that change. Most often, there is an open break full of hostility and recrimination. There are also relationships that exist in name only, from which all intimacy and warmth have fled. A relationship becomes a formality when the women involved in it no longer appreciate each other's individuality. Their interactions with each other become transactions carried on between facades. As you discuss this issue, remember that conformity strangles passion.

Sometimes a situation exists which is more severe than a disagreement over how often to have sex. I have talked with some lesbians who complain that they have no interest in sex at all. They report feeling numb, bored, disinterested, or irritated during sexual encounters. If these women have lovers, they are likely to be especially worried when this occurs. Women who feel that celibacy is second-rate or a waste of time also have trouble coping with a lack of interest in sex.

There are several things that can cause someone to lose her ability to get turned on. Almost all of them are amenable to change.

Are you dealing with a lot of crisis situations? Make a list of all the things that are bothering you and all the problems you are trying to solve. You may discover that you are coping with too many emergencies. It may make more sense that sex has become a low priority.

Are you taking any medication? The drugs used to control diabetes and high blood pressure often have an adverse effect on sexual desire. If you are taking recreational drugs on a regular basis, they can also hamper sexual functioning. Alcohol, stimulants, marijuana, narcotics and several other drugs have been reported to have this effect.

What is the state of your relationship? Repressed anger can stifle arousal. So can familiarity. If your sex life has become too predictable, you may need to try some new things and start taking some chances to wake up your libido.

Try to avoid blaming yourself. Interest in sex will revive when the rest of your life changes enough to make room for it. Such change doesn't always happen overnight.

Concerns About Lubrication

There is no objective standard for measuring whether a particular woman lubricates too much or too little. Everybody has a different quantity and kind of vaginal lubrication. Some women find that their lubrication is more copious at different points of the menstrual cycle. Other women find little or no change.

If you find yourself getting irritated or chafed during sex, your own lubrication needs a little help. Some lesbians who feel their sexual juices are scanty keep a bottle of their favorite lube by the bed. When you are with a new lover, apply it yourself, so that she will know it's there. You may want to tell her the fact that you're a little dry doesn't mean you aren't turned on.

If you feel sloppy or messy during sex, keep a hand towel by the bed or any other surface you use frequently for lovemaking. Use it yourself, so that your partner will know it's okay to blot you. Don't use facial tissues— they shred up into nasty little soggy pieces, and you'll be picking them out of your crotch for the rest of the evening.

Some women's vaginas spurt a noticeable quantity of fluid when they climax. This is called "female ejaculation." Most sex education literature doesn't mention this phenomenon at all. Some authorities believe that women who appear to be ejaculating are actually expelling urine. However, some women who ejaculate insist that the fluid is not urine. It comes from the vagina, not the urethra, although it is thinner than the lubrication the vagina secretes during arousal, and usually has a sour taste.

If you ejaculate, don't feel bad about your body. This is a natural part of the sexual response cycle for some women. If it will put your mind at rest, see your gynecologist to make sure you don't have vaginal or urinary tract infections. Unless you experience involuntary urination at other times (for instance, when you laugh or sneeze), the fluid is probably not urine. If you're still concerned about this, do your Kegels regularly to build pelvic muscle tone.

Keep a plastic sheet on your bed. Have a stack of towels handy and put as many underneath you as you need to soak up the fluid. Let your partner know that you ejaculate *before* you have sex with her. She probably won't reject you, although she may want to know when you are close to orgasm, so she can stimulate you manually instead of orally. Actually, there are lots of women out there who are not phobic about sexual secretions, but revel in them!

Nobody knows why some women ejaculate. Recently, a book has been published about this called *The G Spot* by Alice Ladas, Beverly Whipple and John Perry (Holt, Rinehart and Winston, $11.95 in hardcover). They claim to have discovered an organ called the Gräfenberg spot within the anterior vaginal wall. When stimulated directly, this spot is supposed to trigger a vaginal orgasm for most women and ejaculation in some women. Ladas, et al. speculate that the G spot is a female homologue of the prostate gland, which is located in the male rectum and causes ejaculation when directly stimulated.

I am dubious about this book since the authors seem to have an investment in proving that Freud's theories about the vaginal orgasm have some validitiy. They never describe the sample of women who supposedly were all found to have a G spot, and attempts to replicate their findings have been mixed. No anatomical studies have been done to locate a specific organ which could be a G spot.

However, the book presents an interesting theory and includes lots of personal accounts by women who ejaculate. Because so little has been written on this subject, it is still worth reading.

Ticklishness

One of our odd cultural notions is that women are fragile and, consequently, gentle. Many people assume that lesbian lovemaking is satisfying for women because it is extremely delicate and soft. Some lesbians do prefer to use a very light touch during lovemaking, but it would be a mistake to imagine that all women make love to each other this way.

If you find yourself getting ticklish when your partner touches you, it may be because her touch is not firm enough. Try getting strong with each other. Wrestle, push and pull, exert yourselves!

Ticklishness can also be caused by muscular tension. Some massage can alleviate soreness and free the body to appreciate more stimulation. Being ticklish can be a way to protect yourself if you don't feel relaxed enough or open to being touched.

If part of your body seems permanently ticklish, it may be because it is a very sensitive area. Try thinking of that area as being charged with sexual energy, wanting very badly to be touched, and potentially explosive. At some point when you are already very turned on, invite your partner to touch this very special, high-voltage spot. You may be surprised by the results.

Once somebody starts feeling ticklish, it is often difficult to stop it. Take a break and have a snack or some conversation before you try massage or other ways of assuaging the tickle.

Pain

Most lesbians who find penetration of the vagina or anus painful simply don't include that kind of stimulation in their sexual activity. There are suggestions in the section on partners for lesbians who do want to explore penetration. These suggestions include ways to prevent pain from oc-curring—lots of lubrication, lots of patience, taking lots of time, and put-ting emphasis on how it feels rather than how much you have in.

If you experience severe pain upon penetration and none of the above suggestions helps, you should know that there are some medical problems that can cause this pain. They are listed below. Some of these problems are rather rare, but I have included them anyway as remote possibilities. You may be able to eliminate some of the items on the list, but don't try to diag-nose yourself. If you have any questions, take the list with you to your doctor, and ask her or him to see if any of it is relevant to you.

1. Vaginal infections and infections of the cervix, urethra, uterus or the Bartholin's glands can make vaginal stimulation painful.

2. Hemorrhoids can make anal stimulation or penetration difficult to enjoy. Some women also feel that gentle massage of the rectum helps blood to circulate and increases anal relaxation, both of which promote healing of hemorrhoids.

3. Your hymen could be partially or completely intact. Even some women who have had intercourse still have hymens which are stretched but still in place. You can deal with this by using smaller objects or fewer fingers. If you like, it may be possible to gradually increase the size of what feels good in your vagina by using larger objects or more fingers as the

vagina learns to relax. It is also possible to have the hymen surgically opened. This procedure can be done in a doctor's office. Some lesbians may be proud of their hymens and want to retain them. There is no medical reason to have a hymen dilated or removed if you don't wish to, unless the opening is so small that a speculum cannot be inserted. This would interfere with pelvic examinations and make it impossible for you to get regular Pap smears.

4. Women who are about to experience menopause, are going through or have completed menopause, sometimes have pain or even bleeding during vaginal stimulation. This can be annoying if vaginal stimulation is an important part of your sexuality. Your ovaries are producing less and less estrogen, and this makes the vaginal walls thin and smooth. The amount of lubrication which is then able to pass through the vaginal walls decreases. You can replace this lost lubrication with a lotion or oil, and there are estrogen-based creams that doctors can prescribe to apply to the vaginal walls. Some women do not feel that estrogens should be taken casually. They are very potent substances, and their effects have not been fully researched. Women who do not trust artificial estrogens may prefer to use artificial lubricants. Either way, it's important to keep active sexually. A daily orgasm, either with a partner or with masturbation, will help keep the pelvic muscles in tone and the vagina healthy.

5. During childbirth or rape, the broad ligaments that support the uterus can be torn. These tears are often not detected in a routine pelvic examination. Women who have been injured in this way often complain of a feeling that their insides are falling out. If the vagina or any of the supporting structures are damaged during rape, criminal abortion, childbirth, or a hysterectomy, the scars left behind can be painful if touched or bumped.

6. Pelvic endometriosis is a condition which occurs when the lining of the uterus grows into other areas of the pelvis. This condition can also cause menstrual cramps.

7. Excessive douching or use of irritating soap or deodorant on the vulva can dry out the membranous tissues and cause smarting or burning.

8. Veneral diseases, especially gonorrhea, can infect the cervix, uterus, and Fallopian tubes, and make vaginal penetration painful. Venereal diseases can also affect the rectum. See the section on sex-related health problems for more informaton about VD.

9. Tumors and ovarian cysts are other possible causative factors for vaginal/rectal pain.

Some women also complain that clitoral stimulation is painful. This can have several causes. It is quite common for the glans of the clitoris to be painful to the touch, especially following orgasm. Try more indirect stimulation. It is also possible for material to collect and harden under the clitoral hood. Always lift and clean under the clitoral hood when you wash your genitals. Some women have adhesions—tissue that connects the clitoral glans to the hood and makes free movement of the hood impossible. Adhesions are not always painful and do not necessarily impair sexual functioning. However, a doctor can ease a blunt instrument between the hood and glans and separate the adhesions if they are a problem.

There are other kinds of pain which can occur during sex. Some women experience muscle cramps, especially in the calves, when they get close to orgasm. These women need to avoid positions which place stress on their legs. It helps to flex and relax the muscles as lovemaking progresses. Other lesbians complain of ringing headaches after orgasm. These headaches are usually caused by a shortage of oxygen. Some women forget to breathe as they get turned on. Deep, regular breaths up to and during orgasm will prevent the headache.

Drugs

Any drug that can be smoked, swallowed, injected, inhaled, inserted into the anal cavity or rubbed on the skin has been recommended to me as an aphrodisiac. That includes tetracycline and birth control pills. If an aphrodisiac is defined as a psychotropic substance that always or usually enhances the sexual experience, remember that no such thing exists. However, any drug that alters the way you feel will probably have some effect on your sexuality if you mix lechery with getting high. Sometimes it's the social context that is primarily affected. Sharing drugs with other women can make it easier to meet them, talk with them, or initiate sex. Many drugs also affect physical sensations and the body's capabilities. Tactile stimulation may feel different—more intense, richer.

Drug use doesn't always make a positive contribution to the sexual experience. The problem of serious drug abuse does exist in the lesbian community. A lesbian with substance abuse problems can have a very hard time getting professional assistance. Most treatment programs focus on the male alcoholic or addict. There is also some resistance in the lesbian subculture to admitting that the problem exists. We are in effect trapped by society's view of us as unhealthy women. It can be difficult to demand mental health services without reinforcing that myth.

It is beyond the scope of this book to deal with all the possible effects popular drugs can have on sexual functioning. Such effects vary with the individual user and the dosage and purity of the drug, as well as the context in which it is used. There is a dearth of formal research on drugs and sex. Most of the information about this topic exists in the form of folk wisdom and circulates among people who are fond of recreational drug use. Some of this information is sound and helpful; some of it is inaccurate.

It is not uncommon to find that being stoned affects your ability to have orgasms. Generally speaking, the more loaded you are, the less likely you are to be able to come. You may also lubricate less, get anxious or paranoid, and have trouble relaxing. This may happen because you are afraid of losing control while you are high. It's a good idea to have a safe and comfortable place in which to enjoy being stoned, with companions you know and trust. It also helps to be familiar with your body and its tolerance for various substances. The first time you use a new batch of a particular drug or a whole new substance, try taking less instead of more. You can always take more later if you don't get off, and you may avoid an unpleasant reaction. The availability and quality of illegal drugs are usually unreliable. Avoid buying from people you don't know. Patronize dealers who treat you right.

Some women frequently use their favorite highs to accentuate or alter their sexual experiences. After a while, they come to associate good sex with a particular drug or the general state of being stoned. Let us suppose, just for the sake of argument, that you are such a woman. Your mother knows you would never do such a thing, and I know you would never do such a thing, but I need an example. The drug in question may be alcohol. It may be marijuana or cocaine. One sunny afternoon, you find yourself in a situation where drugs are unavailable. You don't have any. Your partner doesn't have any. Your good friend down the street is cleaned out. Or you may find yourself with a woman who seemed perfectly nice but turns out to be a Seventh Day ova-lachrymose vegetarian who only gets high on days when the ozone count is soaring. You decide to have sex anyway, but you have a hard time getting turned on, and you aren't sure whether you ever came or not. You try to console yourself with an anchovy pizza, and you worry.

It is possible to forget how to get it on without being high. Your body becomes familiar with the sensation of being stoned and associates that feeling with getting turned on and being sexual. If you find yourself with a problem like this, it can usually be dealt with by temporarily cleaning up your act. Have sex without chemical assistance for a while. It's a process similar to learning how to come with a different technique. Your body will readjust, learn to associate sex with stimuli other than the drug you prefer, and start getting turned on again.

It is worthwhile to ask yourself if you have some anxiety or guilt about being sexual that you resolve by getting high. If you have to get stoned before you can get it on, that will erode your self-respect and the affection you have for your partners. Puritanism and homophobia cause a lot of borderline drug dependencies. You would probably enjoy your sexuality (and getting high) a lot more if you could let go of that guilt and anxiety.

Of course, no one else can tell you whether you're a drug user or a drug abuser. You're the only one who knows what effect getting high has on the rest of your life.

Obtaining Professional Assistance

You may have a sexual problem that is unusually severe or of long standing. You have exhausted your own resources, and you feel you need more assistance than you can get from reading educational material about sex, trying self-help exercises, or talking to a friend. When this happens, it's valid to want help from someone who is more skilled at dealing with sexual difficulties than you are—someone who can offer a fresh perspective on your situation.

It can be very difficult to seek therapy. To begin with, there are practical obstacles. Locating a therapist, finding the money to pay for counseling, and finding the time to go can be a slow and annoying process. You may wonder if you are exaggerating the importance of your problem, being self-indulgent or lazy, or risking too much on a stranger with some credentials. You may not know anyone else who has gone for counseling, and you may believe that therapy is only for institutionalized, out-of-control people. Many of us were taught as young people that the appropriate way to deal with an emotional problem is to increase self-control. We may have been made to feel that it is willful or bad to have a problem we don't know how to solve.

There are many different kinds of help available from mental health professionals. Therapy or counseling is not just for people with a diagnosable mental illness. It is possible to learn more effective social skills, change self-destructive patterns in relationships, and ameliorate sexual problems by seeking the appropriate assistance. Effective counseling heals old wounds and helps you feel good about yourself. It is not self-indulgent to want to be happy and healthy.

You will have better chances of finding the kind of help you need if you spend some time shopping around. Call women's switchboards or gay crisis lines and ask them for the names of therapists qualified to deal with your problem. You may want to see someone individually, or you may want to join a group of people working on the same issue. Ask your friends if they know of any competent mental health workers. You can also call city or county mental health agencies and ask for information about the programs they operate. Professional societies for psychiatrists, psychologists or psychiatric social workers sometimes provide referrals.

Once you get a list of names, call up each counselor or group leader.

Remember that you do not have to abdicate any of your power just because you want some professional assistance. You are entitled to ask a therapist the questions that will enable you to decide whether or not they would be good for you. Some questions you may want to ask are

1. What are the fees? Some therapists charge a fixed fee to everyone. Other therapists use a sliding scale that allows clients with low incomes to pay less. A few mental health agencies offer their services for free.

2. What kind of therapy or counseling do they offer?

3. What are their qualifications or training for dealing with sexual issues? Requirements for obtaining a license to do counseling vary from state to state. Very few states require comprehensive training in human sexuality. Try to find someone who is well educated in this area and has some experience working with sexual concerns.

4. Have they ever had lesbian clients? It's important to feel safe with your counselor. You don't want someone who feels lesbianism is a second-rate, neurotic lifestyle. Check out their general attitude toward homosexuality, then ask how much experience they have working with lesbian clients. A well-meaning therapist may not know enough about lesbianism to be able to help you.

Some lesbians hesitate to see a counselor because they are afraid other people will find out that they are lesbians or that they have gone through therapy. Legally speaking, whatever transpires between a counselor and a client is confidential and should not be divulged to third parties. Of course, this is not guarantee of absolute confidentiality. If you need to protect your anonymity, you need not use your real name when you talk to a therapist on the phone or visit her office. You can pay for the therapy in cash and set up appointments in person. Chances are slim that your anonymity will be threatened by seeing a counselor, but some women cannot take even that small chance. Your need for privacy should not prevent you from getting help.

Mental health services for lesbians (and other sexual minorities) are not so readily available as they should be. You will probably have a much easier time finding effective counseling if you live in or near a large city. Rural mental health services are not extensive. Part of the movement for gay liberation is agitating for the social services our community needs. As we become stronger politically, we will be in a better position to demand those services from government agencies. It is also important for lesbians to enter the fields of mental health and sex education, so that we can provide our own sex therapy and general counseling.

HOMAGE TO

Suzanne Ballivet

active around **1945**

Illustrator

6
Youth, Age and Sex

We live in a society segregated according to gender, sexual preference, race—and age. Separate (and largely artificial) universes have been established for infants, school-age children, adolescents, young adults, the middle-aged, and the elderly. Further stratification is enforced within each of these broad categories. Most of us rarely have intimate relationships with people very much older or younger than ourselves. Young people, adults, and the elderly are viewed as having different abilities, needs, and rights. Both young people and the elderly are usually assigned the status of economic dependents, which makes them very vulnerable to social control. Much of that social control focuses on sexuality.

As lesbians, we have a unique opportunity to question traditional assumptions about sexuality. This chapter examines the issue of youth, age and sex from a lesbian perspective.

Sex and Children

Children are believed to be asexual because they are innocent. Oddly enough, the typical child is given close supervision, the intent of which is to prevent sexual play or exploration. The "innocent" little girl will begin to ask questions about sex as soon as she can talk and will display considerable curiosity about her own and other people's bodies. It does not seem likely that sexual curiosity, erotic fantasies, masturbation or sexual play would occur in children if they were genuinely asexual. What we call innocence in children is really ignorance and inexperience. Adults create that ignorance by refusing to answer questions about sex, and they enforce inexperience by punishing masturbation or sexual games.

Children are sexual. Infants in their cribs have frequently been observed exploring and stimulating their own genitals. There is some debate about when orgasm becomes possible. I have talked with lesbians who remember masturbating to orgasm at two years of age. Since sex is such a vital and significant part of the child's experience, ignoring or suppressing it creates guilt and anxiety. It is difficult for a child to love herself if she cannot live in and love her own body. Acceptance and approval of a child's physical self can be expressed in many ways—hugging, kissing, shared nudity, bathing together, backrubs, or playful wrestling.

Most of us learn about pleasure by exploring our own bodies. A child is entitled to this process of self-discovery. Children also feel a strong urge to see and explore other people's bodies. There are a variety of ways to deal with a child's sexual behavior. Some lesbian mothers I have talked to feel that all sexual activity should take place in private. They tell their children it is okay to masturbate but ask them to do it in their own rooms. They may discourage sexual play with other children. Other mothers feel comfortable being with a child while either of them is masturbating or being sexual with other people. Mothers who allow their children to explore sex with their friends usually feel a need to make rules about when and how such activity can take place. One mother I talked to said she did not feel okay about sexual games between children unless the mothers of the other children gave their permission. She frequently talked to the children about what they were planning to do and let them know that any dangerous or nonconsensual activity was off-limits.

The possibility of sex between a child and an adult sometimes arises. Children need to know that they are entitled to say "no" to anyone who wants to engage in sex with them. Some lesbians feel that any sex between a child and an adult is coercive because adults are physically bigger than children and have much more social power. Other lesbians feel that it is not uncommon for an affectionate relationship between an adult and a child to contain an erotic component. They believe it may be possible to express this eroticism in ways that are enjoyable and pleasant for the child. They also believe that children are capable of initiating sexual relationships (with adults as well as other children), since sexual desire can exist in children as well as adults. This is a difficult and controversial issue, perhaps best judged on a case-by-case basis. The horrors of child abuse are a major concern of feminists. However, while protecting children, we should not overlook their right to freedom of sexual expression.

When children ask questions about sex, they need accurate answers in language they can understand. This kind of sex education can be done only by an adult who is well-informed about human sexuality and can discuss it freely. Some of the issues that concern children are masturbation, the meaning of various sex terms, human physiology and reproduction, erotic fantasies, and ethics. In a sexually liberated world, all children would have access to information about the complete spectrum of human sexual behavior. Many lesbians mention a sense of being "different" that was profoundly disturbing to them throughout childhood. Children need to know that there are many acceptable, happy adult lifestyles. This could allay anxiety without forcing any particular choice upon them. Unfortunately, few parents or public sex education programs dispense nonjudgmental information about homosexuality.

Children who are raised in a liberal atmosphere should be told that some children and adults react negatively to any form of sexual expression. They need clear guidelines about when and where it is acceptable to discuss sex or engage in sexual behavior. Mothers should realize that their children won't always agree with them about what is correct sexual behavior or even about facts of human physiology. Children choose to believe what best suits their needs.

Sex and Adolescent Lesbians

In this chapter, "adolescence" refers to the period between childhood and adulthood. This transition in self-image and social position occurs at different ages for different women. "Puberty" is a more specific term that refers to the physiological changes that accompany adolescence. Puberty usually begins between the ages of 9 and 12. For reasons which are not completely understood, the pituitary (a pea-sized endocrine gland located at the base of the brain) begins to produce FSH (follicle-stimulating hormone). FSH causes the ovaries to produce estrogen. Estrogen causes several changes in the internal and external genitals and the whole body. The breasts begin to grow. Hips and buttocks develop a more rounded shape. Pubic and axillary (underarm) hair begins to appear. Hormones secreted by the adrenals (paired glands located just above each kidney) and ACTH (adrenocorticotrophic hormones) from the pituitary gland also stimulate the growth of hair under the arms and on the vulva. Facial acne is probably the result of increased estrogen secretion. Under the influence of estrogen, the labia enlarge. Androgens from the adrenal glands enlarge the clitoris. Estrogen causes the pelvis to become larger and wider. The long bones are growing as well and do not stop growing until about 17 years of age. Estrogen also causes growth of the uterus and vagina. The muscular walls of the uterus enlarge, and the glandular lining develops. The vaginal walls are very sensitive to estrogen. Their thickness is directly proportional to the amount of estrogen being produced by the ovaries. During puberty, the pH of vaginal secretion changes from alkaline to acid, and the vagina becomes capable of secreting lubrication during sexual stimulation.

Eventually, estrogen production becomes cyclical. Menstruation is the result of this cyclical production of estrogen. Menstruation occurs in women, female apes, and some female monkeys. Estrus in other mammals is not accompanied by bleeding. The average human menstrual cycle lasts 28 days. The cycle can range from 26 to 34 days. Menstrual periods commonly last from 3 to 7 days.

The four phases of the menstrual cycle are *proliferative (or preovulatory), ovulation, secretory (or post-ovulatory),* and *menstruation.*

The description below is based on a 28-day menstrual cycle.

Proliferative phase. During this 14-day phase, the lining of the uterus (the endometrium) is reconstructed. The pituitary gland secretes FSH, which increases ovarian secretion of estrogen. The estrogen causes the endometrium to grow until it is about 3.5 millimeters thick. It also causes an ovarian follicle to mature. The ovaries are almond-shaped organs about 1½" x ¾" x 1". Each ovary weighs about ¼ oz. They contain many capsules or follicles, and each follicle contains one ovum or egg. Each woman has a total of about 400,000 follicles that are at various stages of maturity. Current medical belief is that the ovaries do not produce any follicles after puberty. During the proliferative phase, the cervix (the part of the uterus that can be seen and felt at the end of the vagina) produces lots of thin, viscous, alkaline mucus. The vaginal lining grows, reaching maximum thickness during ovulation.

Ovulation. On the 15th day of the cycle, the amount of fluid within the maturing follicle increases until it ruptures and a mature egg (ovum) is released. Some women experience twinges or a vague sense of discomfort when they ovulate. A tiny amount of blood may be secreted via the vagina. The ovum is caught in the fringed end of the uterine (fallopian) tube. This is a remarkable journey, given that the ovum is the size of a needle tip and the opening of the fallopian tube is about as large as a printed hyphen.

Secretory phase. Increased estrogen levels cause the pituitary gland to secrete LH (luteinizing hormone). LH travels through the bloodstream to the ruptured follicle and stimulates the remaining cells to develop into the corpus luteum. The corpus luteum produces more estrogen and progesterone, which causes glands in the endometrium to produce nutrient fluids. This takes place on the 18th day of the cycle. The ovum has traveled down the fallopian tube to the uterus and is nourished by this fluid. The uterus is a hollow, muscular organ shaped like an inverted pear. It usually tilts forward. It is about 3" long, 2" wide at the top, and 1" thick. In this phase, the blood vessels in the uterus proliferate. Progesterone inhibits the flow of cervical mucus and diminishes the thickness of the vaginal lining. When fertilization does not occur, the estrogen and progesterone secreted by the corpus luteum cause the pituitary gland to stop producing FSH and LH. The corpus luteum then ceases to produce estrogen and progesterone and withers away.

Menstruation. Over 3 to 7 days, the endometrium is shed through the cervix and vagina. The vagina is a collapsed muscular tube—a potential rather than an actual space. When not sexually aroused, the vagina is about 3" along its anterior wall and about 4" along its posterior wall. The vaginal lining is like the skin on the inside of the mouth. The menstrual discharge is about 2 oz. of blood, mucus and fragments of endometrial tissue. Some women experience discomfort or pain during their menstrual period. Very little is known about why this pain occurs. Common medical practice is to prescribe pain-killers or tranquilizers without attempting to explore the cause. As the estrogen level continues to fall, the pituitary gland begins to produce FSH again, and the next cycle begins.

Puberty is accompanied by changes in sexual feelings. Very little research has been done in this area, so it is difficult to state which changes are universal, which are the product of socialization or cultural expectations, and which have a biological basis. Some lesbians I have talked to report that orgasms feel different before and after puberty. With the advent of menstruation, sexual desire may become cyclical. Some lesbians described a difference in the quality of sexual desire, saying that it became more intense and more narrowly focused. Other women were not aware of their sexuality at all prior to adolescence and experienced it as a new and powerful force in their lives.

Legally, adolescents are sometimes treated like children and sometimes like adults. The juvenile justice system is often used to punish sexually active adolescent women. Without her full civil rights, the underage lesbian is in a precarious position. If her homosexuality becomes public knowledge, she may be ostracized by her peers, and she may lose any economic or emotional support she obtains from her family. It is very difficult for her to gain access to the lesbian community. Minors are not allowed to patronize lesbian bars, and some social groups are reluctant to admit underage women. Older lesbians can be hesitant to offer friendship or become romantically involved with a younger woman. They fear legal penalties and criticism from other lesbians.

Despite all these difficulties, young women can and do become lesbians. This self-labeling sometimes occurs even before puberty. The established lesbian community needs to reach out to younger gay women. They are our next generation, and straight society is incapable of providing them with assistance in developing healthy lesbian lives. However, older lesbians should not assume they know what is best for adolescent women. Communication with young lesbians about the quality of their lives and consultation with them about their needs must take place if our resources are to be allocated wisely.

Rap groups, foster homes, and counselors are no substitutes for friends and lovers. Sometimes young lesbians find each other and create intimate relationships with women their own age. A young woman usually finds it difficult to support herself financially, find a place to live, obtain an education or job training, and protect her privacy and independence. These practical problems put a strain on any close relationship she forms. But two young lesbians can share common causes, perspectives, and enough love and mutual attraction to overcome these obstacles.

An underage lesbian usually knows many more legally adult lesbians than other minors. Despite social barriers, romantic and sexual relationships are frequently formed between women of disparate ages. Some conflicts are unique to this type of relationship. It may be helpful for lovers in this situation to sort out which conflicts are the product of ageism and which are personal problems.

There are cultural differences between younger and older women— different preferences in music, art, dress, and entertainment. There are also different values—ideas about what is polite and impolite, what is sexually right and wrong, what is politically correct and incorrect. Younger and older women are at different stages in life. They need to make different plans to achieve their life goals. It is common for the older partner to have more money and financial security than her younger partner. This creates a power imbalance which can be a source of resentment. The older partner may fear that her lover will "grow up" and leave her. This can give the relationship a frantic and insecure quality.

Sexually, a relationship between an older and a younger lesbian offers lots of opportunities for frustration and guilt. The older partner may wonder if her young lover is really a lesbian and feel she is corrupting her by introducing her to lesbian lovemaking. She may wonder if she is immature because she has an "immature" partner or worry that her young lover sees her as a mother figure. She may sometimes feel pressure to look or act younger than she is. The younger partner may wonder if she is sexually attractive only because of her age and fear that her lover will lose interest as she grows older. If she has the same amount of or more sexual experience than her partner, she may hesitate to reveal her knowledge for fear of making her lover feel insecure, inhibited, or old-fashioned. Even if her sexual experience has not been extensive, she may feel uneasy with the role of ingenue or novice. She may have to struggle for recognition as a full partner in the relationship and fend off ersatz parenting. If she was the one who initiated the relationship (which is very likely, given the reluctance of older lesbians to have sex with younger lesbians), she may feel guilty for pressuring or manipulating the older woman into a sexual encounter. She may wonder whether the woman would have been interested in her without that pressure.

Such a relationship is also threatened from the outside world. Families and government agencies can disrupt or destroy it. Lesbians who are involved in such a relationship often feel that they would be happier and safer if age-of-consent laws were repealed and federal consenting-adults legislation were enacted. The couples I have talked to feel more accepted

within the lesbian community than anywhere else; however, they also feel
that some lesbians do not take their relationship seriously or that they feel
negative about it.
The rewards of such a relationship come from the women involved and
the feelings they have for each other. In a less homophobic and violent
world, it might be taken for granted that adults would teach adolescents
about the art of sexuality as well as other aspects of life. If adolescents
were not stereotyped as irresponsible, immature and unreliable, adults
might be less reluctant to engage in intimate relationships with them. It
would be clearer that such a relationship is a mutual exchange rather than a
hierarchical, one-way arrangement.

Sex and Old Lesbians

For the purpose of this book, "old age" is the period of a woman's life
which begins with menopause. Menopause is the permanent cessation of
menstruation due to physiological changes associated with aging. It occurs
between the ages of 46 and 50. There seems to be no correlation between
the age of menarche and the age of menopause. A woman who begins
menstruating early is not necessarily going to experience menopause at a
young age. Menstruation is usually irregular for several years before menopause. The pituitary gland continues to produce FSH, but for reasons
which are not understood, the ovaries gradually fail to respond. Eventually
they are producing very little estrogen. The most common symptom of
menopause is the hot flash or hot flush. This is a sensation of heat which
spreads in waves over the face or upper half of the body. Perspiration
and chills may follow. The sensation can last a few seconds or longer. If a
hot flush occurs in the middle of the night, it may awaken the woman experiencing it. Other uncomfortable effects of menopause are headaches,
dizziness, heart palpitations, pains in the joints, and depression. Most
authorities assert that only 10% of women are inconvenienced by climacteric
symptoms. I have been unable to locate any study which would verify this
estimate. Certainly all women are aware of physical changes as they age.
They may have more aches and pains, tire more easily, or lose some physical
strength. The skin wrinkles and becomes dry more easily. Breasts shrink
and change in structure until they may droop. Exercise and good nutrition
can minimize discomfort associated with aging. Some physicians prescribe
estrogen or estrogen/progesterone combinations to replace the hormones
the ovaries do not produce. Some women feel this treatment is safe and
effective in eliminating unpleasant menopausal symptoms. Other women
are suspicious of estrogen replacement therapy (ERT) because the long-
range effects are not known. Lesbians approaching menopause will

probably want to do some research on the latest arguments on both sides
of this debate before taking or rejecting ERT.

Falling estrogen levels affect the sexual organs. The uterus shrinks, and
the endometrium atrophies. The vaginal lining also shrinks. The vagina
produces less lubrication, and the lubrication becomes thinner. Some
women find that vaginal stimulation is uncomfortable or painful. The
vaginal walls may crack or bleed during penetration. Depending on the
severity of this problem, there are several possible solutions. One is to
elminate penetration from your sexual repertoire. You may want to use
smaller objects, fewer fingers, or make penetration less vigorous. Artificial
lubricants can be helpful. Cream which contains estrogen can be prescribed
for application to the vaginal walls. This is a much smaller dose of estrogen
than that prescribed for general menopausal difficulties. Some lesbians
report that frequent masturbation or orgasms from other sources are helpful in keeping the vagina well-lubricated and healthy.

In straight society, old women are viewed as being sexually neuter and
puritanical. Sexual matters are rarely broached in front of old women,
under the assumption that it would offend them. This "polite" silence
keeps old women from perceiving themselves as sexual beings. Fear of ridicule or condemnation prevents many old women from finding sex partners,
obtaining and reading erotic material, purchasing sex toys, engaging in masturbation, or discussing sexual problems and concerns. Fortunately, this
myth has less force in the lesbian community than elsewhere. The white-
haired dyke is often a sex symbol. She is living proof that lesbianism is not
a fad invented by the women's movement. She is living proof that lesbianism is not fatal at an early age. She is often perceived as being sexually experienced, assertive, and very attractive. It's no surprise that "I Like Older
Women" is a popular lesbian button. However, the negative stereotype of
old women has some effect on lesbians. For instance, the women who
thinks nothing of making a pass at a 50-year-old lesbian may hesitate to discuss masturbation with her 50-year-old mother and would be shocked if her
grandmother took a lover. Almost all of us have some anxieties about
aging and wonder whether we will still be attractive and sexually active.

There is nothing ludicrous or unnatural about an old woman having a
sexually satisfying life. That includes our grandmothers, mothers, aunts,
ourselves, our lovers, our daughters, and our friends. Many women experience an increase in sexual desire after menopause. Women who do not
experience such an increase still want and enjoy lovemaking and masturbation. An old lesbian has had time to sample a variety of sexual experiences
and relationships. She may waste less time and suffer fewer disappoint-
ments because she knows what she likes and needs. Far from being sexually
neuter or puritanical, an old lesbian may be a wiser, more skilled and more

tolerant lover than a younger woman.

Older people need more than sexual freedom. Their economic problems have yet to be solved. The typical nursing home is not a warm, comfortable environment for anyone, and the most liberal nursing home is not ready for women's dances or outings to the final playoffs for the lesbian softball league championship. The lesbian movement has struggled to create new social structures to raise children, buy food, obtain justice, get lesbian literature printed, circulate lesbian news, and display our art. Eventually we will probably establish collectively run homes for older lesbians. Young lesbians could learn how to organize for their old age by working with and being close to lesbians who are already elderly.

HOMAGE TO

Gerda Wegener
1885-1940

Illustrator, born in Denmark, worked in Paris

7

Disabled Lesbians

As used here, the term "disability" refers to a broad spectrum of mental or physical difficulties. This includes deafness, blindness, mental retardation, spinal cord injuries, multiple sclerosis, cerebral palsy, and polio. Some disabilities are present from birth or early childhood. Others are the result of an accident or illness experienced later in life. Some of us have disabilities that hamper us for brief periods and then subside, such as back problems. Almost all of us will experience temporary disability at least once in our lives.

The idea that people with disabilities would be concerned about sexuality is new, even shocking, to most able-bodied people. The dissociation between sex and disability is so profound that many doctors routinely advise heart patients or individuals with high blood pressure to refrain from sexual activity. This advice is sometimes given for moral rather than medical reasons. Actually, the need for sexual attention and expression exists in almost everyone, regardless of physical, mental, or emotional capabilities. Usually some way to meet that need can be found, if a tolerant and experimental attitude toward sex is adopted.

Some disabled women prefer other women as lovers or sex partners. They occupy a unique position in the world at large and the lesbian community. Disabled lesbians—like other disabled people—are often dependent on social service agencies for their income and medical treatment. These agencies may discriminate against them or deny them complete assistance because of their homosexuality. The medical profession has a tendency to institutionalize individuals with moderate or severe disabilities. The disabled lesbian who wants an independent life outside an institution may face an uphill battle creating that life. She may have difficulty securing release if she is viewed as a sexual deviant. She may be more dependent on her family than other women are, and fear to put strain on her relationship with them by coming out. If she wants to work, she faces job discrimination. Mobility may be another problem. Women in wheelchairs cannot use stairs. They need ramps, elevators, wide doorways, and handholds or rails in bathrooms. Blind women often have difficulty finding their way about, since they cannot read street signs. A woman who uses crutches, a cane or a walker may not be able to cross the street on one green light. The mobility of disabled women is limited even further by the threat of violence. All women feel this threat, but a disabled woman (especially if she looks like a lesbian) is especially vulnerable to it. Communication can pose another problem. Few people who are not deaf learn sign language. Many people are unwilling to take the time to listen to someone who cannot enunciate clearly. Even if a disabled woman has no speech problems, she may find it hard to catch someone's attention, since many able-bodied people are afraid to look directly at someone with a physical disability.

The lesbian community has begun to develop some consciousness about disability. Many feminist groups try to locate office and meeting space that is accessible to women in wheelchairs. It is becoming more common for women's groups to locate interpreters who can sign speeches and readings for deaf members of the audience. However, even if the lesbian community were completely open to and comfortable for disabled lesbians, they would still experience discrimination in the larger society. That makes it important for feminists and lesbians to work on obtaining full civil rights for people who are physically different.

Before writing this chapter, I talked at length with two disabled lesbians at the Center for Independent Living in Berkeley. They described several issues which they felt were pertinent to the disabled lesbian's sexuality. I have rephrased and condensed what they said and added information from outside sources. Very little has been written about sexuality and disabled women, so the information that follows may seem incomplete. While I have struggled to avoid any well-bodyism in this chapter, it will probably be obvious to disabled lesbian readers that I am writing from an able-bodied woman's point of view. Disabled lesbians are the ultimate authorities on their own sexuality. I hope this chapter will encourage them to write and speak out more on this subject.

Body Image

We have a very narrow definition of attractiveness. The lesbian community recognizes a different kind of beauty from heterosexual society. However, the lesbian ideal—the strong, active, athletic woman—may leave disabled lesbians feeling unattractive.

If her disability was present from an early age, a disabled lesbian's body will have received the attention of doctors and been a source of anxiety and distress to her parents. She may view her body as a problem rather than a part of herself. Women who are disabled later in life may feel angry at their bodies, which no longer behave or perform the way they did before. They may blame their bodies for the accident or injury and feel estranged from them.

A good body image can be built by utilizing the body's talents and abilities as much as possible. It is important for a disabled woman to be as active as she can be and to minimize feelings that her body is inadequate or inferior. Self-acceptance is a difficult state to achieve, but it also forms the foundation for self-love. Some disabled lesbians feel that able-bodied women are afraid to look at them and that consequently they don't notice new clothes or new haircuts. We all need verbal recognition and sincere flattery.

Canes, braces, wheelchairs and other devices intended to assist women with physical disabilities are often designed from a utilitarian rather than aesthetic point of view. Able-bodied women need to become desensitized to the appearance and uses of these mechanical aids. Lesbian erotica is beginning to include images of disabled women and their canes or wheelchairs. This trend will probably do a lot to broaden our notions of what body types are sexually appealing.

Finding Partners

A disabled woman may not think of herself as a sexual person, or she may restrict herself to masturbation because finding a partner seems too difficult and the possibility of rejection too threatening. Disabled women need support from each other and their able-bodied friends to view themselves as sexual women and take the initiative in looking for partners. Simply waiting for the right woman puts too much power in the hands of fate.

A disabled lesbian will need considerable patience and persistence to deal with the following potential problems: (1) Accessibility. Will she be able to travel to and enter the party, dance, or bar? (2) Will the bathroom be usable or accessible? (3) If she is in a wheelchair, will women trip over her or overlook her because she is not at eye level? (4) If she is blind, how will women react to her when she asks directions to the refreshment table, the bartender, or the stairs? (5) Will anyone know sign language? (6) If she uses a cane or is in a wheelchair, will other women laugh or be embarrassed when she dances? (6) Will anyone dance with her?

The disabled lesbians I talked to felt that able-bodied lesbians were reluctant to consider them as potential sex partners or lovers. It was very frustrating for them to take the risk of going out to meet other women if the possibility of sex never occurred to the women they met. It is clear that most able-bodied lesbians need to work on changing their image of disabled lesbians. They go to a gay bar or a concert for the same reason able-bodied women do: to participate in lesbian culture, make friends, and cruise.

Because it can be so difficult to find partners, a disabled woman may hesitate to end an unsatisfactory relationship. She may hesitate to demand changes for fear her lover will leave. This may create a lot of anger that is never communicated directly. The able-bodied partner of a disabled woman may have her own stored-up anger if she feels her partner won't be able to handle a conflict. This overprotection can rapidly create hostility. Some other issues commonly cause problems in relationships between able-bodied and disabled lesbians. One is the guilt the able-bodied partner may feel concerning her lover's disability. If the disability is painful or progressive in nature, she may need professional help to cope with her anxiety and empathy for her partner. She may have difficulty seeing the disability realistically and either create dependency by pampering her partner or make demands her partner cannot meet. The disabled woman may resent the necessity of explaining and taking care of her physical problems or differences. She may wonder whether her lover is secretly ashamed of her or afraid to be seen with a disabled partner.

Some disabled women form relationships with each other. Because they understand each other in a way able-bodied women cannot, such relationships can be very close and reinforcing. Such relationships have their own difficulties. Many disabled women feel some degree of self-hate or unhappiness about their disabilities. It can be difficult to trust another disabled woman or value her as much as an able-bodied partner. If one partner expresses some negative feelings about her life in general or her disability, the other partner may find it difficult to cheer her up rather than join her in depression.

Being aware of potential problems should not obviate the possibility of a relationship or a sexual experience with a disabled lesbian. She is, after all, much more than her disability. She is a unique and perhaps fascinating woman. The friends and lovers of disabled women are fond of or turned on to them because of their intelligence, personality, wit, sexiness, physical beauty, or other valued characteristics. It can be difficult to see a disabled lesbian as a woman rather than a case history, but it is usually achieved not by overlooking her disability but by looking long and dispassionately enough to integrate it into a complete picture of who she is.

Sexual Techniques

Able-bodied lesbians may have a tendency to assume that all disabled women have the same capabilities. Not only are there differences in physical ability among disabled lesbians, there are differences in sexual preference. The communication that should take place about this between a disabled woman and her partner(s) is not so different from the communication that takes place the first time any women have sex with each other. The questions may change, but basically the partners are trying to find out what they are willing or able to do and what they most enjoy. This is not a one-sided process, since the disabled woman needs to become more familiar with her partner's experience and needs.

Some specific disabilities are discussed below. This is not a complete list, nor is the information on sexual functioning and suggestions on technique exhaustive. If you or your partner have a question about sex that this section doesn't answer, try asking your doctor. She may not know the answer, but asking will raise consciousness about the issue. Since so little has been written about sex and disabled women, you may have to find your own answers with patience, experimentation, and love.

Asthma. Some women who have asthma have difficulty being physically close to a partner or allowing themselves to be held and caressed. This closeness makes them feel claustrophobic or anxious about being able to breathe. If asthma is severe enough, sexual activity can sometimes cause an attack of breathlessness. Some asthmatic lesbians take their medication before or during sexual activity to lower anxiety or prevent trouble with breathing. Learning to relax about being close to another woman can also help, since anxiety contributes to asthma. Shallow, quick breating is a natural part of sexual arousal. It is possible to learn to experience this feeling without associating it with an asthmatic attack.

Blindness and deafness. Neither of these conditions commonly has any effect on sexual functioning per se. Blind lesbians need to rely more on verbal and tactile communication during lovemaking than on visual messages. Deaf lesbians need to rely more on visual and tactile than on verbal communication. Sex education materials, feminist literature and erotica are not available on tapes for the blind lesbian.

Diabetes. Some sources report that the medication given diabetic men lowers their sexual desire. I have not been able to locate any information on whether this is true of diabetic women. While diabetes does not lower genital sensitivity, some diabetic women experience repeated cases of vaginitis that interfere with sexual pleasure.

High blood pressure and heart conditions. Some doctors routinely tell any patient with high blood pressure or a heart condition to refrain from any sexual activity. If your doctor gives you such advice, you may want to question her or him about this opinion or ask another doctor for an opinion. If the rest of your life is free from stress and you are responding to treatment, sexual activity that is not strenuous or anxiety-provoking can actually reduce worry and tension and aid recuperation. Some sources report that medication given for high blood pressure lowers sexual desire.

Infantile encephalopathy. This condition appears during infancy. It can take different forms and affect the motor system, personality, perception, learning ability, sensitivity, and emotional control. In severe cases, the individual may be unable to hold objects or walk. The muscles which are supposed to act against gravity may resist being extended. Primitive reflexes may persist beyond infancy. This particular type of physical difference is sometimes called "spasticity." The eyesight, hearing, and perception of spatial relationships are sometimes poor. Sexual arousal can cause spasms to become worse. A mild tranquilizer (usually valium) taken before sexual activity can help prevent this. If the woman affected by infantile encephalopathy cannot control her hands or head movements, she may be unable to use oral sex or manual stimulation to make love to her partner. Manual masturbation may also be impossible. Tribadism is sometimes an alternative, or rubbing the genitals against soft objects. A vibrator placed on the bed and turned on, or a jet of water in the tub, can also be used for masturbation.

Multiple sclerosis. This is a progressive disease with an unknown cause. It takes a long time (years) to develop. The individual affected will sometimes experience symptoms like blurred vision or ataxia for brief periods of time, then these symptoms will vanish. (Ataxia is difficulty regulating the strength and size of movements. Holding things, walking, or picking things up can become difficult.) Multiple sclerosis causes the insulators or sheaths of the nerve fibers of the spinal medulla to deteriorate. The spinal marrow hardens, and sometimes the brain is affected as well.

Because it is so difficult to diagnose, the woman who has multiple sclerosis may have assumed her symptoms were psychosomatic; she may have undergone therapy or severe emotional suffering as a result. The disease may affect the personality, making it difficult for friends or lovers to cope with. The frequent remissions create cycles of hope and despair that are often exhausting to experience.

The disease may or may not affect genital and skin sensitivity. If the genital sensitivity is not impaired, orgasm remains possible. In either case, sexual desire remains strong. Mild tranquilizers may be prescribed to prevent leg spasms during sexual activity. Some medical authorities suggest an operation in which the tendons attached to the spasming muscles are cut, if this problem is especially severe. A woman with M.S. may lose complete bladder control. A partner needs to be able to accept this as part of her physical reality. The partners will need to search for positions which minimize stress on the legs and reduce the possibility of muscular spasms.

Muscular dystrophy. This is a progressive disease which affects the voluntary muscles. Some authorities feel that it is hereditary, at least in some cases. When it occurs in young people, it delays puberty and disrupts psychosexual development. In non-infantile forms, slight hormonal disturbances often appear that can affect the sex drive. Because the voluntary muscles are weak, a woman with muscular dystrophy will probably need some assistance in moving from one sexual position to another. The heart is sometimes affected by muscular dystrophy. In a few cases, the heart is too weak to sustain the effort and excitement of sexual activity.

Polio. This disease is caused by a virus that usually attacks young people. The disease can cause varying degrees of paralysis, usually in the limbs, but does not often affect genital sensitivity. Mobility can be a problem. If the arms are paralyzed and manual stimulation is impossible, oral sex or tribadism are good techniques to try.

Rheumatism. This is a name for several conditions that affect the joints. The affected partner needs to select a position that causes her minimal discomfort. No pressure or stress should be put on affected joints. She may need to take painkillers prior to sexual activity. Muscle contractions or locked joints can sometimes be a problem. If the hands are severely affected, masturbation by hand or manual stimulation of a partner becomes impossible. Vibrators are sometimes useful, and a good position for oral sex is the able-bodied partner kneeling over her lover's face. In one form of rheumatism (Sogren's disease), the mucous membranes become very dry, which of course affects the vagina. Either vaginal stimulation will be undesirable, or the use of artificial lubricants will be necessary for women with this disease.

Spina bifida. This term literally means "open spine." The vertebral arches are not closed. If the opening is small, the spinal cord will not be affected. A child born with spina bifida has a flabby or stiff hump on its back. If the hump contains nothing but skin, spinal membranes, and fluid, and if the spinal marrow is untouched, the hump can be removed. If the hump contains a part of the spinal cord, the cauda equina (nerve fibers running to or from the spinal cord, normally protected by the spinal column) or both, the surgery becomes problematic. If the spinal cord is affected, there are several possible effects: paralysis below the level of the hump, loss of skin sensitivity, loss of control of the bladder and rectum, misshapen hip bones or feet, and loss of genital sensation or the ability to climax. Since many individuals with spina bifida also have hydrocephalus (an increase in cranial fluid), which impairs intelligence, many of them are institutionalized.

The suggestions made below for spinal cord injuries may be of some help.

Spinal cord injuries. Accidents, birth defects, inflammation or infection, tumors or interrupted blood supply can create a transverse lesion or an interruption in the ascending and descending nerves of the spinal cord. The effect of the lesion on the rest of the body depends on its location and on how extensive it is. Generally there is paralysis below the level of the lesion. In the beginning, the paralysis is flaccid. The affected individual cannot move the paralysed muscles. Later on, the paralysis may or may not become spastic, which means some physical movements may be made without being controlled by the affected individual. The sensation of touch or pain may be lost below the level of the lesion. Bladder control is often lost or made less reliable. Some women with spinal cord injuries learn to control urination by pressing or patting on the abdomen and triggering a reflex contraction that empties the bladder. Other women use catheters. A catheter is a small tube which is inserted into the urethra; a bag is used to collect the urine. There are several different kinds of catheters for use on men, but only one for women. Being catheterized increases the chance of vaginal or urethral infection and makes hygiene very important. Sexual partners need to accept the catheter as part of their partner's bodies, understand how it works, and be told what to do if it comes out. Catheters are not designed to be attractive, but they need not prevent sexual activity. It can be difficult for the disabled woman to educate her partner about the catheter or wait for her to become accustomed to it when she already feels self-conscious about it and irritated by its presence. Both partners need to be patient with each other. After a spinal cord injury, menstruation may cease for six to eight months. When periods begin again, they may be shorter and more irregular.

A spinal cord injury does not affect the desire for sex. However, it makes genital orgasms impossible. Sites of the body above the lesion sometimes become very sensitive and can be stimulated and trained to become erogenous zones. The nipples and the back of the neck are two such areas that frequently become sensitized. Some women with transverse lesions like to use vibrators because of the strong, continuous stimulation they provide. A combination of feeling wanted, desire for her partner, her partner's pleasure, their exchange of passion and affection, and stimulation of non-genital erogenous zones can make a sexual experience meaningful and enjoyable for a woman with a spinal cord injury.

A woman with this disability will need assistance moving into sexual positions. Some women like tribadism because of the experience of being held. Other women like to do oral sex, especially if their arms and hands have been affected by the lesion. Sometimes contractions occur in the leg muscles during sexual arousal. Mild tranquilizers can sometimes prevent this.

One concern which accompanies this disability is body image. During lesbian lovemaking, both partners are supposed to be equal and vigorous participants. This ideal leaves out a woman who needs to ask her lover to lift her arms and put them around her. Women with spinal cord injuries often feel that other women are afraid of their bodies—afraid to look at them, afraid to touch them, afraid they might hurt them. Such a woman may need extra reassurance from her partner before she can believe their sex life is satisfactory and her partner's affection is real.

The persistence of sexual need in women with spinal cord injuries demon-

105

strates that human sexuality is not merely a matter of genital juxtapositioning. Sexual response includes the whole body, the heart, and the mind.

Institutions

In this culture, anyone who is different is ostracized. Many physical differences are "handicaps," because our world has been constructed to exclude the disabled. Institutions are ostensibly supposed to provide adequate medical care and a safe, comfortable environment for disabled people. They also relieve able-bodied people of the inconvenience of dealing with people very different from themselves and perpetuate the idea that disability should be stigmatized.

Many disabled women—some of them lesbians—are confined to institutions. Most of these facilities discourage masturbation or actually punish residents who engage in it. Residents may even be prevented from forming close relationships with each other. This denial of the sexuality of disabled women serves no good purpose. Nor is it enough to tell disabled women that they are sexually adequate because they can be passive partners in heterosexual intercourse. This does nothing to reassure a woman concerned about her own pleasure or the pleasure of a female partner.

Erotic materials should be available to disabled women in institutions. Rehabilitation programs exist to teach disabled women how to feed themselves, dress themselves, or read. These programs should include instructions on how to use a vibrator or other technique for masturbation and how to have sex with a partner. If residents require assistance from attendants to masturbate or need help positioning their bodies to have sex with one another, that help should be available. Educational programs for disabled children should include explicit material about sexuality, tailored to fit their physical and emotional needs.

Medical professionals need to be educated about this issue, and the policies of institutions that care for disabled people must be changed. Able-bodied people must stop using these institutions as dumping grounds. Whenever possible, disabled people should have independent lives in their own communities.

HOMAGE TO

Leonor Fini

born in 1908

Painter and Illustrator, lives and works in Paris

8
Variations

There are many different ways to be a lesbian. This chapter describes some sexual specialties that can coexist with lesbianism. It was written for several different interest groups. For some women, their involvement in a particular variation (perhaps group sex or S/M) can be more important to them than the fact that they relate sexually to other women. For other lesbians, a single experience (perhaps a sexual encounter with an animal) can create ripples of anxiety or guilt that affect their day-to-day sexuality. Other lesbians may want more information about a sexual activity to help them decide whether or not to act out their fantiasies about it or to help them understand friends who depart from the lesbian norm.

The sexualities discussed in this chapter are more stimatized than garden-variety lesbianism. This disapproval exists within as well as outside of the lesbian community. Some lesbians find it necessary to draw a line between acceptable and unacceptable sexual conduct. They may feel it is permissible to be a lesbian only if one's sexuality is not unusual or "kinky." The location of the line between normal and deviant lesbian sexuality may be based on personal taste ("I don't like bondage because the idea of being tied up doesn't turn me on.") or moral and political grounds ("Women who do S/M are acting out patriarchal roles.").

We should be wary of making broad statements about the worth or value of another lesbian's sexual style, especially if it involves behavior we don't understand or have never participated in. No erotic act has an intrinsic meaning. A particular sexual activity may symbolize one thing in the majority culture, another thing to members of a sexual subculture or religious sect, and yet another thing to the individuals who engage in it. The context within which an erotic act occurs can also alter its meaning.

While some of these variations may seem unusual, none of them are uncommon, and they have probably always been a part of human sexuality. That does not mean they are desirable or rewarding for everyone. It is much easier for a lesbian to decide whether or not a particular variation is part of her own sexuality than it is to decide whether or not any lesbian ought to enjoy it. Of course, the gross inequities in our society affect sexuality, and no lifestyle or activity ought to escape criticism and evaluation. We should remember, however, that lesbians have been persecuted because we defy heterosexual mores. If we in turn are to enforce sexual prohibitions, surely some compelling reason must be demonstrated for doing so.

107

We should not assume that because we are victims of sexual repression we are free of prejudice. If we carefully consider all the different ways there are to be a lesbian, we must conclude that each sexual specialty is essential to the happiness of some lesbians.

The following variations will be examined (in alphabetical order): sex with animals, fetishes, fist-fucking, group sex, sadomasochism, transsexuality, watersports and scat. This doesn't exhaust all the possibilities but will, it is hoped, encourage more discussion of all dissenting sexual styles in the lesbian community.

Animals

The stentorian term "bestiality" is used to designate giving sexual pleasure to or getting sexual pleasure from an animal. It rarely occurs to the clinicians who use this term that we are animals too. Our chauvinism as a species is further displayed in our use of the terms "beast," "animal," or "brute" for humans who behave in cruel or despicable ways.

The frank eroticism that beasties display can be very arousing to human beings. Other animals seem to be more free than we are about expressing their physical enjoyment and need to be touched. They also have fewer inhibitions about expressing their lack of enthusiasm for things that don't feel good, and will either run away, bite, scratch, or fall asleep when what's happening ceases to be pleasant.

Fantasies that include animals are very common. The sensual attraction of the animal plus the forbidden nature of the experience can make these fantasies very exciting. When it comes to reality, you may have trouble deciding whether you've ever had an experience with bestiality. Does it turn you on to pet your collie? Do you have a cat that insists on lying on your chest while you masturbate? Some experiences with animals are more clearly sexual. Children often explore the genitals of the family pet or allow an animal to smell and lick their genitals. If you have a pet, you may massage its genitals when it comes into heat and can't be allowed to have sex with a member of its own species. You may allow your favorite animal to stay in the room while you masturbate or make love. Dogs become especially interested in sexual noises and smells and may want to taste sexual juices or perspiration on your skin and vulva without any encouragement from you.

Being sexual with animals can cause some anxiety, largely because of the threat of disapproval or ridicule. Other concerns can be dealt with more easily. If you are not compelling the animal to accept your attentions and you are gentle, you will not harm it emotionally or physically. Concerns about hygiene can be alleviated by washing yourself or your non-human, furry friend. Conception cannot occur as a result of sex between humans and animals of other species.

If sex with a particular animal is a regular part of your life, you may wonder whether that's normal. Since we really don't know what people do sexually, that is difficult to determine. It is easier to assess the quality of your life in general and see whether this one experience is affecting it. If you have difficulty forming relationships or initiating sexual encounters with other women, you may wonder whether there is some connection. It is doubtful that eliminating sex with your pet will make relating to women any easier. The social skills lesbians use to find partners are described earlier in this book, along with suggestions for developing and refining these skills. You need not choose between loving women and loving animals. The emotional and sexual content of these two experiences is very different. Women don't have fur, can't purr, and don't bother you to be walked every morning. Animals don't talk, earn their own livings, squeeze fresh orange juice, or write love poems.

To sum it all up, most women have some sexual or sensual feelings about animals at some point in their lives. It is not unusual for these feelings to be expressed. There are few physical risks attached to non-coercive sex with a domesticated animal. However, the threat of social stigma and guilt can make such an experience difficult to enjoy, especially as a regular part of your sexual pattern. Despite the risks, some lesbians feel there is nothing wrong with expressing sexual feelings toward animals or allowing animals to express their sexual impulses toward a human being.

Fetishes

A fetish is any object, substance, or part of the body that is sexually arousing in and of itself. Some of the more common fetishes are leather, rubber, satin, velvet, silk, hair, feet, button-fly levis, boots, spike heels, and feminine underclothes. Just about anything can be a fetish. Its appealing qualities may be the way it looks, feels, or smells. There are different levels of involvement with a fetish. Most of us find some substances, objects, or parts of the body more arousing than others. Some women get especially turned on if their lovers are wearing garter belts and high heels. Some lesbians find denim more attractive than polyester or prefer women with a particular hairdo or body type. Many lesbians have trouble enjoying a sexual encounter if at least one of their fetishes is not present. Others may have a particular thing that epitomizes sex for them and prefer sexual encounters to focus on their fetish. Relatively few lesbians label the things that turn them on, independent of the the person they are owned or worn by, as fetishes. This may be because there is a widespread myth among sexologists, psychologists and psychiatrists that women don't respond to inanimate objects or isolated parts of the body with sexual arousal.

The first step in acting on fetishistic fantasies is to obtain the material or thing that turns you on. Depending on the nature of your fetish, this can be a matter of spending a nickel in a hardware store or sending away to England. Some women, especially those with expensive tastes like leather, learn how to make their own fetish clothing to save money and guarantee that the result is exactly what they want. Fetishes can be very specific. If you like black silk crotchless panties, powder blue bikini briefs won't do. If your thing is denim cut-offs, satin baseball shorts will leave you cold. Some fetishes (leather and rubber clothing and extremely high heels are three of the best examples) have small subcultures built around them. You can find ads for catalogs or clubs in some gay male publications or specialized magazines sold in adult bookstores.

Fetishes are most commonly utilized during masturbation. In the privacy of your own room, you can dress up in the costume of your fantasy or use your favorite implement for stimulation. It can also be exciting to include a partner in fetish play. Ask her if she would like to play dress-up, and discuss the ideas you both have of what costumes are especially sexy. Asking a partner to include a fetish object in sex play (a leather glove, a fur wrap, a monogrammed sterling silver hairbrush) can be done in much the same way you would ask her to try a vibrator or other sex toy. The use of a fetish may be part of a particular fantasy for you that involves roles and dialogue. If this is true, you may want to suggest acting out some sexual dramas to your partner. She may have some scenarios of her own. It is generally easier to find a partner who will play dress-up or use fetish objects than it is to find a partner with a particular physical appearance. Some women may be willing to grow or cut their hair (perhaps even shave it), gain weight, lose weight, or appreciate and turn on to those traits in you. The same publications that advertise catalogs of fetish merchandise may also carry personal ads for individuals seeking partners for specific sexual activities. These ads may be one way for you to find partners who will share your interests.

Some fetishes, especially leather and rubber, are associated with sado-masochism in most people's minds. These sexual specialties can overlap, but they can also be separate and distinct. A woman who finds leather erotic may simply want to wear it when she goes out or during sex with a partner. The smell and feel of the leather are sexually arousing for her, and she has no interest in bondage or pain. Because fetishes and S/M are so often associated, firms that manufacture and sell rubber or leather often sell S/M equipment, and people involved in fetish sex may know or socialize with people involved in S/M.

Fist-Fucking

Upon hearing this term, most lesbians imagine a large, dry fist being forced into a small, unwilling orifice. This is hardly a sensuous image. The synonym "hand-balling" gets a similar response. There doesn't seem to be a descriptive word for putting one's whole hand inside a sexual partner that makes it clear this feels good. For this reason, some lesbians do fist-fucking regularly without calling it anything. Gay men have developed slang terminology and many safety rules for hand-balling, so much information in this section comes from conversations with gay men. Since fist-fucking is becoming more popular among lesbians, it is important to learn from those who have already had a lot of experience with it.

Hand-balling is an extreme form of penetration and should be done carefully. The top (the woman who wants to use her whole hand inside her lover) should prepare her hands. Sharp cuticles and hangnails must be trimmed, and fingernails should be cut as short as possible. An emery board should then be used to file the remaining nail away. If you have enough of a fingernail left to scratch your nose, it could scratch your partner and cause bleeding. A motion with the emery board that goes straight back over the nail toward the wrist works best. Another reason for giving yourself a manicure is that nails can be dirty. Women who like to use just a finger or fingers for penetration should also trim their nails to avoid cuts or infection.

A woman who wants her partner to penetrate her to this extent (the bottom) needs to stay in touch with how relaxed and open her vagina or anus is. It is much more common for women to enjoy vaginal fist-fucking than anal. However, there is no physiological reason why the anus cannot gradually be stretched and relaxed over time until it can contain something as large as a hand. If a woman has had children or is accustomed to maximum penetration, she may need less preparation and relaxation time than a woman who has not had children or is just beginning to enjoy this much dilation.

You must use an artificial lubricant to make vaginal or anal hand-balling comfortable and safe. Crisco is a popular choice, but lubricants that are not water-soluble give some women vaginal infections. Some lubricants like ForPlay which are manufactured for use during sex are water-soluble and can be douched out after sex. Whatever your choice, use a lot of it—several handsful. Be daring! The mess is part of the fun.

This kind of sex works best with constant communication. The top may want to talk out a fantasy that the vagina or anus will open up and actually suck in her hand. The bottom should tell her lover about any irritation, soreness, or tightness, and ask her to back off or provide other kinds of stimulation. She can also reassure the top when the penetration is feeling good and it's time to move ahead. The top needs to rely on her own sense of how relaxed or tight the vagina or anus is, too. While encouraging, flattering, and seducing the bottom into taking her whole hand, the top should not be in a hurry. The important thing is how it feels, not how far in you get.

Some women find that amyl or butyl nitrite causes the sphincter muscles to relax, thus easing penetration. Other drugs which are often used during fist-fucking are MDA, cocaine, and Quaalude. Drugs can enhance the sensations of hand-balling, but they can also increase the risk of injury. The vagina and anus are not very sensitive to pain. Being stoned decreases pain sensitivity even more, making it hard to keep track of potential damage.

If you are exploring anal fist-fucking, you will probably want to invest in a douche hose. A flexible piece of plastic hose can be attached to your bathtub faucet and used much like an enema bag. Adjust the water temperature so that it is not cold (which will make the bowel tense) or hot (which may burn) and fill your rectum with water. To clean out the large intestine, you will need to repeat this procedure five or six times over the course of an hour or so. The bowel should be cleaned for safety as well as aesthetic reasons. Waste products have a gritty texture that can abrade the walls of the rectum. Some people who do anal fist-fucking regularly will either fast the day before a hand-balling session or eat foods which move quickly through their systems without causing constipation or diarrhea.

Another sanitary concern is the micro-organisms that the bowel contains. Some of them cause diseases or infections, so be sure to wash your hands with an antiseptic soap after anal fist-fucking, especially before you do any vaginal penetration.

It is possible for the bowel to be injured without the bottom feeling it. This is less likely, but possible, in the vagina. If any bleeding occurs after you have been fist-fucked, see a doctor immediately. Small tears in the vagina or rectum can be located and stitched. Unrepaired cuts or tears can cause infection, perhaps even peritonitis (an inflammation of the lining of the abdominal cavity). You may want to ask a gay male friend for the name of a sympathetic and knowledgeable physician. If the doctor asks how you were hurt, explain that your sex partner accidentally injured you. They need not press for details before treating you. Sex-related injuries are not rare. A few doctors may ask whether you were sexually assaulted. Thank them for being sensitive to that possibility, and tell them no. It is possible that the doctor you see will let you know she or he disapproves of your sexual activity. Take someone with you for support. Don't let the possibility of disapproval deter you from getting treatment.

A sexual injury can be traumatic as well as physically painful. It can impair trust. You may worry that your partner is not being careful enough, and she may worry about your ability to communicate your limits. The worst thing you can do is keep silent about such an accident and become progressively more suspicious of each other. Talk about the sexual experience that led up to the injury. If either of you was impatient or too stoned, you may want to change your sexual pattern. Remember that when we get turned on we are less sensitive to pain. Stressful sensations in the genitals can be arousing. There are many different kinds of sex-related injuries, and they happen during every kind of sex. This kind of accident is especially scary because the sexual activity is stigmatized. After talking the whole thing over with your partner, you may decide that the incident wasn't anybody's fault.

Fist-fucking can be done safely if both partners take responsibility for following their physical sensations and observing the safety rules given above. It is a good technique for women who really like penetration and can't seem to get enough. If a whole hand will fit inside, there is no logical reason to stay outside. Fist-fucking provides an intense feeling of being entered and posessed that can be felt through the whole body. It is an amazing experience to see and feel your whole hand disappear inside another woman's body. You are simultaneously taking her and having your hand taken in and held. It's like slowly putting on a hot, tight, wet satin glove. The hand naturally closes as it enters the vagina, until the knuckles are pressed up against the cervix.

The top may find it difficult to stay in touch with her partner's vagina or anus and provide clitoral stimulation as well. The bottom may find that her clitoris has become very sensitive and fussy and so prefer to manipulate it herself.

A few lesbians who like fist-fucking have taken to wearing a red hanky in their back pockets (on the right if they are bottoms, on the left if they are tops) to signify this preference. Using colored bandanas to signal sexual specialties may become a lesbian fad.

Group Sex

Chances are that one or both of the following situations has overtaken you during your lesbian career.

(1) You are making love to your partner. You have both hands and your mouth busy. Both of you are going crazy. But there are still apertures left unfilled and sensitive places left untouched. You wonder what it would feel like to have another woman slowly caress your clitoris while you go down on your lover, or you fantasize another woman lowering her cunt onto your lover's waiting eager mouth. The fantasy may make you a little anxious, but you have an explosive orgasm. So does she (maybe while enjoying the same fantasy).

(2) You have a long-term lover you are very close to and very turned on to. Because both of you are sexually active and aware, you become interested in other women. The thought of having your lover leave you to have sex

with another woman is painful and threatening. You do a lot of talking about these erotic attractions to other women, and one day you discover that both of you have a crush on a friend of the family. The crush won't go away. It's a thorny dilemma. Do you and your lover try to ignore this attraction or talk it away? Do you compete for a new flame's attention and destroy your trust for one another? The third woman is in an awkward position, liking and being attracted to both of you, not wanting to cause either of you pain. Wouldn't it be nice if all three of you could somehow work this out—together?

Group sex may be one of the most common lesbian sexual fantasies. But it hardly ever happens (compared to the number of times it could or should happen). One reason for this is the emphasis many lesbians place on coupled monogamy. Another reason is the reluctance many lesbians feel to have sex for the sake of physical pleasure or novelty if they are not romantically involved. Even nonmonogamous lesbians sometimes prefer to take their lovers on one at a time. For these women, casual group sex isn't an option. It can, however, remain a piquant and entrancing fantasy.

If you want to arrange a group sex experience, you are probably going to have to take responsibility for planning and initiating it. It's very common for a group of friends to get together, get high and horny, and just go their separate ways at the end of the evening. Group sex is so taboo that somebody has to be the seductress to make it happen. Since group sex can be a disaster if proper attention isn't paid to anxiety, pride, jealousy, vulnerability, and loneliness, advance planning and preparation are essential. What's the point in having lots of good sex if anger and guilt are going to ruin it the next day?

There are several different ways to initiate a group sex experience. How and when you suggest it has a lot to do with whether or not it will happen. First, assess your own sexual lifestyle. If you have a lover who picks fights with anybody who asks you to dance, it is obvious that other women are going to be wary of your invitation. However, if you are an independent and adventurous type, perhaps with a reputation for being off-beat and polygynous, your offer will be less threatening. If the proposition is being made by you and your lover or best friend, both of you should bring up the possibility of group sex. Then the other woman or women involved will know that both of you want it to happen and feel good about it. Think a little about the other women involved. Would a group sex experience endanger their stability? Are they involved in a sexually exclusive relationship? Is one of them in love with you? If so, will a casual experience that doesn't result in a coupled relationship hurt her? You will have better luck with women who are single or involved in open relationships or with women who are visiting your locale for a brief period of time.

Make your proposal in explicit and sensuous terms. The suggestion will be less startling if it follows an arousing group experience like dancing together, getting stoned, or taking a massage class. You can say something like, "I'm feeling very turned on to all of you, and I'd like to do something about it." or "It would be a real shame if we let all these good feelings go to waste. Let's stay together and get it on."

You may get a mixed response. One woman may be uncomfortable with the idea or too tired to participate and leave the rest of you to carry on. Other women may want to talk about the idea and get some clearer picture of what could happen before saying yes or no. If you are turned down, it is hoped the other women will realize how vulnerable it made you to proposition them and will make their refusals gentle and nonjudgmental. If they accept your invitation, you will probably get a sinking feeling in the pit of your stomach as you say to yourself, "Oh my goddess, it's really going to happen. What do I do now?"

What you do is adjourn to a quiet, private place and do some preliminary negotiation. To begin with, discuss confidentiality. Does anybody want the experience kept a secret? There are several motives for wanting some confidentiality. One is a fear of being viewed as kinky or weird by other lesbians. One of the women present may be taking a holiday from a monogamous relationship. In the latter case, it's essential to tell the other women involved, so that they can decide how they feel about including her. Generally speaking, everyone will feel more free if they don't have to keep what happens under wraps and can do a little discreet bragging about it afterward, but you can't always have that ideal situation. It's okay to keep some things secret in order to protect yourself.

You should also discuss your feelings for one another. If you are especially attracted to one particular woman, you will have to be careful not to make anyone else feel left out. If you have never had sex with each other before, share some information about your favorite ways to be touched or to have an orgasm. If you have any fantasies about how you'd like the evening to go, describe them. One of them could intrigue everybody and become a starting point for the night's activities. This is a good time to trot out your worst fears and get some reassurance that everyone will be good to everybody else and no one will be struck by lightning.

Set up the space where you're going to be having sex. Most beds comfortably accommodate only two women, so you may have to move down onto a carpeted floor and make nests with pillows and sleeping bags. If more than one woman is going to use a vibrator, make sure there are extension cords available. Bring in some bottles of oil or jars of cream to use as lubricant. Towels are a good idea, and something cold to drink. If you have a stereo, you may want to think a little about what music would be ap-

116

propriate.

Talking about what kind of sex everyone wants usually creates a sexy, turned-on mood. You can heighten that mood by dancing; feeding each other sensual foods like strawberries, cheese, or avocado; or partially undressing or putting on erotic costumes.

When it comes to actually getting it on, there are many different ways to handle the logistics. You may want to take turns being the center of attention and let the woman in the middle ask for the kind of strokes she wants. Some women may enjoy masturbating or just watching while other women make love. It can be fun to lie in a circle or side by side and masturbate or buzz off together. You can also break into pairs or other small groups and perhaps change partners later in the evening.

If you are together for very long, you may want to take breaks and talk about what's happening, give each other backrubs, take out dirty dishes, or get something to eat or drink. Ideally, anyone who feels scared or bored or unhappy should say so and be able to talk about what she needs from the other women present.

You may get involved in a group sex situation and begin to feel alienated from the other women present. They may not have done anything to make you feel that way, or you may have had an unpleasant interchange with somebody. Whatever the cause, you aren't having a good time and you want to leave. Group sex etiquette is that you don't leave in such a way that it disrupts other women's fun. Don't walk in on your lover if she's with another woman and announce you are leaving. Don't just take off without some explanation. Everyone will worry about why you left and where you are, and fear the worst. You may have to stay around for a little while until there's a break or you can catch at least one other person and explain that you feel out of it and want to go.

Remember that it may not be necessary for you to leave to make yourself feel better. Group sex parties usually have ups and downs for everyone involved. You may feel depressed and isolated because you're not having sex or you're not getting the kind of sex you anticipated. That may not be true of the whole evening. Find something to do with your energy. Take responsibility for the music, make some fruit salad, check and see whether anybody needs an assistant or a vibrator or a towel. If you don't seem withdrawn or miserable, other women will be more likely to find you interesting and attractive.

Group sex works best if you don't expect the same things from it that you expect from one-to-one sex with your favorite lover. It can take more than one experience with group sex to get used to having other women see you getting turned on and getting off. It takes a while to learn how to cruise or turn down sexual invitations in a group. Adding more women to a situation increases its complexity and risk, so go easy on yourself.

You may want to have a post-orgy workshop. If everyone spends the night, you can do this over coffee and blintzes in the morning. This is a great time to crow a little. Reassure each other that a lovely time was had by all, and congratulate each other on your unconventionality. Thank the women who put out energy to make you feel good. If there were some snags in the evening, talk about what you think went askew and make a suggestion for dealing with it better next time. Remember that a little criticism goes a long way when evaluating an experience as rare and tricky as this one.

It is thoughtful to offer to help with cleaning up. Don't forget to make a telephone call or send a note to your hostess thanking her for organizing the celebration.

Couples who have participated in group sex together will probably need to do their own processing, apart from their discussion with the group. It may take more than one conversation to absorb everything you learned from the experience. To reduce jealousy and make this evaluation easier, some couples have a rule that they will leave group sex parties together and sleep together after it's over. That makes it clear that you are still committed to each other despite your sexual activity with other women.

If you have a social circle that would support such an event, you may want to organize a large group sex party. A social circle of that nature can evolve out of a group of friends who enjoy doing threesomes with each other, or it can be built by a couple who enjoy seducing other women and encouraging open sexual expression. Sex in larger groups of women works a little differently than small groups of intimate friends.

The invitations should be sent well in advance. An appropriate invitation would be a small piece of lesbian erotica with a salaciously worded description of the evening's festivities. Envelopes should be opaque. Specify on the invitation whether dinner, refreshments, or intoxicants will be provided.

It can be difficult to find enough room to make such a party feasible. If a large private home is not available, you may be able to rent space in a gay male bathhouse or a private resort. If you have to spend money to rent space, it is permissible to charge your guests a fee to cover expenses.

It is usually taken for granted that anyone who comes to an orgy has obtained permission from her partner or will handle confidentiality by herself. Couples who come to an orgy together can have different agreements governing their participation. They may wish to have sex only with each other in a public setting. They may agree to have sex with other women only if both of them have a partner. They are responsible for communicating this agreement to potential partners and should do it with some tact.

At large parties, it is rare for a huddle or a group grope to develop.

Women will usually cruise each other, negotiate one-on-ones or threeways, get it on, dissolve the contract, and cruise for another experience. It is bad manners to expect one woman to stay with you the whole evening unless you have a prior agreement to that effect. It is also bad manners to lose your temper if someone approaches you or to be rude when making your approach. Low pressure is the key to a pleasant experience. If you begin to massage someone's neck and she moves away, let her go and look for someone who is available. If a woman starts dancing around you and you are not interested, smile and say, "I'm taking a break," or "Sorry—not now." It's handy to be able to say what you want in a brief sentence: "I'd love to eat your luscious cunt," or "Does that gorgeous ass of yours crave some attention?" It's usually easier to proposition someone from a top or active space, since it makes you less vulnerable.

This experience is not yet readily available to most lesbians. However, large group sex parties for women are becoming more frequent, popular, and accepted. Several good things could come about if group sex parties were a lesbian institution. The level of frustration and alcohol consumption in lesbian bars could be drastically reduced. It would be easier for women to have casual sex in an honest, comfortable, non-manipulative way. It might even increase the lifetime of coupled relationships. If your lover can go to a group sex party for her extracurricular excitement, it may be less threatening for you than having her establish an ongoing sexual relationship with another woman.

Sadomasochism

This sexual variation is surrounded by a lot of fear and distortion. Relationships in which one partner physically abuses the other or dominates her emotionally are often described as sadomasochistic. The newspapers routinely refer to sex murderers or rapists as sadists. Armchair psychologists are fond of labeling friends who frequently get involved in situations that cause them distress or threaten their survival as masochists.

Unhealthy relationships, violent crimes with a genital or sexual component, and self-destructive behavior do exist. But in this section a distinction is made between coercive or suicidal activities and sexual sadomasochism. Sadomasochism is defined here as an erotic ritual that involves acting out fantasies in which one partner is sexually dominant and the other partner is sexually submissive. This ritual is preceded by a negotiation process that enables participants to select their roles, state their limits, and specify some of the activities which will take place. The basic dynamic of sexual sadomasochism is an eroticized, consensual exchange of power—not violence or pain.

One of the many myths about sadomasochism, or S/M, is that lesbians don't do it. S/M is stereotyped as a gay male or heterosexual activity. It's true that lesbians don't have bars or private clubs that cater to an S/M-oriented clientele, nor do we have magazines full of sex ads and snapshots of lesbian dominatrixes. But there are lesbians who have decided to act on their persistent and powerful S/M fantasies, or who would like to if an opportunity arose. S/M among lesbians is underground rather than nonexistent. Hostility toward S/M from within and outside the lesbian community keeps it underground.

Anti-S/M feelings among feminists have some legitimate sources. We are still fighting an entrenched psychoanalytic concept that says that women are naturally masochistic and passive. This concept is used to justify the sexual, social and economic exploitation of women. The ugly idea that women encourage, cooperate with, and secretly enjoy rape or sexual abuse is a companion piece of misogyny.

This anti-woman propaganda can make a lesbian who has S/M fantasies feel very bad about herself. Is her libido cooperating with the enemy? Has she somehow failed to take back her power as a woman? Actually, having an S/M fantasy and dealing with second-class status in a male-dominated society are very different things. Women work at low-paying jobs because they must survive and those jobs are often all that is available. An S/M fantasy is a choice made out of a field of possible erotic themes. Saying "yes, mistress" to a lover who has you beside yourself with pleasure is not the same thing as saying "yes, sir" to a boss.

Some feminist theoreticians equate the role of top, or sadist, with masculinity and male privilege and equate the role of bottom, or masochist, with femininity and the low status of women in this culture. They see S/M as a logical extension (perhaps the epitome) of sexism, and suggest that it is caused by guilt about sexual feelings and anger or hatred of one's sexual partner.

The dominant role in S/M sex is not based on economic control or physical constraint. The only power a top has is temporarily given to her by the bottom. Thus, that power is always limited by the needs and capabilities of the bottom. The dominant role can be expressed by using feminine costume and mannerisms as easily as it can be expressed using a masculine mode of expression; or a top can be androgynous. The same holds true for the submissive. The bottom need not be self-destructive, nor is she genuinely helpless. She is likely to be very aware of her own sexual fantasies and preferences and exceptionally good at getting what she wants. The power she loans to her sexual partner is not permanently lost, nor does it inhibit her ability to maneuver and succeed in the rest of her life. Both partners benefit from an S/M exchange because both of them obtain sexual pleasure from it.

Calling sadomasochism sexist is similar to calling an army or a boarding school homosexual. There may be erotic feelings and sexual activity between members of the same sex in a prison, the military, or a sex-segregated school. But those feelings and activities are quantitatively and qualitatively different from those of individuals who freely choose a homosexual identity. The lesbian who self-identifies as a sadomasochist uses roles, power exchanges, and intense sensations for sexual gratification. She is very different from that class of individuals (male) who use social institutions, police powers, and economic inequity to force half of humanity (women) into a subservient position.

If S/M is the result of male domination, why is it stigmatized rather than being the official form of sexual interaction? A better case can be made for viewing sadomasochism as a sexual minority. Job discrimination, public ridicule, harassment on the street, and violence are the threats that S/M people who disclose their sexuality face. The women who engage in S/M refuse to accept the standard definitions of what sex should be or how it should be done. S/M is a form of sexual rebellion. It is represssed for many of the same reasons that homosexuality is repressed. It is nonreproductive, denies any correlation between maleness and sexual control or femaleness and sexual passivity, and utilizes non-genital objects as foci of desire.

Psychoanalysts used to say that lesbians were narcissistic, had a paranoid fear of sexual penetration, and were immature and neurotic because they had avoided marriage and motherhood. Arguments that suggest S/M is caused by sexual guilt follow similar lines. There is no evidence that sadomasochists were made to feel any more guilty about their sexuality as children than other people were, and there is also no evidence to support the assertion that they feel resentment or hatred toward their partners.

It is often misleading to use one's own values as a framework for interpreting other women's behavior. What looks dangerous or violent in an S/M encounter has probably been carefully planned and executed. S/M is a language of passion with its own conventions, signals and sexual techniques. In the material that follows, components of sadomasochism will be described. This will probably be most helpful to lesbians who are already doing S/M sex or women who would like to explore it. It may also be enlightening to lesbians who have a more academic interest in the topic. The most accessible images of S/M are found in commercial pornography. This material often portrays nonconsensual activities and may show people doing things that are not safe. Most S/M people do not play that way. Great attention is given to the safety, comfort and arousal of the bottom, or submissive. Contrary to myth, women who prefer S/M sex often have close and loving relationships. Traditional erotica distorts S/M in much the same way that it distorts lesbianism. It is hoped that this section will present a more accurate picture of how S/M lesbians find partners, have sex, resolve conflicts and express affection in the context of an S/M relationship.

Communication. Because S/M is so controversial, it can be a diffcult thing to broach to your lover or suggest to a casual sex partner. It is often easier to begin the discussion on an abstract level rather than to blurt out, "Why don't you pretend I'm your slave tonight?" You can ask your partner what she thinks of S/M in general, give her some S/M erotica like *The Story of O, Nine and a Half Weeks,* or portions of *A Woman's Touch* to read, or suggest she read this chapter and get her opinion on it. This kind of discussion can give you some idea of how she feels about S/M on a theoretical level, but it may not tell you whether or not she has fantasies about it or has had any experience with it. It is also possible that she will give you a negative or indifferent opinion of S/M if she has not thought much about it or wants to protect herself from criticism.

You can educate her about S/M and provoke her curiosity; but at some point, if you want to actually do it, you'll probably have to speak directly about your needs. A good way to start this discussion is to ask her whether she ever has any S/M fantasies and would she be shocked if she discovered that you have them. If her response is reassuring, explain yourself in more detail. You might want to say something like, "I've had S/M fantasies for years and years, and I trust you enough to want to explore them with you. I am really curious about what it would be like to have you tie me up or tell me what to do in bed." Another possible introduction is, "There are times when I feel so much passion for you that I really want to possess and own you. Would it scare you if we pretended sometime that you belong to me, so that I could express some of those feelings? Is that something you might enjoy?"

She may respond with an instantaneous, firm "Yes!" or she may need to talk it over and think about it before agreeing to experiment. Once the decision is made, take some time to familiarize one another with your expectations and fears, and work out some limits within which the scene or session can take place. One way to do this is to make three lists. One is a list of sexual things (S/M and non-S/M) that you have done and enjoy. The second is a list of sexual things you are curious about and might want to try. The third is a list of sexual things you do not want to do—activities that are off-limits. Switch lists and see how many items you have in common. The material on roles, bondage, pain and humiliation that follows can give you more ideas for your adventure.

When you start exploring S/M, you will probably find that it brings up some unexpected and powerful feelings. You may get in touch with old hurts, buried pain, power you never knew you had, or discover you want things that surprise you. It's often necessary to take breaks during a scene to drop the roles and talk about your reactions. This is especially important if you feel alienated from your partner or if she is concerned because you have been incoherent or crying. Subsequent scenes will be improved if you follow a session with a conversation about what went well, what could have gone better, the effects it had on your self-image and emotions, and the ideas it gave you for next time.

Some S/M fantasies involve a situation in which the bottom protests and resists. She may wish to pretend she is being captured, subdued, or seduced. If it is part of your lover's role to cry, "No! No! Stop! Please stop!" you will need to know when she is playing and when she really means it. You should agree upon a code word (sometimes called a safe word) that neither of you will use accidentally. This can be a word like "pickle" or "rosebud." If either of you uses the safe word, it means you want the action to stop. You can also simply ask for a break.

It is possible that, after careful preparation and a diplomatic invitation to sample the delights of dominance and submission, your prospective partner will turn you down. If she is a casual partner and you have someone else you can ask, or if your interest in S/M is minimal, you can probably accept her refusal without too much angst. If she is a primary or monogamous lover, or if she tells you S/M is sick and your suggestion is offensive, you will probably suffer from self-doubt and conflict.

Remember that there is nothing wrong with asking someone if she would like to share a particular sexual experience with you. That includes sucking on her toes, squirting whipped cream on her clitoris, and spanking her perfect round behind. If she doesn't want to participate, it doesn't mean your fantasies are evil or weird. It means she doesn't want to participate, that's all. A rejection designed to make you feel bad about yourself is unfair and undeserved. Many women would react with hostility to a sexual proposition from another woman, and we all know there's nothing wrong or bad about such a proposition.

Confronted with a primary or monogamous partner's refusal to engage in S/M, you have several choices. You can try to change her mind. It is possible that you can do this by continuing to bring up the subject and talking over her objections. However, you will probably feel frustrated and impotent during this process and resent her for having so much power over your sexuality. You may be able to arrange a compromise. One possible solution is for you to find another partner or partners to do S/M with. She may be willing to talk out S/M fantasies while you are making love or masturbating. There may be sexual techniques which are on the border between vanilla and S/M sex (biting, hair-tugging, holding the other woman down,

123

vigorous penetration, anal sex) that she enjoys and can agree to do more
often.

You and your partner should remember that relationships do end over
issues like this. Sex is one of the most important aspects of a relationship.
If the sex is not satisfying for both partners, it is reasonable to change the
relationship. It can be very painful to break up with a lover or change a romantic relationship into a friendship, but sometimes it is necessary. Few
things cause more anger than sexual frustration. Remaining lovers when
you are sexually incompatible can damage any respect or affection you have
for one another.

Roles. You may already know which role you want to adopt when you
start talking about doing S/M for the first time. Your choice may be based
on sexual fantasies in which you identify or empathize with one role much
more strongly than the other. Your choice may be based on experience.
With a novice partner, the more experienced woman often decides to play
top, at least in the first few encounters, because she is more familiar with
S/M technique. If both of you are inexperienced and neither of you has a
strong preference, you can agree to play for a little while and then switch
roles.

There are many different approaches to adopting a role. You may want
to keep things simple and have one of you merely give orders or tie the other
woman up and then make love to her. You may want to use some S/M
etiquette and institute some rules that forbid the bottom to look at her top
or require the bottom to address her as "mistress" or kneel when she enters
the room. You may want to pretend you are characters in a particular fantasy. Some popular characters are teacher and student, parent and child,
doctor and patient, mistress and servant or slave, priest and penitent, Amazon warrior and captive, and interrogator and prisoner. You may want to
improvise a dialogue and events, or you may use a script both of you have
agreed to before the scene.

Each role has its own difficulties, responsibilities, and rewards. The
woman on the bottom has to trust her partner a great deal. She will probably need reassurance that her top is going to be careful, respect her limits,
and really want to take the power she is given. The woman on top is
probably going to wonder whether her bottom takes her seriously, especially if she is an inexperienced dominant. Many tops find it helps them
to assume their role with more style and confidence if they dress for the
part. The top is also reassured if she knows that her partner is turned on
and enjoying what is going on and doesn't find it abusive or violent. The
bottom is responsible for being obedient, for carrying out her top's orders
with dispatch and grace, for being as aroused and sexually available and

desirable as possible, and for letting her top know when she is physically un-
fortable or needs a break. Hands or feet that are falling asleep, a muscle
cramp, an itchy nose, a hair on your tongue, or feeling chilly are turn-offs
that should be corrected before the scene progresses. The bottom is also
responsible for being responsive—for revealing her feelings and reactions in
explicit detail to the top. The top is responsible for constructing a scene that
falls within the bottom's limits, although it is permissible to stretch her
limits if she suddenly discovers the capacity to go further than she ever has
before. Half of the responsibility for safety falls on the top's shoulders.
Safety includes the bottom's physical and emotional state. The top should
not attempt things she does not know how to do. After a scene, the bottom
has to be returned to a pre-session consciousness. Her autonomy must be
reinstated.

Partners in an S/M scene often wonder what the other woman gets out of
it. Switching roles can be educational. The bottom's reward is sexual pleasure and catharsis. Her pleasure comes from being dominated, from experiencing intense physical sensations and forbidden emotions, and from
having her sacrifices witnessed by the top. The top's reward is the affirma-
tion of her power and the sexual service she receives from the bottom. She
participates vicariously in the delight and distress of her submissive. Knowing that another woman is willing to trust you, give herself up to you, and
suffer for you is a heady experience.

There are some common concerns about S/M associated with each role.
A woman who prefers to play bottom or submissive may experience some
anxiety about how much she likes to give in to her top. She may wonder
just how far she will go and fear for her independence and self-control.
This anxiety usually fades over time as she continues to explore S/M and
finds it does not impair her ability to function in the rest of her life. It also
helps if she can talk over her fears with her partner or partners and if they
offer ample evidence that they do not want to exploit or injure her. A lesbian masochist may also be concerned about the social status of her role,
both because masochism is associated with femininity and because bottoms
tend to outnumber tops. Being part of a supportive group of other S/M
lesbians can alleviate concerns about status. Both partners are essential if a
scene is to work well. A good bottom is equal in status to a good top. Bottoms who are concerned about finding partners sometimes decide to play
top occasionally so that they won't feel stuck or deprived if a dominant
partner is not available.

A woman who prefers to play top or dominant can also wonder just how
far she will go. This anxiety can be exacerbated by the cultural association
of sexual sadism with violence and brutality. While the masochist worries
about being of lower status than a top, the top worries about being accused

of coercive or damaging behavior. The difference between a top and a violent individual lies in their motives and the source of their pleasure. A top's pleasure is linked to the pleasure of the submissive. If the submissive is not turned on, the top doesn't get off. As long as that link is intact, a dominant lesbian can be reassured that she will not exceed her submissive's limits. Tops also sometimes feel pressure to perform, because there are many available submissives. A top needs to insist on the right to have sex only with those women she feels attracted to or interested in.

Lesbians who do not prefer one role over the other are often called switchables or duals. They complain that they are not take seriously and often feel pressure to choose and stick with one role. Chances are that they will also be pressured to play top and will feel that their needs to submit or bottom out go unacknowledged. It is perfectly valid to wish to choose your role based on the situation and your partner or your needs of the moment. It is also valid to wish to have both sides of your desire gratified. In fact, most S/M lesbians switch roles.

Bondage. Tying up your lover is probably the most popular and least talked about sexual game. For women who associate physical restraint with literal enslavement, bondage is not a turn-on. The point of the game is to temporarily place your partner at your mercy, not to convert her to a piece of property. The phrase "at your mercy" implies that a high degree of sensitivity and consideration must be present for this game to work.

Before you tie up a partner or otherwise restrain her, there are some simple safety precautions to be observed. Be careful of wrist and ankle joints. Wrap a hand towel or scarf around the joint, and do knot-tying on top of the padding. Be careful not to leave restraints on so long that hands or feet fall asleep. The bottom must take responsibility for moving to keep blood flowing into extremities and should let her top know when they feel cold or numb. Quick massage of hands and feet can prolong the amount of time bondage can be tolerated, but half an hour is probably the longest time most beginners can comfortably endure restraints. If you are playing top, be sure the knots you tie can be undone easily, or have something handy to cut your ropes. Avoid nylon rope, since it tends to slip, making the bondage tighter. Plain cotton clothesline is excellent. Leather cuffs that buckle and have rings for attaching rope or chain are wonderful for protecting vulnerable joints. Unfortunately, they cost $30-40 a pair at leather shops. You will probably want to experiment with cheaper rope before making a major investment.

Some women have very specific bondage fantasies that involve one position (being tied standing up or being tied spread-eagled to a bed) or one type of restraint (perhaps the chains and leather have a higher erotic value than the cotton rope, or perhaps she prefers silk ties). Tying someone to a bed can be done even if it is not a four-poster by utilizing the legs. You can also put hooks in a wooden frame or put them into the baseboard or floor. A chin-up bar placed in a doorway or a discreet ornamental hook (perhaps concealed by a hanging plant) can be used for standing bondage. You can also tie one hand to each doorknob of the bedroom door or lash her to a chair.

Another form of restraint that allows a lot of freedom of movement is a collar and leash. These can be purchased cheaply at any pet store. Send her out to find a collar that will fit. Some of them have buckles that lock. Some are in pastel shades of leather, with fancy rings and rhinestones.

Handcuffs can be put on quickly and do not involve a lot of fussing with knots. If you get a pair of handcuffs, spend a few more dollars for a pair that can be set in one position, preventing them from closing tighter and tighter. Be sure to find out how your particular pair works—where they can be unlocked and how to set them in place. And get a spare key.

If you use *anything* that locks, make sure that you have the key before you snap it shut. If your fantasies involve using chains and locks, get a set of padlocks that all respond to one key. Several tiny padlocks, each with its own tiny key, are too much to deal with in the heat of passion.

If you are a novice dominatrix, you may be intimidated by all the expertise you are expected to display. A hint to enhance your mystique: blindfold her. An ace bandage or a black bandana works very well and will leave her in utter suspense as to what you are going to do next. You can untangle ropes and hunt for keys while you snarl sexy threats at her to cover the noise.

You may want to restrict her verbal as well as physical and visual responses. You can tie one knot in a bandana, put the knot in her mouth, and tie it around her head, or purchase a specially constructed gag. A leather thong threaded through a soft rubber ball makes an effective gag. However, ask special permisson before you put one on her. The gag has a symbolic meaning that many submissives need to give additional consent to. Some women do not enjoy being gagged at all. Never gag anyone who is drunk or has any problems breathing, and never gag her so tightly that she literally cannot make a sound. Provide her with some means of stopping the action if she can't say the safe word. Ask her to make her whole body go limp and unresponsive if she wants the action to stop.

A few final safety suggestions are to never put pressure on someone's neck, never leave a person who is in bondage alone, and never put a restrained woman on her stomach on a soft surface. Never lift someone by her wrists or ankles. Suspension can be done with a mechanical hoist, but this is an advanced game you should probably learn how to do from a more experienced S/M person.

If you find physical restraints crude and unsophisticated, or if you get stuck with a chance to play a hot scene when no equipment is available, you may want to experiment with psychological bondage. Order your bottom to hold a certain position. Display her for your admiration, or place her at your advantage. Use a firm, soothing rap to make her feel admired and controlled.

Some women try bondage once or twice, find it uninteresting, and drop it from their repertoires. Other women like to use restraints when they are in a special mood or with only one partner. For other lesbians, being tied up or tying up a partner is a regular event in their sex lives. Bondage can be a light game, the expression of some serious and rigid roles, and can go along with several different fantasies. Not everyone who enjoys bondage also enjoys pain or other S/M games. S/M preferences can be as specialized and varied as any other sexual preference.

Physical stress and pain. A common objection to S/M is, "I want sex to feel good. I just don't see how pain can be erotic." S/M is usually associated with pain. As a matter of fact, it is quite possible to play with dominance and submission without including physical stress or pain in the sex. There are a variety of ways to express the dominant and submissive roles— verbal orders, bondage, and costume. For some S/M lesbians, certain kinds of physical discomfort or pain can become erotic if they are expressions of the dominant and submissive roles.

What is pain? Common synonyms are suffering and distress. The medical definition identifies pain as a warning signal given by the body in response to damage or harm being done to the organism. How and why we experience pain has not been explained completely, in physiological or psychological terms. It is difficult to provide an objective definition of pain because it is a subjective sensation. Depending on the context, any stimulus can impart pleasure or pain. To an athlete trying desperately for points seconds before the end of the game, a serious injury may not hurt at all. If you are angry with a woman who insists on embracing you, her touch can be irritating to the point of being painful. Intense sensations experienced during arousal are not painful in the same sense as a stubbed toe or cut finger. For one thing, arousal alters the ability to perceive pain. We become less sensitive to pain as we approach orgasm. Also, a lover biting your nipples or smacking your behind is not damaging or harming you.

Most of the women who enjoy intense sensations or rough sex don't label their behavior S/M. Many of us find bruises or scratches the morning after some fine sex and don't remember how we got them. Using an object like a nipple clip or a whip to produce sexual pain is crossing some kind of line.

Having your partner nibble on your cunt until it hurts is all-American enthusiasm. Having her put a clothespin on one of your inner lips is sado-masochism. The difference between these situations doesn't lie in the sensations produced; it lies in the self-awareness of the participants.

Discomfort, stress or actual pain can contribute to some women's sexual pleasure. First of all, these sensations increase tension, speed up breathing, and reproduce or intensify many of the physiological changes associated with arousal. This is also a way to express trust or devotion to a lover (if you are accepting pain from her hands) or take her on an all-encompassing, transcendental trip (if you are administering the stress). Breaking through mental and physical barriers creates a feeling of elation. Some lesbian masochists describe themselves as feeling more powerful and self-confident as they learn to tolerate and enjoy higher levels of pain. The drama of giving and receiving pain can become a ritual that leads to catharsis.

There are other reasons for undergoing physical suffering than the sensations involved. Some lesbians who do S/M like to give or receive marks that will last beyond the session and serve as a reminder of it. These marks are usually limited to small bruises or scratches. On occasion, a top will give her bottom a permanent or quasi-permanent mark, such as a scar or a pierced ear or a tattoo. These permanent marks are tokens of the relationship and can be compared to an exchange of rings or vows.

During an S/M scene, the focus is on emotional effect and sexual pleasure, not on physical damage. Consequently, S/M lesbians are always looking for new ways to experience intense sensations without creating undesired marks or injuries. Some of the most common techniques and toys are described below, along with some safety precautions.

A good general rule is to keep communication open. The line between arousal and turn-off can be quite thin. The bottom needs to let her top know whether an activity is approaching or exceeding her limits. The top should know what she is asking her bottom to do for her. Ideally, she has either experienced the game herself as a bottom or has exceptional empathy with the woman she is playing with.

Whips and paddles. Remember that sensitivity to pain decreases as the level of arousal increases. Build slowly. Start by doing sensuous things with your toy. Stroke the skin. Tickle. Talk about what you are going to do. If you have a leather cat-of-nine-tails, wrap her face in it and order her to breathe in the smell of leather. If you have a riding crop, slide it between her legs and run the tip of it along her nether lips. Strike lightly, then with more force. Intersperse your blows with breaks so that she can catch her breath and you can rub the reddened skin. Never strike someone's face, head, neck, or throat with a whip or paddle. Avoid the area below the rib cage and above the hips, since the internal organs have no protection and ribs are fragile. If she is on her stomach, you should never hit the area between her shoulder blades and the top of the buttocks, or you may injure the spine. The breasts, buttocks, thighs, and bottoms of the feet are good areas for this kind of stimulation. If you have never used a whip before, try it on a pillow to make sure you can hit what you are aiming at. Riding crops are easiest for novices to handle. If you use a cat, you should know that most of the force will be in the tips of the lashes, and wherever the tips land will hurt the most. You can put pillows on either side of your submissive and hit so that the tips fall on the pillows. Don't forget to ask about marks before you get started. If she doesn't want any, go slow and easy. It is relatively easy to mark someone who has not been whipped before. Over time, a bottom becomes progressively more difficult to mark.

Enemas. Filling the rectum with warm water provides a feeling that is more extreme than simple anal penetration. The slower you let the water flow, the more your bottom will be able to retain. In an S/M context, giving someone an enema symbolizes taking control over her excretory functions. Deciding when and if someone will be allowed to relieve herself represents a lot of power.

Clips and clamps. A wide variety of clips and clamps are available in grocery stores, the housewares departments of chain stores, and stationery shops. Experiment with them to see what you can tolerate and what you can't. Clothespins are good to start with, since they are cheap and readily available. You can use a pair of pliers to spring them if they feel too tight. Clips can be placed anywhere you can get enough loose skin to hold them. Generally, the bigger the bite, the less it will hurt. Clips should not be left on for more than 20 minutes. After they have been on for a little while, they hurt less, because the tissue has gone numb. Flicking them lightly will start circulation again, and feeling will suddenly return. Be prepared for a surge of sensation when the clamp is removed. It can feel good to lick, press or rub the area where the clip was. One way to use clips is to agree to reward the bottom if she will wear them for a certain period of time. Her reward can be an orgasm, a tangerine, or a chance to lick your cunt.

Dildoes, vibrators and ass plugs. These are toys that can be used outside an S/M situation. Used in a scene, they become magic implements that possess the bottom at the top's whim. You may want to use a vibrator on your slave in the context of a fantasy that you are going to make her come. You may want her to wear a dildo in her vagina or a plug in her ass while she performs some simple task for you. It generally takes some training to get the ass to open up enough to accept a plug. Ass plugs are generally diamond-shaped. The anal sphincter closes around the narrow neck of the plug, holding the larger part of it in place. Several different sizes are available at most adult bookstores. You may want to devise a belt or harness to keep dildoes and plugs in place.

Candle wax. Cigarettes or matches can cause infected burns. It is possible to use heat to produce pain without causing a burn. Candles without perfume or scent, which are not made of beeswax, are the best kind to use. They are called plumber's candles and are available at hardware stores or backpacking and camping stores. The feeling of hot wax spattering the skin is shocking but brief. By the time the bottom reacts to the pain, the feeling is gone.

Other objects with S/M potential are ice cubes, rabbit fur, masking tape, plastic dog-grooming brushes, and velvet. A glove of rabbit fur and velvet can make a submissive shiver when it is passed over freshly spanked buttocks. Masking tape, wrapped around hairless areas of the body, can be slowly or rapidly peeled off. Plastic pet brushes fit into the palm of your hand can be used for light scratching or harder stimulation. Ice cubes can be used to tantalize someone. If she is tied and blindfolded, she may not be able to tell the difference between hot wax and ice. An interest in S/M can eroticize your local hardware store. Every little gadget you see in the housewares section takes on a new meaning.

Being stoned can alter a bottom's ability to take pain. She may be able to take more, and she may be able to take less. It will certainly make communication more problematic. Tops should be especially cautious of playing when they are high. It isn't always unsafe or disastrous to do S/M while you are using drugs, but it can have negative results. Use your best judgment.

Another thing that alters a bottom's perception of discomfort and stress is her feelings about her partner. If you do not trust her or feel turned on to her, you will not be able to take much pain from your top. It is important to give yourself over to people only when you feel safe with them. You don't have to perform certain acts in order to be a good bottom. There's nothing wrong with saving complex or intense games for the next time or the next woman.

Humiliation. In an S/M context, humiliation is defined as a deliberate lowering of the bottom's status. This lowering of status is not permanent, and its purpose is to increase the sexual excitement of the bottom as well as the top. The bottom may be treated as if she were an object, an animal, a slave, or the top's inferior. The top may order the bottom to become a table so that she can rest her boots on her back. She may pretend the bottom is her dog or horse, put her into a harness appropriate to that role, then lead her through a ritualized exercise intended to demonstrate the bottom's animal nature. She may make her drink from a dish on the floor, or she may ride on her back. The bottom may be treated as if she were purely sexual or genital and be teased and shamed for the intensity of her sexual need. Some physical sensations or activities may be experienced as humiliating by the bottom, such as receiving an enema, licking the top's anus, having her buttocks or breasts exposed, wearing feminine items of clothing, cleaning part of the house, not being allowed to masturbate, or having other women witness her submission.

Humiliation is the emotional or psychological counterpart of physical discomfort or pain. A top who is not physically powerful can be quite domineering if she can think of new and effective ways to humiliate the bottom. Because humiliation can have as great an effect as pain, limits need to be understood and respected with both techniques. Physical pain experienced during an S/M scene can make the bottom aware of how she handles pain in other situations—suffer stoically, protesting out of proportion to what is happening in order to make it stop, giving it too much importance because she is afraid of it. Humiliation can make the bottom more aware of her feelings of worthlessness or helplessness. It is important for the top to treat her submissive with gentleness and respect after a scene of this nature and make if very clear that the insults and jibes were dealt out for erotic purposes only.

Most of us feel some guilt or shame about being sexual and may have insecurity about our worth as human beings. S/M is one way to acknowledge those feelings when they occur in a sexual setting, and it is often useful for resolving them. The bottom who derives pleasure from being shamed or abased is triumphing over that degradation. The negative feelings we have about sex and ourselves are often treated like dirty secrets. Liberated women aren't supposed to feel that sex is bad or worry about being promiscuous sluts. The top acts as a confessor and interrogator, uncovering these secrets, assigning concrete punishment for vague crimes, and releasing the bottom from her obligation to suffer guilt.

Adults in this society are made to feel extremely competitive and endangered. All of us are urged to struggle, succeed, and defend ourselves against the ambitions of others. This creates a great fear of defeat or weakness and a paradoxical yearning for such defeat, if it will mean respite from competition. For some women, this vicious circle can be broken through S/M. The top defeats the bottom, reduces her to the status she fears, then makes it possible for her to derive pleasure from it. This reduces anxiety to a manageable level, at least in the short run.

Women who play top often mention the pleasure they feel when they violate society's injunction to be passive, weak, or powerless. Playing top is one way for these women to resolve anxieties they have about being swept away or conquered. Sexual power is no substitute for political or economic power, but it can be a stabilizing force and a source of strength.

Although the effects of S/M may be therapeutic, it should not be mistaken for therapy. Therapy is intended to produce long-term changes in personality and behavior. S/M has a short-term goal: pleasure.

Finding support. It is important for members of any minority to make contact with others who share that status. S/M lesbians can feel isolated and oppressed within the lesbian subculture. A lesbian who enters a dyke bar feels validated by the presence of so many other gay women. An S/M lesbian who enters the same bar is acutely aware of the fact that she cannot wear leather, handcuffs, a dog collar, or other S/M regalia in that bar without shocking most of the patrons. Lesbians sometimes patronize gay male leather bars because of this alienation. Some men's bars will refuse to admit women. Others will accept women who are in S/M costume, especially if they are taken there by gay male friends who are part of the established clientele. A gay male leather bar can be a friendlier place than a lesbian bar, but an S/M lesbian is not likely to meet other women there.

You may wonder whether you are limiting yourself by pursuing your interest in S/M. Remember that lesbians are often accused of limiting themselves because they are interested in only half of the human race. Getting what you want isn't limiting, it's rewarding. If it becomes possible for you to get as much S/M sex as you want, you may still find you have an interest in and need for vanilla sex. S/M need not engulf you. You can explore as much or as little as is safe and healthy for you.

Transsexuality

Material on transsexuality is included in this book because some pre-operative female-to-male transsexuals live as lesbians before they realize they are transsexuals, and some post-operative male-to-female transsexuals choose a lesbian lifestyle.

There is currently a lot of discussion in the feminist press regarding the legitimacy of surgery and reassignment as a method of treating gender dysphoria. (Gender dysphoria is the clinical term for the feeling that one's true sex is not consistent with one's body.) Some women believe that male-to-female transsexuals are really men who can't accept their homosexuality or their femininity. They believe that as social sex-roles become less rigid and homosexuality becomes more acceptable, the number of biological males desiring sex reassignment will decrease. Some women also believe that male-to-female transsexuals who call themselves feminists and lesbians are really neither, and that a biological male remains a male even after surgery. Because of this, they wish to exclude male-to-female transsexuals from women's bars, organizations, and events. Little or no mention has been made in the lesbian or feminist press of female-to-male transsexuals.

It is certainly true that some men who have intense guilt about being homosexual think that they should have been women, and so do some men whose appearance or mannerisms are effeminate. However, most clinics that treat gender dysphoria have a screening program to separate these individuals from those who will be reassigned to their sex of preference. Surgery and reassignment won't help a man who loves other men as a biological male, nor will it be of use to an effeminate man who identifies as male and simply has behaviors that aren't socially acceptable.

It is also true that the genetic sex of an individual cannot be altered. Females have xx chromosomes; males have xy chromosomes. No surgery can alter that. If one defines gender as a simple matter of chromosomes, transsexuality is a charade.

However, the feelings and experiences of transsexuals should not be ignored when this issue is discussed. Transsexuals describe very clear, strong feelings of having the wrong body. These feelings are usually present from early childhood. Many transsexuals experience severe emotional distress and confusion as a result. If they reveal these feelings, they are often ridiculed or persecuted by peers and family members. Some transsexuals do not masturbate or have sex with partners because they cannot accept their genitals or the rest of their bodies as a part of their real selves.

Some transsexuals attempt to cope with their feelings about their inappropriate gender by adopting a homosexual lifestyle. The myth that homosexuals are people who really want to be members of the opposite sex is widespread enough to make this seem a plausible choice. Living as a homosexual usually doesn't solve a transsexual's problems. A biological female who wants to relate to other women and have sex with them as a male is not a lesbian. Neither is a heterosexual male-to-female transsexual a gay man. The question of gender identity—i.e., which sex someone believes herself or himself to be—is a separate issue from sexual orientation—i.e., whether someone prefers male or female sex partners or can enjoy sex with both men and women. If this were not so, homosexuality would not exist. Biological males would always prefer biological females as sex partners, and vice versa.

Most transsexuals experience a feeling of isolation and difference that is even more intense than that felt by gay men and women prior to coming out. When a transsexual discovers that there are other individuals who have the same conflicts about their genders and that there is a chance to resolve those conflicts and live as the sex they perceive themselves to be, it seems like a miracle.

It is obvious that anyone who chooses to undergo this process must be very serious about wanting sex reassignment. To begin with, the treatment is expensive. It can cost thousands of dollars. A few transsexuals can obtain financial assistance from social service agencies. Reassignment can take years to complete. Most professionals who deal with gender dysphoria insist that their patients live as the sex they perceive themselves to be for at least a year prior to final surgery. Thus, the transsexual must face the hostility and ignorance of government agencies, landlords, friends, relatives, and employers before any permanent alteration to his or her body is made. (Female-to-male transsexuals are an exception in that they usually have the fatty tissue removed from their breasts and the nipples repositioned prior to living as men.)

In addition to living and dressing as the gender of their preferences, transsexuals take artificial hormones. Male-to-female transsexuals are given estrogens. These stimulate breast development, alter the shape of the hips, and create some other changes in the body. In addition, male-to-female transsexuals usually have electrolysis treatments to permanently remove facial and body hair. Female-to-male transsexuals find that the androgens they take stimulate the growth of facial and body hair and create more musculature in the upper body. They may also enlarge the clitoris and deepen the voice.

Some transsexuals stop at this point. Surgical alteration of the genitals is a painful and radical process. Some transsexuals feel that until the operation has been improved they do not wish to undergo it. For those who choose to complete the process, there are several different procedures for altering the genitals. All result in male or female genitals of slightly different appearance. The male-to-female transsexual is castrated. The skin from the outside of the penis is left intact and is reversed and tucked back inside the body to form an artifical vagina. Female-to-male transsexuals are given penises. One common method is to create a skin graft from the lower abdomen to the thigh, cut the graft at the thigh, and shape it into a phallus. The clitoris can be left in place to provide sexual sensation. There are many more male-to-female transsexuals than female-to-male, so the operation for the former is a better developed procedure.

In addition to the expense and pain of surgery, transsexuals who are gay must stay in the closet during their entire treatments. Most professionals will refuse to provide sexual reassignment to gay transsexuals. While the transsexuals conceal their sexual orientation from their doctors and psychologists, they often conceal their genetic sex from the gay people they socialize with. They are thus in the closet all of the time.

When a transsexual is present in a group of lesbians, everyone involved has to think about the issue of how to define a woman. Is it the ability to reproduce? If so, are genetic females who use birth control, lesbians who refuse to have children, or women who have had hysterectomies no longer women? Is it dressing and behaving in a feminine manner? Many genetic women choose not to do this. Is it a common conditioning or indoctrination into our culture's stereotype of womanliness? If so, will we no longer be women when sex-role stereotyping ceases to exist?

Male-to-female transsexuals are certainly not women in the same sense that genetic females are. They do not share our history of socialization into femininity. However, by choosing to live as women, they have lost a significant amount of their male privilege. Choosing to love as lesbians costs them their heterosexual privilege. They share in our status as second-class citizens.

Some transsexuals differ from genetic females in appearance. They may be taller than most women or have bigger hands and deeper voices. This can make it even harder for genetic females to read and accept them as women.

Do male-to-female transsexuals belong in the lesbian community? Should a lesbian continue to be friends or lovers with an individual who decides she is a female-to-male transsexual? How you feel about this issue depends on your definintion of gender, your definitions of feminism and lesbianism, and the extent to which you can empathize with a transsexual.

It is disturbing to see women turning against one another over this issue. Some women feel that transsexuals are invading the women's movement and place the blame for conflict and strife on them. Other women place the blame on those who cannot tolerate transsexuals, pointing out that there are very few male-to-female lesbian transsexuals. Some women suggest that it would be better if transsexuals formed their own movement and community. It is difficult to see how this could be accomplished. How much does a radical lesbian transsexual have in common with a heterosexual transsexual who wants a ranch house in the suburbs, a husband who commutes to the city, and four adopted children? Most transsexuals want to fade into the majority culture and forget all about their lives prior to sex reassignment. The small number of transsexuals and the fact that they are scattered all over the country are further obstacles to the formation of a transsexual community.

It is difficult to see how an attempt to bar transsexuals from the women's movement or the lesbian community could succeed. After all, the label "feminist" is not copyrighted. There are even men who use it to describe themselves, and there are homophobic straight women who define themselves as feminists. Many transsexuals are not readily distinguishable from genetic females. Do we want to start doing tests for genetic sex as a prerequisite for admittance to an all-women's dance? If we're not going to do something like this, the only transsexuals anyone will object to are the ones who go public or get caught. They will be excluded for honesty, not for transsexuality.

The issue of transsexuality is closely related to the feminist demand for control over our own bodies. Since feminists support free availability of safe abortion and birth control, and since feminists support civil rights for homosexual men and women, why can't feminists support the free determination of gender? It is possible that the transsexual individual knows her or his own sex better than society does, just as a lesbian knows where her love and lust naturally flow—toward other women.

Questions like, "Do I believe this person is a woman?" and "Do I trust this person?" can be answered only on an individual basis. Demanding that all transsexuals go away for the good of the movement sounds a lot like straight feminists freaking out over visible lesbian feminists. Some of us probably want transsexuals to go away for the same reason that we might want any people different from ourselves to go away. We don't understand them, they challenge our basic assumptions about life, they confuse issues we'd rather keep simple, and they scare us.

Watersports and Scat

"Watersports" is a slang term for sexual play that involes urine or enemas. "Scat" is a slang term for sexual play that involves excrement.

Piss and shit can be associated with the genitals and eroticized. They are commonly treated as taboo substances, produced in privacy and never handled or examined. This attitude toward waste products is so deeply ingrained in some people that they are unable to eliminate waste if there is a chance that someone might see or hear them. Humans seem to be constructed so that anything forbidden or secretive can become sexually exciting; or perhaps there is a cultural tendency toward making anything which is potentially erotic forbidden and secret.

Being required or forbidden to produce piss or shit has links with childhood discipline and maternal care. Children often play with their urine or excrement or interpret eliminating waste as a pleasant, sexually stimulating experience. Playing with piss can be a playful, childlike experience. Urinating on someone or at her command involves a loss of control and inhibition that is often an exciting, liberating experience. Because piss and shit are equated with filth, they can also be used as symbols of humiliation. Controlling your partner's elimination of waste is an intimate experience that can make her feel helpless, accepted, and cared for.

Urine is sterile. It is possible to drink the urine of a healthy person without harmful effect. Drinking a large quantity of urine could cause a little nausea because urine contains urea. Drinking large quantities of water will flush the extra waste out of the system.

Excrement is not sterile. It contains bacteria, viruses, and other microorganisms. Hepatitis, shigella, amoebic dysentery, and other infectious diseases can be transmitted via oral contact with the feces of a woman who has such a disease. If ingesting shit is a sexual game you play, you should monitor your health and the health of your sex partners with great care.

A good investment for anyone who enjoys watersports or scat is a rubber sheet to protect the floor or your bed. If you find the plastic, sticky feel of the sheet unpleasant, put a cotton sheet on top of it. The shower or bathtub is a good place for doing watersports or scat, especially for squeamish beginners, because the urine or excrement can be washed away. Some foods, like coffee and asparagus, discolor urine and give it an unpleasant odor, so the top in a watersports scene may want to avoid those foods.

HOMAGE TO

Margit Gaal

active around 1921

Illustrator

9
Sexually Transmitted Diseases

While doing research for this chapter, I ran into the following myth again and again: lesbians don't get VD. Many lesbians believe this, and unfortunately so do many health officials. There is very little written about sexually transmitted diseases that is specifically for lesbians, nor are medical health workers well-educated about this issue. Liberal public health pamphlets about VD mention heterosexuals and gay men; lesbians are omitted. This is dangerous to the health of lesbians.

This myth may have its origins in the notion that women are not really sexual, that lesbian relationships are not sexual, and that there is thus no possibility of contagious diseases or pests being transmitted. It may also have resulted from the notion that sex with men is dirty and sex with women is clean. The truth is that a woman can get any contagious disease during sex with a woman if her partner has that disease.

I encountered another difficulty in obtaining information for this chapter: the attitude of the general public toward sexually transmitted diseases. They are perceived as being divine punishment for promiscuous or immoral sexual behavior. Very little federal money is allocated to research the causes and treatment of venereal disease, and very little money is spent on treatment for it. Gonorrhea has reached epidemic proportions in the United States—something that the public would never tolerate if the disease were not associated with sex. There is no immunization for either syphilis or gonorrhea, yet the organisms which cause them have been known for quite a long time. This attitude toward VD results in poor diagnosis and can make it very difficult for someone to go for treatment.

It may seem to you that the subject is too depressing and doesn't belong in a sex-positive book. I think it is irresponsible for any sexually active woman to avoid becoming fully informed on the subject. The health of your partners, as well as your own well-being, is at stake.

Some remarks on general hygiene and prevention are given here, along with some descriptive material on specific sexually transmitted diseases. I have tried to indicate where sources give conflicting information and where I am making educated guesses. Current medical research may have outdated portions of this material by the time you read it, so don't ignore other sources of information on VD. In addition to telling you what is known about the cause of each condition, I have described the conventional medical treatment and alternative, natural or herbal remedies. I am not a

139

139

physician or an herbalist; thus, I make no guarantees about the safety or effectiveness of any cure mentioned. If you think you may have a health problem, check with someone experienced in diagnosis and treatment for assistance.

General Hygiene and Disease Prevention

Some of the information that follows has already been given in other parts of this book. It is repeated for speed-readers. I suggest you make yourself feel scholarly and virtuous and read the whole thing.

Be clean. Always wipe from front to back after urinating or defecating. This keeps waste products out of the urethra and vagina. Wash your vulva with warm water every day or oftener. Don't use feminine hygiene sprays; they can be irritating, dry out mucous membranes, or cause allergic reactions. Clipping your public hair short will minimize odor. A healthy vagina does not smell bad. Unpleasant odor could be a warning symptom of a vaginal infection. Bubble baths and commercial douching solutions can also be irritating. You don't need to douche at all, since the vagina cleans itself out with small daily secretions and keeps itself chemically balanced. If you still feel the need to douche out of paranoia or narcissism, don't do it oftener than once a month. Plain tepid water is best. You can also use 4 tablespoons of white, distilled vinegar in 2 quarts of water. Other kinds of vinegar have sugar in them, which promotes yeast growth. One tablespoon of white, distilled vinegar and 2 tablespoons of plain health food store yogurt in 1 quart of water is another good douching solution. Avoid flavored yogurt, which contains sugar. When you douche, don't hang the bag any higher than your waist, and let water into the vagina slowly. Avoid bulbs, syringes, and other squeeze devices. Water that is forced into the vagina can be pushed into the uterus or the abdominal cavity. (However, this would take a great deal of pressure.) Pregnant women should never douche. While bathing or showering, don't forget your clit. Pull back on the clitoral hood and clean under it with a soft washcloth. After you rinse off, dry your genitals thoroughly. Avoid pantyhose and nylon panties. They don't let the vulva breathe. Cotton panties are good; so are no panties at all (provided you wear skirts or change your slacks often). Don't share douching equipment or sex toys used for penetration with another woman. Don't put anything in your vagina that has been in your or another woman's anus. Don't use one bag for both enemas and douching.

Pay attention to your sex partners. Avoid having sex with women with poor health or bad hygiene. Don't let anyone with sores around the lips go down on you. If your partner has dirty fingers, sores, or unusual-looking warts, her fingers shouldn't go inside your vagina or anus. Try to get a first name and phone number from everyone you have sex with, so you can let them know if you are diagnosed as having a sexually transmitted disease. If you ever have sex with a male partner, be aware that it is much easier to contract gonorrhea from a man than from a woman, and use some form of birth control. It takes ten minutes to buy some condoms and spermicidal foam in a drugstore. You don't need a prescription, and used together they are 90% effective. You may feel silly purchasing these items while wearing a DYKE button on your lapel, but you'll feel a lot sillier filling out forms in an abortion clinic.

Include tests for VD in your regular checkup. When you get a Pap smear, request a blood test for syphilis and a vaginal culture for gonorrhea. If you suspect that you have a venereal disease, don't offer yourself as a sexual partner, and get immediate treatment. If you have sex with lots of different women, get the tests two or three times a year. It's not a bad idea to get yearly tests for syphilis and gonorrhea even if you are monogamous. These are serious diseases that can usually be cured quickly. You may not know what your monogamous partner did when she went home for Christmas.

Do self-examinations of your breasts. Almost none of the lesbians I've talked to does this simple exam on a regular basis. This is hard to explain, since the exam takes about 10 minutes and can save your life. No one should expect her doctor to automatically detect any changes in her breast tissue. Breasts come in all different sizes, shapes, and textures. You are the woman most likely to detect changes and abnormalities in your own breasts.

After menopause, women should examine their breasts on the first day of each month. Before menopause, do the self-examination a week after your period. Your breasts will usually not be swollen or tender then. Women who have had hysterectomies will probably be taking artificial hormones and should check with their doctors to see how often they should examine their breasts. Establish a pattern so that you don't forget, and don't put off doing it.

The self-exam has three steps. Start in the shower or bathtub. Soap up your hand and breasts. Put one hand behind your head. Use your left hand to examine your right breast, and vice versa. Bring your fingers together and use them to flatten, press and move gently over every part of the breast. Check for any lump, hard knot, or thickening.

Step two should be done in front of a mirror. Let your arms rest at your sides and look at your breasts. Raise your arms over your head and look again. See whether you can detect any changes in the contour of each breast. Are there any signs of swelling, a dimpling or stippled pattern on the skin, or changes in the nipple? Do the nipples point in radically different directions, or does one nipple appear to be crooked? Rest your hands on your hips and press down firmly. This will flex your chest muscles.

Examine your breasts again for any of the changes described above. The right and left breast are rarely exactly the same size, so don't worry about any size difference, unless there is a change.

For the third step, find a comfortable place to lie down. Put a pillow under your shoulder. Place your hand on that side under your head. This flattens out the breast, distributing tissue evenly on your chest. Using the fingers of your other hand, press gently in small circular motions. Make small circles moving in toward the nipple. You will probably feel a ridge of firm tissue in the lower curve of your breast. That is normal. You should make at least three circles, each about an inch apart from the previous one. Repeat this procedure for the other breast.

The last thing you should do is gently squeeze the nipples between thumb and forefinger. A discharge, whether it is clear or bloody, should be reported to your doctor.

If you do find a lump or thickening that doesn't seem ordinary, make an appointment with your doctor or a clinic and get it checked out. Postponing an examination will only make you more anxious. Most lumps are not cancerous. Some women tend to get benign lumps, called cysts, which appear and disappear within one menstrual cycle.

Learn to do pelvic self-examinations at a feminist health clinic. Pelvic self-examination is not just for heterosexual women. It can help lesbians keep track of their menstrual cycle, changes in the vaginal walls or secretions that may signal infections, or cervical polyps.

Are you a DES daughter? DES is an abbreviation for diethylstilbestrol, one of the first synthetic estrogens. During the 1940s and 1950s, it was prescribed for pregnant women who were in danger of miscarriage. Around 1953, it was discovered that DES did nothing to prevent miscarriage, but many doctors continued to prescribe it to their patients until 1971. In 1971, the FDA banned the use of DES, because a link had been discovered between the drug and a rare form of vaginal cancer. Prior to 1970, vaginal cancer was a very rare disease that almost never appeared in women under 50. Since that time, hundreds of young women whose mothers were given DES during pregnancy have been found to have vaginal cancer.

If your birthdate falls within the appropriate range, you should ask your mother whether she was given any prescription drugs during any of her pregnancies. She may remember taking medication but not remember what it was. You have a legal right to get this information from her medical records, if they have been retained by private physicians, clinics, or hospitals. Depending on the policy of the people you contact, you may or may not need a lawyer's assistance to see your mother's medical records.

A standard Pap smear and vaginal examination does not reveal the harmful effects of DES. A device called a colposcope, which lights and magnifies the walls of the vagina, is used to detect abnormalities. A Schiller test, which involves painting the entire vagina with a stain that reveals the presence of abnormal cells, should also be administered. These tests are expensive. If your mother was given DES during pregnancy, the colposcope exam should be repeated for you every six months.

DES also affects male children. The most common effect is infertility. If you are a mother who was given DES, both your male and your female children should receive special medical attention.

Many DES daughters do not develop vaginal cancer. However, abnormal vaginal cells may be present, and regular medical examinations will be necessary. This creates stress and anxiety that can be difficult to live with. Mothers also feel guilty and helpless when they realize that drugs they were given during pregnancy may have an adverse effect on the health of their children. DES mothers and daughters need more than regular medical examinations to deal with their anger and fear. For some women, this will mean meeting and talking with other DES daughters and mothers, and perhaps getting involved in doing public education on DES or other medical problems pertinent to women. Some individual counseling can also be useful.

Because vaginal cancer was so rare prior to the wide-scale use of DES, treatments currently being used for it are experimental. Vaginal cancer is treated by using progesterone suppositories, surgical excision, cauterization or radiation. DES daughters must avoid any further exposure to estrogen and specifically to DES, which is still being used by some doctors as a "morning after pill" to start menstruation when a woman suspects she may have conceived. Estrogens are also found in contraceptive pills and are prescribed for some women going through menopause.

Lesbians are often estranged from their families. It can be very difficult to ask your mother whether or not she was given DES. If you feel there is any possibility that you are a DES daughter, you may want to consider getting the tests without re-establishing family ties.

This tragedy was created by the American medical establishment's indifference to women. Prescribing DES for miscarriage was a massive medical experiment using our bodies as unconsenting subjects. We all need to obtain as much information as possible about the side effects of drugs and new medical practices—in other countries as well as our own. Tests on laboratory animals do not always reveal all the potential dangers for humans, and such test results are often ignored. Regulatory government agencies are often partially controlled by the businesses they are supposed to regulate. We need to think twice before taking any pill a doctor prescribes.

If you would like more information about DES, contact DES Action

National, c/o Coalition for the Medical Rights of Women, 1638 "B" Haight, San Francisco, CA 94117 or call (415) 621-8032.

Sexually Transmitted Diseases

Pests. Three kinds of sexually transmitted pests that appear most frequently are lice, mites of scabies, and pinworms.

LICE

There are three kinds of lice. They are all spread by physical contact, so their appearance does not mean you have filthy habits. It just means you got close to somebody who had them. Although lice are a nuisance, they can be disposed of fairly easily. Since treatment varies with each type, the types are discussed separately below.

Crabs live almost exclusively on the pubic hair. Pubic hairs are spaced differently from other body hair. The distance between hair shafts just happens to be perfect for this louse. It grabs hold of two hairs and digs in. It stays put, laying its eggs right where it is, and it usually doesn't move onto clothing or bedding. If you have oral sex with someone who has crabs, you may wind up with a few eking out a difficult existence on your eyebrows, but this doesn't often happen. You can usually self-diagnose crabs because they are visible to the naked eye. They look like tiny freckles. The eggs are very small crooks or nodules on the hair. But before you see them, you'll feel them. They produce an intolerable itching in your crotch.

Crabs are almost always transmitted via sexual contact. Adult lice can live only three days without a host. Eggs live for only two weeks. They are hardly ever spread by toilet seats, towels, bedding, or clothing.

To get rid of them, you are going to have to poison them. You have a couple of choices. A-200 Pyrinate can be obtained without a prescription. Kwell smells nicer and isn't so harsh, but you need a prescription. A third medication is called Cuprex, but it stings. Avoid it unless you want to punish yourself.

Follow the directions on the product you choose. Wash your underwear, sheets, towels, bedding and pants in hot water. Sexual partners and members of your household should examine themselves or use the medication along with you. If you don't get everybody treated, you'll catch lice again from someone else in your social circle.

You can also shave off your pubic hair. Deprived of a home, the pests are with you no more. Use a mild soap or shaving cream and be careful not to cut yourself. You may want to trim the hair short before shaving, to

avoid clogging your razor. When you finish shaving, the outer lips will swell. You may have some ingrown hairs, which will itch. Some herbal potions recommended for itching are
  1. Slippery elm infusion. Bring one cup of water to a boil. Add 2 teaspoons slippery elm powder. Simmer for 20 minutes. When the solution cools, apply it to the area with fingers or cotton.
  2. Corn starch, buttermilk, or wheat germ oil can be applied to the itching area.
  3. Stinging nettle. Boil 1 cup of water, add 2 heaping tablespoons of stinging nettle and simmer for 20 minutes. Let cool, strain, and splash onto the area.

Body lice are commonly called cooties, which may spoil memories of that game you played as a child. Body lice feed on all parts of the body and live in the seams and hems of clothing and bedding. They lay their eggs there as well. You can tell them from crab lice by looking to see where they are. If they are in the seams of your pajamas (the eggs look like little gritty granules) and not in your crotch, you have cooties—not crabs. You will itch in several different areas, instead of in just your pubic area.
  Body lice can be transmitted during sex but are more easily transmitted by sharing clothing or bedding. If they are discovered, the whole house and everybody in it needs to be treated. Body lice can carry typhus, trench fever, and relapsing fever, so don't procrastinate.
  Everybody should use Kwell. Make sure you spread it over EVERY INCH of your skin. Leave it on for a full 24 hours. You will have to destroy heavily infested bedding or clothing and disinfect the house. Other items of clothing or bedding should be steam-cleaned and treated with insecticide. Send everything away to be cleaned before you use the Kwell, so that you don't reinfect yourself. When you wash the stuff off 24 hours later, have clean clothes and bedding to use.

Head lice are the reason your mother didn't want you lending anybody your comb. Head lice live on the roots and the long end of the hair. Many doctors have the idea that middle-class, white people don't get lice, and they misdiagnose cases of itchy, crusty scalp as eczema or a rash. Head lice spread most easily during group living situations. Luckily, they are relatively rare. They will not spread to pubic hair or other parts of the body.
  You can use Kwell shampoo and steam- or dry-clean any hats or head scarves. Anyone you live with or a sexual partner should be inspected by a doctor. Include pillowcases, combs and brushes in your cleanup. Head lice lay more eggs than crabs or cooties, so shampoo thoroughly. Reinfestation is common.

MITES OF SCABIES

The mite (Sarcoptes scabiei) is much smaller than a louse. It burrows into the skin, leaving tracks that look like grayish black streaks, at most ¼" long. When the mite lays its eggs, a tiny blister about the size of a pinhead appears. Blisters often occur in groups, as the eggs hatch and new mites mate and burrow again. The mites leave feces pellets beneath the skin that provoke an allergic reaction.

The itch produced by mites can drive you to tears and make work or sleep impossible. Scratching seems involuntary; but by scratching, you carry eggs and larvae under your fingernails to infest new sites of your body. The mite has a preference for the thinnest, most sensitive skin. The vulva, nipples, armpits, the skin inside the elbow and covering the elbow, the ankles, instep, and the skin between the fingers are favorite places.

Scabies can be transmitted by sleeping with or having sex with an infected person. In rare cases, the mites travel from dogs to humans. However, you should not treat an animal with Kwell. Take it to a vet. The mite that causes common mange in dogs is of another species and won't spread to humans.

Mites can be misdiagnosed as severe eczema or impetigo or labeled a psychosomatic condition. If you have symptoms listed above, ask your physician to check for mites of scabies.

Kwell is used to treat scabies. Use the lotion, not the shampoo. After a hot, soapy shower, apply lots of the lotion to every square inch of your body below the jaw. Do not miss any area, or you will have to do it all over again. Leave it on for 24 hours. Do not wash your hands. Trim your fingernails very short, and get lots of Kwell underneath them.

Some sources say mites cannot be transmitted by bedding. Others say that they can. Since this is such a miserable problem, do a complete laundry and have clean clothes and bedding to use when you wash off the Kwell. You will continue to have an allergic reaction and itch for two or three weeks, so knowing that your laundry and clothes are clean will reassure you. Also, have housemates and sex partners treat themselves, even if they have no symptoms.

Check yourself for red marks, burrows, or blisters. If you find any, repeat the treatment.

Kwell is a powerful insecticide. Some women are allergic to it. If you apply Kwell and your skin becomes red or itches severely, wash off the Kwell and consult your physician for a different medication. Be sure you don't get any in your eyes or mouth.

Some women refuse to use Kwell, even for mites, and resort to herbal remedies. Such remedies are often not as powerful as chemicals or drugs and don't work as quickly. An herbal remedy depends on the quality and freshness of the herbs, your diet and health, and the skill used in selecting the appropriate herb. If you do use an alternative remedy for any sexually transmitted disease, have sex partners or housemates use it as well, to prevent reinfection.

One herbal remedy for mites of scabies is to steep 2 teaspoons of juniper berries in 1 pint of boiling water for ½ hour. Divide the solution into 4 parts. Drink one part 4 times a day. Repeat the recipe and bathe in the solution for the itch and to drive out the parasites. Another suggested remedy is to wash with green soap to open the burrows, then make an ointment and rub it on the affected areas thoroughly. Do not change underwear or bathe for three to four days, then boil all clothes and bedclothes. The ointment consists of ¼ teaspoon of zinc sulfate, sulfur flowers, basillion, castor oil, and gum styrax.

PINWORMS

These parasites are also called threadworms. They are tiny white worms, a little thicker than sewing thread and about ½″ long. They are most commonly found in the large intestine but can also cause vaginal irritation. Many people have them and don't know it. The most common symptom is an itchy anus. The worms are most active at night and during the full moon, moving around and laying their eggs. This produces the itch.

If you suspect you have pinworms, the doctor will probably ask you to apply some scotch tape to your anus and then stick it on a glass slide. The slide is examined under a microscope to see whether any eggs are present. You may have to do this for two or three days to make sure you pick up any sign of them.

If pinworms are diagnosed as present, you and everybody in your household and all sex partners should be treated. Pinworms are transmitted very easily, usually on the hands. Remember to wash your hands after using the bathroom, to avoid reinfecting yourself.

The herbal remedy for pinworms is to eat a clove of garlic every day for three days. On the third day, drink a cup of senna and peppermint tea. Make the tea by covering ½ teaspoon of senna leaves and ½ teaspoon of peppermint leaves with one cup of boiling water. Brew in a covered pot for 3-5 minutes. Sweeten with honey if you like. The garlic weakens the worms, and the tea is a laxative that washes them out. Repeat the treatment in a week to get rid of larvae which have recently hatched, and again in another week.

Antepar and antiminth are drugs prescribed for pinworms. Both are mild and effective. They should be taken again in a week to kill larvae.

Vaginal pinworms can be drawn out by sitting in a sitz bath with 1 ½ cups of epsom salts added per gallon of water. You should do this twice a day for three days and apply zinc oxide ointment to the opening of the vagina, the anus, and the perineum. You will need a prescription for the ointment.

Vaginal infections. Several different organisms can cause infections in the vagina. Because many different micro-organisms live in the vagina, it can be difficult to diagnose which one is causing a problem. Some symptoms of a vaginal infection may resemble gonorrhea or syphilis, so always ask to be tested for these diseases in addition to less serious conditions. Never treat yourself with a home remedy before making sure what kind of infection you have. Most vaginal infections unfortunately have a tendency to recur.

MONILIA
This type of infection is caused by the yeast Candida albicans. This yeast is present in a healthy vagina. Bacteria and the slightly acid pH of the vagina normally keep it under control. Taking antibiotics, the pill or other steroid drugs, pregnancy, getting tired or run-down, menstruating, douching excessively, diabetes (the yeast feeds on the glucose in a diabetic's urine)— any of these things can cause a population explosion of Candida albicans.

The textbook symptoms of a yeast infection are a vaginal odor like that of rising bread, a thick white discharge that sometimes resembles cottage cheese and may cling to the inner lips, itching and swelling of the vulva, and perhaps pain or burning when you urinate. Symptoms are not always this clearcut. A yeast infection is diagnosed by culturing the discharge. The culture should be taken when you are not menstruating.

The yeast infection may cure itself if the cause of it goes away. A doctor will give you an antibiotic in the form of a vaginal suppository or a cream that contains nystatin. These drugs will kill vaginal bacteria as well as yeast, so while you are taking them you should cut down on your sugar intake and eat health food store yogurt to replace the acidophilus bacteria that naturally control yeast. You can also douche with Lactinex, an over-the-counter douche that produces lactic acid favorable to the growth of bacteria.

Some alternative remedies are listed below.

1. Garlic suppositories: Peel a clove of garlic. Don't nick it, or it will burn. Place it in the middle of a piece of gauze about a foot long and 3 or 4 inches wide. Fold the gauze to make a tampon. You can dip the end of it in vegetable oil to make insertion easier. Change the tampon every 12 hours for three to five days.

2. Yogurt douche: Use 4 tablespoons of plain yogurt to 1 quart of warm water. Douche with this solution twice a day for five days or until the symptoms disappear, plus a few more days. You can use a vaginal applicator (sold to apply spermicidal foam) to insert 2 tablespoons of plain yogurt into

the vagina; keep it in place with a tampon. You can also open the vagina with a speculum and then spoon the yogurt in.

3. Acidophilus: Put 2 tablespoons of acidophilus yogurt culture and 2 tablespoons of white, distilled vinegar in 1 quart of lukewarm water. Douche twice a day for 2 weeks.

3. Gentian violet: You can buy this at a pharmacy and douche with a few drops of it in a quart of lukewarm water. You can also get suppositories with a prescription. This works very well, but the gentian violet stains everything it touches bright purple. Wear sanitary napkins after you douche or insert the suppository.

Yeast infections can be transmitted between sexual partners, so don't share douching equipment or sex toys. Don't put your fingers inside your own vagina and then inside your partner. One source I read indicated that yeast infections can occur in the throat as a result of having oral sex with an infected partner. This happens very rarely. It can be treated with oral doses of nystatin drops or gentian violet.

TRICHOMONIASIS

This vaginal infection is caused by flagellates, one-celled parasites formally known as Trichomonas vaginalis Protozoa. Sources indicated that trich was difficult to give to a female sex partner. I suggest taking precautions just to be safe. Some authorities state that trich cannot be transmitted by wet towels, bathing suits, or washclothes, while other sources stated that it could. Don't share these items with an infected partner, just to be sure.

Like yeast, the trichomoniasis protozoa are found in healthy vaginas. The mechanism which causes it to become a health problem is not understood. Research should be done on this problem, since a natural control for trich could be discovered. This would be especially nice since the preferred drug for trich, Flagyl, is under suspicion as a carcinogen, and since women who have had trichomoniasis contract gonorrhea more often than women who have not.

Classical symptoms for trich are a yellow or yellow-green discharge that smells foul rather than yeasty. The liquid may be thin and bubbly. The vulva swells; the labia become inflamed, red, raw and itchy. Trich can also cause urinary tract infections if the discharge gets smeared into the urethra. It is common to have a yeast infection at the same time as a trich infection.

Flagyl, the drug your gynecologist will automatically try to give you, is a powerful and very expensive drug which has been patented by one drug company. It is also known as metronidazole. You cannot take it if you have blood diseases, peptic ulcers, a disease of the central nervous system, or another infectious disease besides trich. Flagyl kills some of the white blood cells and will impair your body's defenses against another disease. If one course of the treatment doesn't get rid of the trich and you have to take Flagyl again, your doctor should do a white blood count before, during, and after the second treatment. Don't drink any alcoholic beverages while using Flagyl. Side effects of this drug include darkening of the urine, nausea, cramps, diarrhea and dizziness. It can also set up the right vaginal conditions for you to get a yeast infection. If you are pregnant or nursing, you should take Flagyl suppositories rather than oral doses of the medication.

By the time this appears in print, tinidazole may be on the market and in use to treat trich. This drug (like Flagyl) has caused gene mutations, birth defects and cancer in laboratory animals. Some feminist health workers feel that women should avoid taking either of these drugs.

Trich is such a miserable infection that few women want to put up with it while they search for alternative remedies. If you feel up to it, try vaginal suppositories such as Floraquin or vaginal gels. The garlic suppository and the vinegar-and-acidophilus douche described under Monilia are sometimes useful. An antiseptic called Betadine is available in most drugstores. One tablespoon of Betadine in one pint of warm water can be used as a douche twice a day for 3 days, then once a day for 7 days. If it is irritating, use it less often. On the 4th day, douche with yogurt as well. Repeat the yogurt douche every 2 days until the treatment is finished. This helps prevent the yeast infection that often accompanies trich.

If you have a mild infection, your doctor may be willing to prescribe a lower dosage of Flagyl or tell you to take it for fewer days than normal. However, if you don't get rid of the infection, it will just come back. If you are taking a reduced dosage of Flagyl, take tub baths, use the suppositories nightly, wear loose clothing (since exposure to air destroys the parasites), and avoid tampons, douching, and deodorant sprays.

NON-SPECIFIC VAGINITIS

Occasionally a doctor is not able to pinpoint any one organism as being the cause of a vaginal infection. The usual procedure is to give you a sulfa cream or suppository like Vagitrol, Sultrin, or AVC Cream. Symptoms of non-specific vaginitis can include a white or yellow discharge, possibly streaked with blood. The walls of the vagina can be bubbly with fluid and perhaps covered with a coat of pus. Early symptoms of non-specific vaginitis can resemble cystitis (discussed later on).

Some sources suggest that non-specific vaginitis is caused by bacteria. A bacterium called Hemophilus vaginalis has recently been isolated as the cause of a vaginal infection that resembles trichomoniasis. The discharge tends to be creamy white or grayish. This bacterium is diagnosed using a wet mount—a mixture of vaginal discharge and a saline solution that is examined under a microscope. If you have a persistent vaginal infection that can't be diagnosed, ask your doctor to check for this organism.

Hemophilus (and non-specific vaginitis) can be passed to your sexual partner, so she should watch herself for symptoms. It is possible for two or more sexual partners to pass a vaginal infection back and forth indefinitely, if both are not treated. Nitrofurazone (also called Furacin) or sulfa suppositories are prescribed for Hemophilus.

Alternative remedies are listed below.

1. Douche with 2 tablespoons of white, distilled vinegar in 1 quart of warm water 3 times a week for 2 weeks. Add a clove of crushed garlic for really stubborn infections.

2. Douche twice a week for 2 weeks with 2 osha roots and ½ oz. of alum root, boiled in 1 quart of warm water for 30 minutes.

3. Use the garlic suppository described in Monilia.

4. Cover 1 teaspoon of goldenseal and 1 clove of minced garlic with 1 quart of boiling water. After it cools, douche daily with the solution for 1 week.

Viruses. Some viral infections are usually transmitted via sexual contact. Two of these, hepatitis and herpes, are described below.

HEPATITIS

Hepatitis is an inflammation of the liver. There are two basic kinds, type A ("infectious hepatitis") and type B ("serum hepatitis"). There is also a third type, non-A non-B, about which very little is known.

The early stages of hepatitis resemble the flu. Jaundice, a yellowing of the eyes and skin, occurs in about half the cases. The urine may turn dark and stools may become light-colored. Because the liver is not able to detoxify the blood as well as it does when it is healthy, the sufferer usually experiences severe mood swings. The disease is, diagnosed with a blood test called a liver profile.

Type A is usually transmitted by contact with the fecal matter of an infected person. This can happen during oral-anal contact ("rimming") or if your fingers go into your mouth after they've been in somebody else's anus. This can happen quite easily if you use spit for lubrication or if you need some saliva to dilute a water-soluble lubricant like KY that's dried up. Non-sexual methods of transmission include drinking water that has been contaminated by human sewage or eating shellfish from such water.

Type B is transmitted by contact between infected body fluids (saliva, semen, blood, urine, vaginal secretions) and your bloodstream. This can happen quite easily during sex through small cracks in your mouth, vagina or anus. It can happen more easily by sharing hypodermic needles.

If you have hepatitis, you will probably need complete bed rest for about six weeks, and you may feel fatigued for up to a year. You should not prepare other people's food, and your own dishes, towels, razors, etc., should be kept separate from theirs. You will probably need to use your own bathroom or disinfect it after you use it. You should not use any alcohol or drugs. Your appetite will probably be poor, but it is important to eat high-calorie, high-protein meals to keep depression at a minimum and give your body energy to fight the disease. Your doctor will give you a diet that can fulfill these requirements without being too hard on your liver.

A few people who have Type B become carriers. They can infect other people and have a high risk of developing liver cancer or cirrhosis. This makes it important to see a doctor, find out which kind of hepatitis you have, and find out whether you have developed an immunity to the disease or are still carrying it.

A gamma globulin shot, administered immediately after exposure to Type A, can confer short-term immunity. And a vaccine, Heptavax, is available for Type B. The vaccine is administered in three doses, costing about $100 altogether (not including doctor's fees). It's expensive, but get it if your sex life, drug habits or place of employment (hospitals) put you in a high-risk category.

Once you've had hepatitis, you should not be a blood donor.

HERPES SIMPLEX TYPE 2

There are several kinds of herpes viruses. Type 1 herpes simplex causes cold sores on the lips and around the mouth. Type 2 causes a similar blister on the genitals, inside the vagina, and sometimes on the cervix. Herpes is very common, and there is no known cure. About one-third of the people who get herpes (either type) suffer from painful and frequent recurrences of the disease. This makes it very important for women who have herpes to avoid passing it on to others.

After exposure, the sores take two to twenty days to appear. They may initially look like pimples. They have red caps and spring up in groups. They may appear on the inner and outer lips and spread to the thighs, buttocks, anus and perineum. They also appear on the vaginal walls and the cervix. You may have flu-like symptoms (a low-grade fever and enlarged lymph nodes). The vulva swells, and the sores are very painful. You may find it impossible to sit with your legs together or walk. Urination can be painful and increase itching. You may need sedatives to help you sleep, as well as some medication for the pain.

Recurrences tend to be less severe than the original outbreak of the disease. The length of time between recurrences tends to increase as you age. Recurrences can be provoked by overexposure to the sun, a minor fever, anxiety or tension, fatigue, irritation of the genitals, ovulation, hormonal imbalances, menstruation, excessive intake of caffeine, speed or birth control pills. If no open sores are visible, you are probably not infectious. During bouts of the disease, you should not have partner sex.

Your body never completely gets rid of the herpes virus, even if you don't suffer recurrences of the sores. There is some suspicion that women who have had Type 2 herpes have an increased risk of cervical cancer. Therefore, even if you have had only one episode of the disease, be sure to get your Pap smear and pelvic exam on a regular basis, and tell your doctor you've had herpes.

Herpes is usually diagnosed simply by the appearance of the sores. It is occasionally misdiagnosed as venereal warts, a rash, or syphilis, usually by medical personnel who haven't seen herpes before. An expensive blood test can be done to see whether you have antibodies in your system against the herpes virus. This would indicate that you have been exposed to the disease. Other less reliable tests include the Tzank test, which involves examining the discharge from the sores, and a viral tissue culture. A colposcopy can be done for the vagina or cervix to see whether you have herpes there.

Herpes is usually transmitted by genital contact with the sores. The virus may be carried on fingers from the sores to healthy genitals and cause infection. Type 1 herpes occasionally infects the genitals, or Type 2 can infect the mouth and from there infect another woman's genitals. Because of this crossover between Type 1 and Type 2 herpes, never let anyone with cold sores go down on you.

Treatment for herpes is aimed at relieving the symptoms. The blisters should heal in two to six weeks. Be careful not to scratch the sores. You could infect them. If urination is painful, try sitting in a bathtub full of cold water to urinate. When the sores are wet, they don't hurt as much. However, this slows healing; so pat yourself dry when you get out of the tub. Some dressings for relieving pain are given below.

1. Calendula tincture. You can buy this in a health food store or make it from pot marigolds. Pick fresh flower heads and pack them tightly in a glass jar. Cover them with ethyl alcohol (the kind you can drink). It is available by prescription, or you can substitute vodka or tequila. Shake it once a day for 14 days and then strain off the liquid. Dilute with 10 times as much water. Use as often as desired.

2. Use a sun lamp at 18 inches from the infected area. Leave it on for 30 seconds four times a day for three days. You can increase this to 1 minute 3 times a day for 3 days, and then to 2 minutes 3 times a day for 3 days.

3. Aloe vera gel can relieve the pain and help healing.

4. The doctor may give you topical steroids, antihistamines, BHA, or other drugs for healing.

Some non-prescription analgesics that I have heard make herpes feel better are Camphophenique, Blistex, Xylocaine, and Nupercainol.

Do not touch the sores and then touch another part of your body without washing your hands first. It is very easy to spread the virus to another site. The eyes are especially vulnerable. Wash your hands as soon as you wake up in the morning, before you rub your eyes, and do not put contact lenses in with saliva.

You may be able to avoid recurrences by figuring out what triggers them. Avoid becoming fatigued or getting colds. If sunburn, fever, or ovulation cause recurrences, take an aspirin to lower your body temperature. People over 30 rarely get new cases of herpes, so it may be that some immunity is acquired over time.

Women with herpes should be aware that they can infect an unborn child. If active sores appear during the last week of pregnancy, the fetus can come into contact with the virus during delivery. The virus may travel up through the cervix and infect the fetus. Some authorities report that a mother who contracts herpes before pregnancy or during the first 6 months will build up enough antibodies to pass them on to the fetus, but this is not a certainty. An infected infant may be born blind, mentally defective, have psycho-motor disabilities, or die of severe infection and hemorrhage. Since the mortality rate for babies who pass through an infected birth canal is 60%, your gynecologist will recommend that you be delivered via Caesarean section if you have active sores during late pregnancy.

Gonorrhea. This is the number one infectious disease in this country. Over 2 million people get gonorrhea every year. Most of them don't know they have it. Most of the people who have it and don't know are women. If it is detected early enough, gonorrhea can be treated with antibiotics. Unfortunately, the two tests used to detect gonorrhea in women (gram stain and vaginal culture) are not reliable. This makes it important to ask for a test for gonorrhea every time you get your Pap smear and pelvic exam.

This disease is caused by the gonococcus bacteria Neisseria gonorrhoeae. It is difficult to grow in the laboratory, since it survives only under very specific conditions. It prefers wet, warm, mucous-lined surfaces—the genitals, rectum, and throat.

For women, the symptoms of gonorrhea may include a vaginal discharge, an itchy or uncomfortable urethra, discomfort before and after bowel movements, diarrhea or a feeling of fullness when the rectum is actually empty, or a sore throat. You can contract gonorrhea and have no noticeable symptoms. If you do have symptoms, they show up 2 to 5 days after contact with an infected person.

There is some controversy over how and when gonorrhea is transmitted. At one end of the spectrum are authorities who insist that the bacteria are too fragile to be transmitted via inanimate objects or during any sexual act other than heterosexual intercourse, anal intercourse, or fellatio. At the other end of the spectrum are authorities who feel gonorrhea may be transmitted if infected vaginal discharge is carried on the fingers to the genitals and who believe the bacteria swim in the perspiration that coats the skin during sex to reach sites where they can fluorish. One source that I read stated that the gonococcus bacteria can linger on the external vulva after initial exposure and during that time can be transmitted to the throat of a woman who has oral sex with the infected individual. Another source stated that the bacteria near the vaginal entrance would be killed by exposure to air. Since the bacteria do not grow on the vaginal walls but cluster on the cervix and then enter the uterus and Fallopian tubes, it would be difficult (according to this authority) to catch gonorrhea by having oral sex with an infected woman.

The information is muddled because of the lack of research on sexually transmitted diseases and the fact that most medical people do not have a clear idea of how lesbians make love. Since our health is at stake, I suggest that we err on the side of caution. Vaginal lubrication produced by sexual arousal would come into contact with an infected cervix and might contain gonorrhea bacteria. Infected vaginal discharge could spread gonorrhea to the rectum. For this reason, it may be a good idea to have your throat cultured, your rectum cultured, and a vaginal culture made, along with a Pap smear. Don't bother with a gram stain test; it is next to useless. Get a culture. If it shows up negative and you have reason to believe you have gonorrhea (that is, a sex partner has been diagnosed as having it), repeat the test in a couple of weeks to be sure. Pregnant women should always be tested for gonorrhea. Babies can get the bacteria in their eyes when they pass through an infected birth canal. The tests are available free at public health VD clinics. You may have to argue with the doctor to get them, since most doctors prefer to diagnose gonorrhea in women by testing their male sex partners. The tests used for males are much more reliable.

If you are diagnosed as having gonorrhea, the treatment is a single large dose of penicillin. If you are allergic to this antibiotic, others will be prescribed. If you were ever fitted with an IUD and for some reason haven't had it removed, you will have to do so before taking the penicillin. For some unknown reason, the IUD hinders the antibiotic within your uterus. The dosage of penicillin is so high that even women who are not allergic to the drug may develop a skin rash, itching, swelling of the face or difficulty in breathing. If any of these allergy symptoms develop, go immediately to an emergency room and get treatment.

Women who have had a hysterectomy should get a urethral culture, as well as vaginal, rectal, and throat cultures.

If gonorrhea is undetected, it does damage to the reproductive organs. About 20% of the women who have it experience an abdominal spread of the bacteria. It affects the uterus, the Fallopian tubes, and the ovaries. It almost always causes sterility, since the resulting scar tissue blocks the Fallopian tubes. In the abdominal cavity, it can create symptoms that resemble PID (pelvic inflammatory disease) or acute appendicitis.

An immunization for this disease should be developed, and a nationwide screening program should be instituted to wipe it out.

Syphilis. During the 16th century, there was a continent-wide epidemic of syphilis in Europe. It was a much more virulent disease than the form we encounter today. Syphilis would run its course in a matter of weeks and almost always kill its victims. Authorities theorize that only the milder strains of syphilis kept their victims alive long enough to transmit them to another host. The more potent strains killed themselves off, along with the people who contracted them.

Syphilis is not as prevalent as gonorrhea. However, 90% of the women treated for syphilis do not remember seeing any of the primary symptoms. The only good way to defend yourself against this sexually transmitted disease is to get a blood test for syphilis along with your Pap smear. If you are very active sexually, you should get this test at least twice a year.

Syphilis is caused by a spirochete bacterium that (unlike gonorrhea) can penetrate the skin by a corkscrew action. It will usually enter the skin where sexual contact was the most vigorous. Where the bacteria enter, the skin becomes swollen and inflamed. The first visible sign of syphilis is a chancre that appears from 9 to 90 days after exposure. It can look like a pimple, a blister, or a sore. It is usually smaller than a dime. The chancre is painless. It does not bleed or drain pus. It does not smell, and it looks clean. Chancres can appear wherever the spirochete enters the body—on fingers, lips, breasts, the vulva, or inside the vagina, around the anus or inside the rectum. They are often overlooked because of their location or ignored because they do not hurt. The chancre disappears after a few weeks. While it is visible, any contact with it is probably going to pass on the disease. This is referred to as the primary phase of syphilis. A blood test will not show up as positive during this phase, but fluid from the chancre can be examined under a dark-field microscope for spirochetes.

After the chancre disappears, the disease is referred to as "secondary syphilis." During this second stage, which occurs 3 to 8 weeks or longer after the chancre disappears, you will probably have a rash. This can look like pimples, heat rash, measles, or consist of larger bumps the size of a pea. These can appear on the genitals, at the site of the chancre, or in other areas of the body. The spirochetes spread throughout the body during the this phase. They can cause syphilitic warts, which are large and fleshy, are usually on the genitals, and ooze a fluid that is almost as infectious as the chancre. These warts are called condylomata lata. They can become infected, which will make them smelly and sore. Syphilis can also cause blisters on the head, which can make patches of hair fall out. Palms and soles of the feet can show dark callouses that itch and dry up to become scabs. Secondary syphilis can mimic the flu. A mucous patch may appear in the mouth, cheek, tongue, or vagina. The mucous patch is grayish-white and may form dime-sized ulcers. They do not hurt; but if they appear on the vocal cords, they can cause hoarseness. Secondary syphilis can spread to the liver and cause jaundice—a rare effect.

These symptoms will also go away without treatment. However, the syphilis is not cured. After the second stage, it becomes latent. It will show up on a blood test. Otherwise, there are no symptoms; and you are not infectious. During its latent phase, syphilis can be passed to an unborn child. The spirochetes cluster around a vital organ in your body and may damage it severely.

In the fourth phase (tertiary syphilis) the bacteria do severe damage to about one-third of those who go untreated. Tertiary syphilis imitates nearly every severe disease. The bacteria destroy normal tissue and replace it with scar tissue called gumma. Gummas can replace large chunks of the liver, skin surfaces, tongue, bones, etc. Spirochetes can obliterate capillaries in the brain and cause insanity.

If detected in this stage, the disease can be halted in its progress by antibiotics, but the damage already done cannot be reversed.

Syphilis, like gonorrhea, is treated by a single large dose of penicillin. Some people take prophylactic doses of penicilin prior to sex with strangers or group sex events. This usually does nothing but build their resistance to the antibiotic, since they hardly ever take the right kind or amount of the drug.

Syphilis and gonorrhea confer no immunity. You can get them again and again.

Minors can be treated without parental consent everywhere but in Puerto Rico and Wisconsin. If you are a minor and need to be tested for a sexually transmitted disease, call the department of public health and ask for the number of the VD clinic. You can also find the VD clinic through hotlines or crisis counseling services. Call them up and ask them about their policy on treating minors. Make sure the treatment is confidential. If you have to go to a private physician, use an assumed name and take enough cash to pay the bill. Call the doctor in advance to find out how much it will be. Generally, you will get better treatment from a specialized clinic, and the public health clinic should be free. If you cannot locate treatment with a guarantee of confidentiality, get tested and treated anyway. Depending on your relationship with your family and their attitudes about sexuality, this may be a harrowing experience. But the damage these diseases can do to your body is much worse than family disapproval.

Most public VD clinics are used to dealing with gay men. They may not be too thrilled about your homosexuality, but they shouldn't hassle you. Take a friend for support. They will probably ask you for the names of your sexual contacts, and you are required by law to help them with this information if you can.

Venereal warts. Genital warts are caused by a virus. This virus is called condylomata acuminata, to distinguish it from condylomata lata (syphilitic warts). Venereal warts tend to ulcerate and become infected, which means they become very painful and smell bad. They can be spread to a sexual partner and are likely to spread from one genital area to another.

Genital warts are soft, pink, fleshy growths on the skin of the external genitals. They sometimes appear inside the vaginal entrance, on or around the cervix, and around the anus. They sometimes appear to be on stalks and may fuse until they look like pink cauliflower. Any vaginal infection will cause the warts to become infected. Depending on where they are growing, they can make defecation painful or even cause bleeding. They can also cause urinary retention and irritation of the urethra. If they are not treated, they are disfiguring and very painful. There is some evidence that they may cause skin cancer if left untreated.

The conventional medication for genital warts is tincture of podophyllin. This ointment should be washed off 4 to 6 hours after application. It can burn if applied too heavily. You will probably need several applications before the warts lose their blood supply and begin to slough off. Doctors also use electrocautery (burning the warts off after applying a local anesthetic), freezing them, or removing them surgically.

Be sure your doctor tests you for syphilis. Also be sure you are checked inside the vagina and anus for internal warts. Venereal warts are sometimes mistaken for cervical polyps.

Avoid sex with your partner(s) until the warts have disappeared and your doctor gives you an all-clear.

Chancroid, granuloma inguinale, and lymphogranuloma venereum. Rugged individualists, take heart. You can get VD without following the common herd. These three venereal diseases were recently discovered (about 100 years ago), are rarely seen, but may be increasing. Not much is known about them, so the information given will be brief.

These diseases were first seen in tropical climates. The causative organisms seem to flourish in hot, wet parts of the world. However, they are turning up farther and farther north.

CHANCROID

This disease mimics some stages of syphilis. It is caused by the bacillus Hemophilus ducreyi. It does not spread throughout the system but stays in the pelvic and groin area. Its first symptom is an ulcerated sore which appears where the bacillus entered the body. It progresses from a small, reddened area to a blister that rapidly ulcerates. It finally becomes a smooth, round ulcer with a ragged red area around it. A small amount of pus drains from it, unlike the dry chancre of syphilis. It also hurts, unlike a chancre. The chancroid can appear on the anus, thighs, vulva, and occasionally the hands or mouth. It rarely affects the vaginal walls or cervix.

As a result of fighting this infection, the lymph nodes may become inflamed and infected. The lymph nodes in the groin are especially vulnerable. An infected lymph node is called a bubo. The chancroids may cause large abscesses in the groin that break through the skin and drain pus. At this point, the sufferer has a fever. If the lesions are allowed to spread, they disfigure the genitals; but they are so painful that most people seek medical help long before they reach that point.

Chancroid is diagnosed from a smear of the pus or other liquid in the ulcer, a culture of that material, or a biopsy. Tests for syphilis should also be given, since the ulcer and the chancroid can be confused. Chancroid is treated with oral doses of sulfa drugs. Infected lymph nodes have to be drained. The affected individual should refrain from sexual activity with partners until she is rid of the disease.

GRANULOMA INGUINALE

There is some debate about whether or not this disease can be transmitted during sexual contact. Since it is a serious condition, someone who has been diagnosed as having granuloma inguinale should refrain from sexual activity with partners.

"Granuloma" means an excessive growth of scar tissue. "Inguinale" refers to the groin. A peculiar bacterium called the Donovan body, known in the textbooks as Donovania granulomatis, invades the tissues of the groin and causes continuous scarring and obliteration of normal tissue.

The disease first appears as groups of blisters. They quickly ulcerate and become a fleshy, elevated mass. The ulcers are grainy. They spread to ad-adjacent areas of the groin. Contact with thighs or buttocks can spread them there. One source stated that they may be spread by oral contact to the mouth and lips. These blisters are almost always painless, and for that reason they may be ignored. However, they do not disappear the way a chancre will. They continue to spread and will leave a large mass of scar tissue in the groin, if they are not treated.

The disease is diagnosed from its unique appearance or by taking a biopsy or smear and checking for Donovan bodies under a microscope. Treatment is oral doses of antibiotics. It takes longer to get rid of this disease than other sexually transmitted conditions. Any destruction of pelvic tissue that has taken place prior to treatment cannot be reversed.

LYMPHOGRANULOMA VENEREUM
This disease is caused by a chlymydia organism that has been described as being halfway between a virus and a bacterium. The incubation period is thought to vary from a few days to several months. A small blister may appear where the organism entered the skin. This blister is likely to go unnoticed. The organism spreads to the lymph nodes in the groin and causes them to become infected. These buboes may drain through the surface of the skin. The groin swells, is tender and may be painful. There may also be chills, fever, and a general feeling of poor health and discomfort.

Without treatment, all the lymph nodes in the groin and thighs become involved. Swollen buboes and backed-up lymph fluid engorge the whole lymphatic system. The vulva and thighs swell in a kind of elephantiasis. The skin of the vulva may become discolored, ulcerated, or be covered by wart-like growths. These long-term consequences take months to develop, however; and the disease may halt of its own accord at any stage and disappear.

Later complications include the deterioration of urinary and rectal functions. The lesions may even become malignant and develop into skin cancer.

The test for lymphogranuloma venereum resembles a TB test. An antigen for the disease is injected. Forty-eight to 72 hours later, the injection is examined to check for a reaction. Fluid from a bubo can also be cultured and then examined for the causative organism.

Antibiotics are given orally to arrest the progress of the disease. Tissue damage cannot be reversed.

Non-Contagious Medical Problems Affecting The Genitals

Three medical problems are described that affect the genitals but cannot be transmitted to a sexual partner.

Bartholin's gland abscesses. The Bartholin's glands are at either side of the vaginal opening. They are too tiny for their openings to be seen. No one is sure exactly what their function is. They may contribute a small amount of lubrication during sexual arousal. The glands are blind pockets. Their only outlet is to the vulva. Vigorous vaginal penetration or poor hygiene can push normal skin bacteria into the glands.

If they become infected, the glands swell. They can reach the size of grapes. They become red and painful to the touch and may drain pus. The infection can occur in either or both glands. Urination and any kind of vulval or anal stimulation becomes painful. A low-grade fever and a general feeling of discomfort and misery may result from the infection.

A doctor will clean and drain the glands. Antibiotics can be given to control the infection. Usually the swelling will subside without affecting the appearance of the genitals. However, this sort of infection is liable to recur. Be aware that you cannot tolerate vigorous vaginal stimulation, and be extra careful of genital hygiene. Insist that your partners treat your vagina gently, or avoid engaging in vaginal penetration.

Hemorrhoids. These distended, swollen varicose veins in the anus or lower rectum can cause pain at defecation and vaginal or anal penetration. Any pressure put on them can make them bleed or cause infection, depending on how sensitive they are.

If your hemorrhoids give you only minor difficulty and you really like anal sex, use a lot of a sterile lubricant. KY jelly is the old standby. Severe hemorrhoids should get medical treatment. Be aware that rectal gonorrhea infections can act on hemorrhoids and aggravate them. It probably wouldn't hurt to get a culture for gonorrhea when you see your doctor.

There are many possible causes for hemorrhoids. Constipation is one. Another is tension or stress. Some people under pressure react by getting backaches, kinks in their necks, Charley horses, or ulcers. Other people may clench or tighten the anal sphincter and rectum, putting stress on them. Women with hemorrhoids should avoid becoming constipated and straining for a bowel movement. A warm water enema can be better for you than constipation. Gentle anal sex that feels good—an anal massage—can help blood to circulate in the tissues and may promote the healing of hemorrhoids.

Cystitis. Cystitis is a bladder infection. Manual stimulation of the genitals that irritates the opening of the urethra or pushes bacteria into the urethra can cause such an infection. The germs may stay in the urethra or travel back to the bladder. Cystitis can also be caused by a trichomonal vaginal infection or by careless wiping after a bowel movement. Intestinal

162

bacteria like Escherichia coli multiply like mad in the bladder, which normally contains no bacteria.

Cystitis can also develop while you are being treated for other problems. Surgery on the genitals or reproductive organs, childbirth, or catheterization can provoke bladder infections. There is also a theory that cystitis develops more frequently in women who urinate infrequently. Little girls are supposed to be able to wait longer to "go" than little boys. Adult women often find that the restroom at their place of employment is inconveniently located or that trips to the restroom are frowned upon by their employers. This puts a strain on the urinary tract that may aggravate or contribute to a case of cystitis.

A bladder infection must be treated. If the infection travels into the kidneys, you will have a very serious medical problem.

The first symptom of cystitis is usually a change in your urinary pattern. You will suddenly need to urinate every few minutes. When you do, the urine will spurt out. Your urethra may itch or hurt. The urination will feel uncontrolable or spastic. Some women report a burning sensation or pain above the pelvic bone, or describe a peculiar, heavy urine odor when they first urinate in the morning. There may be traces of blood or pus in the urine.

Soaking in a hot tub several times a day and using hot water bottles on your abdomen and back will give you some symptomatic relief. Avoid coffee, tea, alcohol and spices, since these will irritate the bladder. Drink lots of water, enough to get yourself urinating plentifully every hour.

Cystitis is diagnosed by examining a urine specimen. A clean urine specimen can be obtained even if you are menstruating, by inserting a catheter into the urethra. Drugs frequently prescribed are Gantrisin, tetracycline, ampicillin and nitrofurantoin. These antibiotics must be taken for about two weeks, but symptoms should disappear in a couple of days. If they don't, check back with your doctor. The bacteria causing your infection may not respond to the antibiotic you were given. You can try a different kind. Remember that antibiotics sometimes cause vaginal infections, so use the preventive measures described under MONILIA.

Health food store cranberry juice (made without sugar) can keep your urine at the right pH to fight the infection. Four ounces of juice every four hours is the recommended amount. Vitamin C in large doses can also be helpful. Orange juice, while it contains Vitamin C, is excreted from the body at too alkaline a pH to be useful.

Some women have recurring bouts of cystitis. A visit to a urologist is recommended to check for abnormalities in the urinary tract. Some women find that having the urethra enlarged helps cure their cystitis. Other women find it necessary to change their habits to prevent recurrences of the infection.

Phenapithazine paper can be obtained at a drugstore and used to test the pH of your urine. It should be between 5.0 and 5.5 to prevent infection. The pH level can be manipulated by drinking cranberry juice. Your doctor may be able to suggest other dietary changes that would be helpful. You should be very careful of genital hygiene. It may be necessary for you to avoid vaginal penetration. Before any kind of sexual activity, you should make sure you and your partner have clean hands. Make sure that any objects used in sexual play are also clean. You should plan to get a urine test every 3 to 6 months. If your travels take you away from medical help, there is a drug called Pyridium that relieves the symptoms of cystitis but does not affect the bacteria. However, it turns urine bright orange, so you will have to be careful to avoid stains.

Some women report feeling very restless at night when their cystitis flares up. This is also described as insomnia or a feeling of panic. It is not an unusual experience, even though few medical textbooks mention it.

An infection mentioned earlier, Bartholin's glands abscesses, can cause cystitis. Pus from the infected Bartholin's glands can be smeared into the urethra. If you have this sort of problem, some doctors suggest removing the Bartholin's glands. This operation is painful and takes about a month to recover from. There is conflicting evidence about whether or not it is effective in eliminating cystitis.

There is a relatively rare form of cystitis that is not caused by bacteria. It is usually found in women who have gone through menopause. Lowered levels of estrogen cause changes in the mucous lining of the lower urinary tract. This condition is called interstitial cystitis, or Hunner's ulcer. It is very difficult to treat. Post-menopausal women with cystitis might ask their doctors to check for this condition.

As I mentioned earlier, new information about sexually transmitted diseases appears in the medical literature all the time. Women who want to be well-informed should keep up with new developments.

HOMAGE TO

Mariette Lydis
1894-1970

Painter and Illustrator, born in Austria

10
Passion: An Afterword

This book has focused on sexuality, which is just one aspect of the lesbian lifestyle. Sex is a suppressed topic in our society, and the repression of lesbian eroticism is a major component of the oppression of women. I wanted to write about lesbian sexuality in explicit detail because I wanted to combat the separation of woman from woman and return some of our power to us.

But I did not come out at the age of 17 because I thought it would make me a better feminist, nor did I come out because I had sex with women and discovered it was better than sex with men. I came out because I fell in love with another woman. We never made love—we were never lovers. But the intensity of that passion was all I needed to tell me I was indeed a lesbian. It was so incandescent, so all-consuming, that I could not possibly have mistaken my feelings for mere affection.

Knowing I was a lesbian transformed the way I saw, heard, perceived the whole world. I became aware of a network of sensations and reactions that I had ignored my entire life. Each time a woman walked by me, sat by me or talked to me, my response to her included a pulse of potential arousal. I can't adequately describe how good it made me feel about myself when I finally started noticing and really looking at other women.

The system doesn't simply deny women economic or political power. It denies them a vision of their own fury and glory, the feeling that each of them is a thundering river pouring into and joining other women until they are a flashflood that will carry everything in its wake. The world denies us a chance to be heroes for one another, to rescue and care for and worship each other.

There are lesbians who adore and never touch another woman. There are lesbians who choose to love just one woman and create whatever perfection is possible with her. There are lesbians who yearn for every woman they see, who give themselves to love and lust at every possible opportunity. We all share the knowledge that women are fine, strong, delightful, beautiful— and incredibly desirable. We share a rebellious passion for the disinherited one, woman.

HOMAGE TO

Clara Tice
1888-1973

Illustrator, born and worked in U.S.A.

Resource List

This resource list is not comprehensive, but it will suggest some places you can go for more information about various aspects of lesbian sexuality. Some of the information, especially prices and addresses, may be outdated by the time you read this. Not all the material listed here is produced by lesbians or deals exclusively with them. I have tried to indicate any reservations I have about particular items on the list. Unless otherwise indicated, all books listed are paperbacks.

Audiovisual Aids

The Multi-Media Resource Center, 1525 Franklin St., San Francisco, CA 94109, (415) 673-5100, free catalogs, one for A/V material and one for books. They make and distribute a wide variety of films, slides, and other educational material for use in sex education classes, therapy groups, and in other professional settings. Among their lesbian films are *Holding, In Winterlight*, and *We Are Ourselves*. They also have films on female masturbation, and they distribute Tee Corinne's color slides of the female genitals, which come with a teaching guide. Many of the books mentioned here can be ordered from them.

Anal Sex

Anal Pleasure and Health: A Guide for Men and Women, Jack Morin, Ph.D. $9.50 plus $1.50 postage, Down There Press, Box 2086, Burlingame, CA 94010, 1981.

Disability

Sexuality and the Spinal Cord Injured Woman, Sue Bregman, $6.00, Sister Kenny Institute, Abbott-Northwestern Hospital, Research and Education Dept., Office of Continuing Education, 2727 Chicago Ave., Minneapolis, MN 55407.

Not Made of Stone, Dr. K. Heslinga, $18.25, Charles C. Thomas, 1974.

Toward Intimacy: Family Planning and Sexual Concerns of Physically Disabled Women, Task Force on Concerns of Physically Disabled Women, $4.95, Human Sciences Press, 72 Fifth Ave., New York, NY 10011, 1978.

The Source Book for the Disabled, Gloria Hale (ed.), $15.95, Holt, Rinehart and Winston, 1982.

All of these books have a strong heterosexual bias.

Guide Books

Gaia's Guide, $9.50, 132 W. 24th St., New York, NY 10011. A lesbian guide to the U.S.A., Canada and other countries. Updated yearly.

Places of Interest to Women, $5.25, Ferrari Publications, Box 16054, Phoenix, AZ 85011. Excellent lesbian guide to U.S.A. and Canada, updated yearly.

The Gayellow Pages, $10, Renaissance House, Box 292, Village Station, New York, NY 10014. A guide to lesbian and gay bars, organizations, businesses, etc. Updated yearly.

Health

Our Bodies, Ourselves, 2nd edition, Boston Women's Health Collective, $8.95, Simon and Schuster, 1979.

A New View of a Woman's Body, Federation of Feminist Women's Health Centers, illustrated by Suzann Gage, $8.95, Simon and Schuster, 1981. Includes beautiful color photographs of the cervix at various stages of the menstrual cycle.

How to Stay out of the Gynecologist's Office, Federation of Feminist Women's Health Centers, illustrated by Suzann Gage, $6.95, Peace Press, Inc., 3828 Willat Ave., Culver City, CA 90230, 1981.

Lesbian Health Matters!, Mary O'Donnell, Val Leoffler, Kater Pollock and Ziesel Saunders, $3.75, Santa Cruz Women's Health Center, 250 Locust St., Santa Cruz, CA 95060, 1979. An excellent, nonjudgmental book that no lesbian household should be without.

Freedom from Menstrual Cramps, Dr. Kathryn Schrotenboer and Genell J. Subak-Sharpe, $2.95, Pocket Books, 1981.

The Advocate Guide to Gay Health, R. D. Fenwick, new edition updated by Nathan Fain, $6.95, Alyson Publications, Box 2783, Boston, MA 02208. Has a bias toward gay male health and includes some silly statements about lesbian sexuality ("Women don't do *that!*"), but has good information on sexually transmitted diseases, especially the current medical crisis over acquired immune deficiency syndrome (AIDS).

STD: A Commonsense Guide to Sexually Transmitted Diseases, Maria Corsaro and Carole Korzeniowski, $5.25, Holt, Rinehart and Winston, 1980.

The Herpes Book, Richard Hamilton, M.D., $4.95, J. P. Tarcher/Houghton Mifflin Co., 1980. The most reassuring book available for the herpes sufferer or her partner. However, Hamilton puts too much emphasis on the patient's responsibility to reduce the disease's severity by having the correct attitude toward life and wellness.

DES: The Complete Story, Cynthia Orenberg, $6.95, St. Martin's Press, 1981.

The Handbook of Alternatives to Chemical Medicine, Terri Teague and Mildred Jackson, $5.95 from Terri Teague, Box 656, Oakland, CA 94694, 1975.

Witches Heal: Lesbian Herbal Self-Sufficiency, Billie Potts, $8, Hecuba's Daughters Inc., Box 488, Bearsville, NY 12409, 1981.

The National Gay Health Directory, 2nd edition, $3 from the National Lesbian and Gay Health Conference, 1981.

Lesbian Sexuality

Loving Women, the Nomadic Sisters. Currently out of print. Hopefully a new edition will be out by the time you read this. A warm, witty sex manual. Check your local women's bookstore.

The Joy of Lesbian Sex, Dr. Emily L. Sisley and Bertha Harris, $10.95, Fireside/Simon and Schuster, 1977. This book should be read with a grain of salt. The authors distort lesbian sexuality to make us look good.

A Woman's Touch, Cedar and Nelly (eds.), $4.75, Womanshare Books, Box 2922, Eugene, OR 97402. Lesbian erotica. Includes images of disabled lesbians.

Sapphic Touch, Jeanine Karen and Sue Skope (eds.), $6, Pamir Productions, Box 40218, San Francisco, CA 94140. Lesbian erotica.

Graphic Details, Bev Balliett and Patti Patton, $4.50, Starr Publications, Box 5586, Phoenix, AZ 85010. Lesbian erotica.

Lesbian/Woman, Del Martin and Phyllis Lyon, $2.95, Bantam, 1972. One of the first books to appear about lesbians written by lesbians. A classic.

The Rights of Gay People, E. Carrington Boggan, Marilyn G. Haft, Charles Lister, John P. Rupp and Thomas B. Stoddard, $3.95, Bantam, 1983 (revised edition). This is an ACLU handbook. Includes information for transsexuals and transvestites.

Masturbation

Liberating Masturbation, Betty Dodson, $5 from Dodson, Box 1933, New York, NY 10116, 1974.

Preorgasmic Women

For Yourself: The Fulfillment of Female Sexuality, Lonnie Garfield Barbach, $2.95, Signet, 1975.

Sadomasochism

Coming to Power: Writings and Graphics on Lesbian S/M, Samois (ed.), $7.95, Alyson Publications, Box 2783, Boston, MA 02208, 1982.

S/M The Last Taboo, Gerald and Caroline Greene, $2.95, Grove Press, 1974.

Sex Toys

You can order vibrators from the following women-owned businesses:

As You Like It, 4411 Geary, Suite C3, San Francisco, CA 94118. Catalog
$2.

Come to Your Senses, 321 Cedar Ave. S., Minneapolis, MN 55454. Catalog
$2.

Eve's Garden, 119 W. 57th St., Room 1406, New York, NY 10019. Catalog
$3.

Good Vibrations, 3416 22nd St., San Francisco, CA 94110. Catalog $.50.

You can order vibrators, dildoes and other sex toys from the Xandria Col-
lection, Box 31039, San Francisco, CA 94131. Their catalog is $3. This is
a straight business, but very reputable and reliable. All their merchandise is
tested, and they will not sell your name to other companies. Very discreet
and confidential.

Transsexuality

Man and Woman Boy and Girl, John Money and Anke A. Ehrhardt, $5.95,
 The Johns Hopkins Univerity Press, 1972. This book is important because
 it tells you what social scientists think of gender, sex roles and transsexuality. Not a good book from the transsexual's point of view,
 however.

The Center for Special Problems, 2107 Van Ness Ave., San Francisco,
 (415) 558-4801, does work with transsexuals. They may be able to provide referrals for other parts of the country. Also check the *Gayellow
 Pages* for transsexual services.

Women's Sexuality

Human Sexual Response, William H. Masters, M.D. and Virginia E. Johnson,
 $5.95, Bantam.

Understanding Human Sexual Inadequacy, Fred Belliveau and Lin Richter,
 $2.95, Bantam, 1970. A popularization of Masters and Johnson's research.
 It includes a good, simple description of the female sexual response cycle.

The Nature and Evolution of Female Sexuality, Mary Jane Sherfey, M.D.,
 Vintage, $2.45, 1973. A very detailed, technical work on female sexual
 functioning. Luckily there is a glossary of the medical terminology.
 Sherfey has some strange ideas about mutiple orgasms. She believes pre-
 historic women spent all their time having sex, so multiple orgasms had
 to be repressed before civilization could begin. Otherwise, an interesting
 and unconventional book, worth the struggle to read it.

The Hite Report, Shere Hite, $3.95, Dell, 1976. Documents the diversity
 of women's sexuality.

The Playbook for Women About Sex, Joani Blank, $4, Down There Press,
 Box 2086, Burlingame, CA 94010. Includes some heterosexual material.

Labiaflowers, Tee Corinne, $3.95, Naiad Press, Box 10543, Tallahassee, FL, 32302. This used to be called *The Cunt Coloring Book.* Fun as well as educational.

Young People

Young, Gay and Proud!, $2.95, Alyson Publications, Box 2783, Boston, MA 02208.

The Rights of Young People, Alan Sussman, $2.50, Avon, 1977. An ACLU handbook.

VERY IMPORTANT NOTE: When you order a book by mail, include $1 for postage.

Index

Note: A variety of sex terms is used interchangeably throughout the book. Not all these slang terms are indexed. Indexed terms tend to be conservative, although not necessarily clinical.

Bottom role, 111-112
see also Roles; S & M
Brain damage, 157
Breasts, 11, 39, 42, 93, 104, 141-42
Bruises, 37, 127-28
Burns, 130
Butch, 58-59
see also Roles

Caesarean, 154
Calendula tincture, 153
Camphophenique, 154
Cancer, 142-143, 158, 160
Candida albicans, 148-149
Candle wax, 130
Carcinogens, 150, 154
Castor oil, 147
Castration, 134
Casual sex, *see* Group sex
Catharsis, 14, 124, 128
Catheters, 104, 162
Cats, *see* Animals
Celibacy, 54, 57, 67, 133, 158
Censorship, 14-18
Cerebral palsy, 97
Chancres, 152, 156-157, 159-160
Child abuse, 16-17, 88
Childbirth, 80, 154, 162
Children, 15-17, 67, 87-89, 105, 108,
136-137, 157
Chlymydia organism, 160
Climacteric, *see* Menopause
Climaxes, *see* Orgasms
Clips and clamps, 129
see also Sex toys
Clitoral stimulation, 21, 38, 52, 80, 113
Coalition for the Medical Rights of
Women, 144
Code word, *see* Safe word
Codes for sex, 58-59, 113
see also Variations
Cold sores, *see* Chancres
Coloscope, 142-143, 153
Coming out, 58, 60-61, 67
Communication, *see* Contracts; Limits;
Negotiations; Sex problems
Communication about sex, 65-69, 72, 75,
100, 117
Communication about fantasies, 12,
121-123
Communication and sign language, 98

Communication during sex, 46-47,
111-112, 128, 130
Condylomata lata, 158
Confidentiality, 68, 84, 115, 157
see also Privacy
Conflicts and problems about sex, 71-84,
92
see also Communication; Patterns of
sexual response; Sex techniques
Consent, 16-17, 67
Contracts, 57, 76
Control, 3, 73, 82, 118-119
see also Power; S & M; Surrender
Cooties, 145
Costume, 6-8, 13, 58-59, 109-110, 119,
123, 127, 131
see also Roles
Crabs, 144-145
Cramps, menstrual, 23, 80, 91
Cramps, non-menstrual, 41, 81, 150
Cunnilingus, *see* Oral sex
Cuprex, 144
Cycle of communication, 69
Cysts, 80, 142
Cystitis, 150, 161-62

DES, *see* Diethylstilbestrol
Dancing, 36, 39, 115-116
Deafness, 97, 101
Defection to straight life, 58
Depression, 60, 93, 100
Desire levels for sex, 76-77, 94
Deviants, *see* Sexual minorities
Diabetes, 77, 100-101, 148
Diarrhea, 150
Diet, *see* Nutrition
Diethylstilbestrol, 142-144
Dildoes, 50-52, 125-126
see also Penetration, Sex toys
Disabled women, 69-70, 96-105
Disability, temporary, 97
Discharge, 6-8, 142, 148-150, 154-155
Discrimination, 59
see also Hygiene
Diseases, sexual, 139-160
Dizziness, 93, 150
Dodson, Betty, 27
Dogs, *see* Animals
Dominant partner, *see* S & M
Domination, 6-8, 118-132
Donovan body, 159-160

180

A NOTE ON LESBIANS AND AIDS

Although most lesbians have heard that there is a deadly new disease called AIDS (an abbreviation for Acquired Immune Deficiency Syndrome), the impact it has had on our lives has been for the most part vicarious, when gay male friends became ill or passed away. Few of us have altered our own sexual practices or feel much anxiety about AIDS touching our lives directly.

If there was a vaccine to protect us against this disease, or a cure for people who had contracted it, this attitude would be quite valid. But because AIDS is fatal, and because the entire issue of sexual transmission of disease between women is under-researched, it is very important for all lesbians to know more about AIDS and carefully consider whether or not to change some of their sexual practices. Lesbians are probably at less risk for getting AIDS than any other group. However, individual lesbians can still be endangered. If you know that engaging in "unsafe sex" might give you a vaginal infection, you may decide that the risk is worth it. But nobody should risk getting AIDS.

A basic difficulty in evaluating how much lesbians should worry about AIDS is the fact that the Centers for Disease Control (CDC), which is in charge of keeping statistics on the disease, does not ask women who have been diagnosed with AIDS about their sexual orientation. But from data collected in New York and other states, we know that some of the women who have AIDS are lesbians. In most cases, doctors have decided that these women got AIDS by sharing needles during recreational drug use. Only about 7% of the total number of the people with AIDS in this country are women. However, this figure is probably not accurate because all AIDS cases are under-reported and because it does not occur to many doctors to test a woman for AIDS.

AIDS is transmitted when a sick person's blood or other body fluids enter your bloodstream. This means that lesbians who share needles (whether those needles are used for intravenous drug use, piercing, or tattooing) are at the same high risk for AIDS as any other population of shooters. After blood, the body fluid that seems to contain the highest concentration of human immunodeficiency virus (HIV), the virus thought to cause AIDS, is semen. So lesbians who have sex with men—perhaps because they work in the sex industry, perhaps because they wish to become pregnant—are also at risk for AIDS.

HIV has been found in small amounts in vaginal secretions, and is probably found in high concentrations in menstrual blood. We don't know if cunnilingus or penetration performed with fingers and hands are an efficient way to transmit AIDS. Many factors such as the condition of your immune system, the type of sex you have, the amount and type of body fluid you are exposed to, and whether a person with AIDS is in a contagious phase of the disease can also affect whether or not transmission occurs. Since the virus can exist in a woman's blood and sexual fluids, it seems reasonable to assume that it can pass from her to another woman during lesbian sex. There is one published case in the medical literature of sexual transmission of AIDS between women, which apparently occurred when blood was exchanged (M. Marmor, L. R. Weiss, M. Lyden, S. H. Weiss, W. C. Saxinger, T. J. Spira, and P. M. Feorino, "Possible Female-to-Female Transmission of Human Immunodeficiency Virus," *Annals of Internal Medicine,* vol. 105, Dec. 1986, page 969.

If you have been in a mutually monogamous relationship for the last five to seven years, there is little or no chance that you and your partner can give each other AIDS, and you do not need to follow "safer sex" precautions unless one of you has vaginitis or some other STD. If you had a blood transfusion between 1979 and 1985, have sex with multiple partners, or if you have a history of heterosexual activity or sex with IV drug users of any gender, or if you have shared needles yourself, you should consider adopting the following safer sex guidelines. Safer sex is also recommended for women who feel a lot of anxiety about AIDS or their health in general, since it is one way to alleviate that anxiety and will also prevent the transmission of any STD.

As this new edition of *Sapphistry* goes to press, this information is current. But further research may uncover new facts about AIDS. So supplement this by keeping abreast of new developments.

1. HIV cannot pass through latex. Rubber or vinyl gloves will prevent any virus in your partner's vaginal secretions or blood from entering your bloodstream via cuts on your hands or abrasions caused by filing your nails for fisting. Use a water-based lubricant like KY when you use any rubber product. Oil-based lubes like Crisco can weaken latex.

2. Your mother probably told you to always share your toys. Well, mother was wrong (again). It's safest to have your own set of insertables and reserve them for your own use. After use, clean them. *This is essential if they are going to be shared.* HIV is fragile. It can be killed by brief contact with Betadine, boiling water, 70% rubbing alcohol, hydrogen peroxide, the spermicide nonoxynol-9, or a solution of one part bleach in nine parts water. You can also use condoms to help keep your dildoes clean.

3. Dental surgical supply houses sell thin squares of latex (called "dental dams") which can be used during oral sex to prevent disease transmission. This is an especially good idea if your partner is menstruating. You can get them in flavors like mint, vanilla, or chocolate. Putting some water-based lubricant on the side of the dam that touches your partner's body will transmit more sensation. When you take a break, throw the dam away. If you start having sex again, use a new dam. This will prevent your picking it up and licking the wrong side by mistake. Dental dams can also be used during rimming (eating somebody's ass).

4. If you have sex with a male partner, insist on using condoms from start to finish. During intercourse, supplement the condom with a spermicide which contains at least 5% nonoxynol-9. This spermicide has been shown to kill HIV in test tubes. When a condom is applied, you should leave a little room at the tip to catch semen. This will prevent breakage during ejaculation. It's a good idea for the man to hang onto the base of the condom to prevent it from slipping off. He should withdraw as soon as he has come, to prevent leakage. Condoms should not be reused.

5. If you want to get pregnant, and you are at risk for AIDS, consider getting the test for the antibody to HIV. (This test is described more fully in item 9, below.) There is some evidence that having a baby puts enough stress on the mother's immune system to aggravate HIV infection and make it worse. The AIDS virus can be transmitted from the mother to her child, either via the placenta, the birth canal, or through breast milk. Semen donors for alternative conception should be tested twice for the HIV antibody, at three- to six-month intervals, since there may be a gap of several months after exposure to the virus before enough antibodies are produced to be detectable. A donor should practice safe sex between tests.

6. Use lubricant that comes in a tube or squeeze-bottle. If you stick your hand in an entire container of lube, it is contaminated and should be discarded after sex. If you are using a large can of lube for something like anal fisting, fill up a bunch of little paper cups and stick your hand in those, instead of the original container.

7. Leather toys are difficult to clean. A leather dildo should always be used with a condom, and never shared. If a leather item which has gotten blood on it is set aside for a few weeks, any virus present may die. However, there is no medical evidence to substantiate this. Dry-cleaning leather probably kills HIV. To be absolutely safe, any blooded item which cannot be cleaned should probably be used on only one person.

8. IV drug use with sterile needles that are not shared does not transmit AIDS. It's the contaminated blood in needles, syringes, cottons, and cookers that can make you sick. You should clean all of your paraphernalia before each use, since you can never be sure someone else didn't borrow your works. Cottons are impossible to clean without removing the dope, and should be thrown away if you want to be absolutely safe. Never use anybody else's cottons. Never trust spikes that you've bought on the street to be sterile. Use rubbing alcohol, bleach that has been diluted with nine parts of water, or plain boiling water to clean them. If you are using alcohol or bleach, draw the liquid into the syringe and squirt it out several times. Take off the spike and let it soak for 15 minutes, along with your cooker. Rinse your syringe completely— you don't want to inject bleach or alcohol! If you are using boiling water, take everything apart and boil the syringe, plunger, and needle for fifteen minutes. Don't forget to boil the cooker, too. You might not want to use boiling water on plastic syringes since it can make them sticky inside.

9. A blood test can be performed which will detect the presence of antibodies to HIV. This test is mostly used to screen donated blood, and it serves that purpose very well. But it is problematic for individuals who are concerned about AIDS and their personal health.

The first problem is that test results which are not kept absolutely private can result in your losing health insurance, experiencing job discrimination, housing and other kinds of discrimination, etc. You should never take this test at a center which does not allow you to remain absolutely anonymous. Anonymous testing means that you don't give your name, so you can never be linked to the test results. Instead, you are given a number, and you call in to learn your results. Confidential testing sounds similar, but it is not. If you give the test center your name, it is possible that your test results will be released because of a subpoena, snooping, or through simple malice and stupidity.

The second problem is the difficulty of interpreting the test results. It is a test for exposure to the virus only. If no HIV antibodies are found, it may mean that you were exposed to the virus, but your body has not had time to make antibodies (or is no longer able to do so). And it doesn't mean that you can't be exposed to AIDS the next time you have unsafe sex or share needles. If your test result is positive, it probably means that antibodies to HIV were detected. A very small number of tests are false positives. Factors other than the presence of HIV antibodies existed which caused your test result to be misinterpreted. The CDC currently estimates that about one-half of those people who test positive will get AIDS or an AIDS-related condition (ARC). But nobody knows how to tell if any particular individual will go on to develop troublesome symptoms of HIV infection.

This makes a positive test result very difficult to cope with. If you intend to take the test, make sure you have access to counseling. Because of its limited value and potentially devastating effects, most doctors recommend that you *do not* get tested for HIV antibodies unless you know you are in a high risk category, want to become pregnant, or are so worried about having AIDS despite being in a low risk category that the overwhelming probability is that test results will be negative, and put your mind at rest.

There is another disease that is every bit as dangerous as AIDS, and that is AIDS phobia. During the best of times, there has been tension between lesbians and gay men. AIDS has the potential for increasing the distance between us, and making it even more difficult for us to support one another for being queer in a very homophobic world. The questions I have gotten from lesbians who are concerned about being invited to eat dinner or stay at the homes of faggot friends make it clear that lesbians can be as ignorant as straight people about the impossibility of casual transmission of AIDS. Touching someone with AIDS, kissing them, sleeping on sheets they have used, and using the same toilet will not give you AIDS.

There always have been, and sadly probably always will be, lesbians who feel that our way of loving is superior to the nasty things that gay men do. This sort of "lesbian supremacist" often believes that if it weren't for gay men, lesbians wouldn't experience much oppression at all. AIDS exacerbates this attitude because it has given bigots an excuse to intensify anti-gay discrimination, harassment, and violence. When lesbians take this kind of heat, it seems incredibly unfair. The fact that some gay men are in effect male separatists who are completely ignorant about lesbian lives and our needs and political issues makes things even worse. Some lesbians who have been asked to donate money or time to AIDS organizations wonder, with good reason, if the majority of gay men would have any interest at all in fighting a disease that struck down dykes.

These divisions can make women who do AIDS work or women with close ties to the gay male community feel isolated from other lesbians. They may be afraid to talk about how difficult it is to take care of sick people or educate the public about sex and drugs and AIDS. They may be reluctant to express their grief at the loss of loved ones, which can make it harder to stop mourning. Bisexual women have always been scapegoated for the presence of "male venereal diseases" in the lesbian community, and their status now—no matter how much they love women, no matter how much they contribute to lesbian institutions—is even more tenuous.

But all this is becoming a moot point. No matter how resentful we are, no matter how deeply we deny its effect on our lives, AIDS is not going to go away. There may never be a miracle cure or a vaccine. Whether we like it or not, AIDS affects our lives just as deeply as it does our gay brothers and every other high-risk group. Most people who want to use AIDS to justify anti-gay actions don't know—and worse, don't care—that very few lesbians have the disease. We have learned to our sorrow that any action taken against a gay man can be used as a precedent for taking action against a lesbian. The struggle against AIDS discrimination, demands for better treatment for people with AIDS, and obtaining funding for educating the public about AIDS prevention have to become part of the lesbian agenda.

We must also deal with the problem of drug abuse in the lesbian community, and that is impossible to do without confronting racism, our insane drug laws, and the brutal economic disparity in America, the poverty and despair that allow fortunes to be made from traffic in narcotics and other illicit drugs. The lesbian who is most at risk for AIDS is not the stereotypical white, middle-class women's studies major. She is a woman of color, she is poor, she is a prostitute, she is a mother, she has men in her life, she is an addict, she may not think of herself as a lesbian. But she is also likely to be your friend, your lover, your co-worker, the next woman you buy a beer. There are closets within the lesbian community, and if we are going to stop AIDS, we must open those doors without fear and without anger.

FOR MORE INFORMATION

The San Francisco AIDS Foundation, 333 Valencia St., Fourth Floor, San Francisco, CA 94103. Enclose a long, stamped, self-addressed envelope. (415) 863-AIDS. They operate a toll-free hotline in Northern California, 800-FOR-AIDS. TDD: (415) 864-6606.

Gay Men's Health Crisis, Box 274, 132 West 24th Street, New York, NY 10011. (212) 807-6655.

The above organizations can refer you to an agency doing AIDS work in your community.

A few of the publications of
THE NAIAD PRESS, INC.
P.O. Box 10543 ● Tallahassee, Florida 32302
Phone (904) 539-9322
Mail orders welcome. Please include 15% postage.

CHERISHED LOVE by Evelyn Kennedy. 192 pp. Erotic
Lesbian love story.   ISBN 0-941483-08-8 $8.95

LAST SEPTEMBER by Helen R. Hull. 208 pp. Six stories & a
glorious novella.   ISBN 0-941483-09-6   8.95

THE SECRET IN THE BIRD by Camarin Grae. 312 pp. Striking,
psychological suspense novel.   ISBN 0-941483-05-3   8.95

TO THE LIGHTNING by Catherine Ennis. 208 pp. Romantic
Lesbian 'Robinson Crusoe' adventure.   ISBN 0-941483-06-1   8.95

THE OTHER SIDE OF VENUS by Shirley Verel. 224 pp.
Luminous, romantic love story.   ISBN 0-941483-07-X   8.95

DREAMS AND SWORDS by Katherine V. Forrest. 192 pp.
Romantic, erotic, imaginative stories. ISBN 0-941483-03-7   8.95

MEMORY BOARD by Jane Rule. 336 pp. Memorable novel
about an aging Lesbian couple.   ISBN 0-941483-02-9   8.95

THE ALWAYS ANONYMOUS BEAST by Lauren Wright
Douglas. 224 pp. A Caitlin Reese mystery. First in a series.
                                       ISBN 0-941483-04-5   8.95

SEARCHING FOR SPRING by Patricia A. Murphy. 224 pp.
Novel about the recovery of love.   ISBN 0-941483-00-2   8.95

DUSTY'S QUEEN OF HEARTS DINER by Lee Lynch. 240 pp.
Romantic blue-collar novel.   ISBN 0-941483-01-0   8.95

PARENTS MATTER by Ann Muller. 240 pp. Parents'
relationships with Lesbian daughters and gay sons.
                                       ISBN 0-930044-91-6   9.95

THE PEARLS by Shelley Smith. 176 pp. Passion and fun in
the Caribbean sun.   ISBN 0-930044-93-2   7.95

MAGDALENA by Sarah Aldridge. 352 pp. Epic Lesbian novel
set on three continents.   ISBN 0-930044-99-1   8.95

THE BLACK AND WHITE OF IT by Ann Allen Shockley.
144 pp. Short stories.   ISBN 0-930044-96-7   7.95

SAY JESUS AND COME TO ME by Ann Allen Shockley. 288
pp. Contemporary romance.   ISBN 0-930044-98-3   8.95

LOVING HER by Ann Allen Shockley. 192 pp. Romantic love
story.   ISBN 0-930044-97-5   7.95

MURDER AT THE NIGHTWOOD BAR by Katherine V. Forrest. 240 pp. A Kate Delafield mystery. Second in a series.
ISBN 0-930044-92-4   8.95

ZOE'S BOOK by Gail Pass. 224 pp. Passionate, obsessive love story.   ISBN 0-930044-95-9   7.95

WINGED DANCER by Camarin Grae. 228 pp. Erotic Lesbian adventure story.   ISBN 0-930044-88-6   8.95

PAZ by Camarin Grae. 336 pp. Romantic Lesbian adventurer with the power to change the world.   ISBN 0-930044-89-4   8.95

SOUL SNATCHER by Camarin Grae. 224 pp. A puzzle, an adventure, a mystery — Lesbian romance.   ISBN 0-930044-90-8   8.95

THE LOVE OF GOOD WOMEN by Isabel Miller. 224 pp. Long-awaited new novel by the author of the beloved *Patience and Sarah*.   ISBN 0-930044-81-9   8.95

THE HOUSE AT PELHAM FALLS by Brenda Weathers. 240 pp. Suspenseful Lesbian ghost story.   ISBN 0-930044-79-7   7.95

HOME IN YOUR HANDS by Lee Lynch. 240 pp. More stories from the author of *Old Dyke Tales*.   ISBN 0-930044-80-0   7.95

EACH HAND A MAP by Anita Skeen. 112 pp. Real-life poems that touch us all.   ISBN 0-930044-82-7   6.95

SURPLUS by Sylvia Stevenson. 342 pp. A classic early Lesbian novel.   ISBN 0-930044-78-9   6.95

PEMBROKE PARK by Michelle Martin. 256 pp. Derring-do and daring romance in Regency England.   ISBN 0-930044-77-0   7.95

THE LONG TRAIL by Penny Hayes. 248 pp. Vivid adventures of two women in love in the old west.   ISBN 0-930044-76-2   8.95

HORIZON OF THE HEART by Shelley Smith. 192 pp. Hot romance in summertime New England.   ISBN 0-930044-75-4   7.95

AN EMERGENCE OF GREEN by Katherine V. Forrest. 288 pp. Powerful novel of sexual discovery.   ISBN 0-930044-69-X   8.95

THE LESBIAN PERIODICALS INDEX edited by Claire Potter. 432 pp. Author & subject index.   ISBN 0-930044-74-6   29.95

DESERT OF THE HEART by Jane Rule. 224 pp. A classic; basis for the movie *Desert Hearts*.   ISBN 0-930044-73-8   7.95

SPRING FORWARD/FALL BACK by Sheila Ortiz Taylor. 288 pp. Literary novel of timeless love.   ISBN 0-930044-70-3   7.95

FOR KEEPS by Elisabeth Nonas. 144 pp. Contemporary novel about losing and finding love.   ISBN 0-930044-71-1   7.95

TORCHLIGHT TO VALHALLA by Gale Wilhelm. 128 pp. Classic novel by a great Lesbian writer.   ISBN 0-930044-68-1   7.95

LESBIAN NUNS: BREAKING SILENCE edited by Rosemary Curb and Nancy Manahan. 432 pp. Unprecedented autobiographies of religious life.   ISBN 0-930044-62-2   9.95

YANTRAS OF WOMANLOVE by Tee A. Corinne. 64 pp.
Photos by noted Lesbian photographer.   ISBN 0-930044-30-4   6.95

MRS. PORTER'S LETTER by Vicki P. McConnell. 224 pp.
The first Nyla Wade mystery.   ISBN 0-930044-29-0   7.95

TO THE CLEVELAND STATION by Carol Anne Douglas.
192 pp. Interracial Lesbian love story.   ISBN 0-930044-27-4   6.95

THE NESTING PLACE by Sarah Aldridge. 224 pp. A
three-woman triangle—love conquers all!   ISBN 0-930044-26-6   7.95

THIS IS NOT FOR YOU by Jane Rule. 284 pp. A letter to a
beloved is also an intricate novel.   ISBN 0-930044-25-8   8.95

FAULTLINE by Sheila Ortiz Taylor. 140 pp. Warm, funny,
literate story of a startling family.   ISBN 0-930044-24-X   6.95

THE LESBIAN IN LITERATURE by Barbara Grier. 3d ed.
Foreword by Maida Tilchen. 240 pp. Comprehensive bibliography.
Literary ratings; rare photos.   ISBN 0-930044-23-1   7.95

ANNA'S COUNTRY by Elizabeth Lang. 208 pp. A woman
finds her Lesbian identity.   ISBN 0-930044-19-3   6.95

PRISM by Valerie Taylor. 158 pp. A love affair between two
women in their sixties.   ISBN 0-930044-18-5   6.95

BLACK LESBIANS: AN ANNOTATED BIBLIOGRAPHY
compiled by J. R. Roberts. Foreword by Barbara Smith. 112 pp.
Award-winning bibliography.   ISBN 0-930044-21-5   5.95

THE MARQUISE AND THE NOVICE by Victoria Ramstetter.
108 pp. A Lesbian Gothic novel.   ISBN 0-930044-16-9   4.95

OUTLANDER by Jane Rule. 207 pp. Short stories and essays
by one of our finest writers.   ISBN 0-930044-17-7   6.95

SAPPHISTRY: THE BOOK OF LESBIAN SEXUALITY by
Pat Califia. 3d edition, revised. 208 pp. ISBN 0-941483-24-X   8.95

ALL TRUE LOVERS by Sarah Aldridge. 292 pp. Romantic
novel set in the 1930s and 1940s.   ISBN 0-930044-10-X   7.95

A WOMAN APPEARED TO ME by Renee Vivien. 65 pp. A
classic; translated by Jeannette H. Foster. ISBN 0-930044-06-1   5.00

CYTHEREA'S BREATH by Sarah Aldridge. 240 pp. Romantic
novel about women's entrance into medicine.
                                           ISBN 0-930044-02-9   6.95

These are just a few of the many Naiad Press titles — we are the oldest and
largest lesbian/feminist publishing company in the world. Please request a
complete catalog. We offer personal service; we encourage and welcome
direct mail orders from individuals who have limited access to bookstores
carrying our publications.